ENDORSEMENTS

"Before we let the radical left tear down all the statues of our American founders, we need to read F. Leroy Forlines's insightful book, *Secularism and the American Republic*. This book is a powerful reminder that, while far from perfect, those extraordinary men who prayerfully created our great republic crafted the greatest experiment in human government in history. Thank God for this book, and for these United States of America!"

—MIKE HUCKABEE, *Former Governor of Arkansas, Talk Show Host*

"This Forlines volume, including attendant essays by Sergent, Sheldon, and Bracey, is a treasure. I wish I'd had it on hand when I was teaching my church-state relations courses. Clear spoken and incisive, the book brings assiduous research to bear on the confusion stemming from the judicial malpractice, however well intentioned, embedded in the *Everson* and *McCollum* decisions. Forlines makes his case for 'reasonable accommodation' over against 'absolute separation,' deploying etymology, epistemology, history, and good, plain common sense along the way—words fitly spoken for our day on this crucial issue."

—MARK COPPENGER, *Retired Professor of Christian Philosophy and Ethics, Southern Baptist Theological Seminary*

"Thanks to the efforts of the Welch College Press, we are extremely fortunate to have the benefit of the late F. Leroy Forlines's careful and nuanced discussion of the varied meanings of 'secularism' as applied to the early Republic, and by extension, to today's America. There is much misunderstanding and misconception on this point. But as Forlines makes memorably clear, there is an important distinction between the founders' and framers' idea of a secular *state*—meaning a polity operating independently of ecclesiastical authority—and *secularism* as a master ideology superseding all religious assertions and commitments. To embrace the former was most emphatically *not*, and never has been, to embrace the latter. We stand desperately in need of a fresh recognition of that fact, and Forlines's book is a wonderful place to begin that necessary work. The future of religious liberty in this country may depend on it."

—WILFRED M. MCCLAY, G.T. *and Libby Blankenship Chair in the History of Liberty, University of Oklahoma*

"Who would have thought that a theologian would write about political theory? And do such thorough research and careful analysis? And make it interesting and informing to boot? That's what Leroy Forlines has done, showing that the First Amendment to the Constitution of the United States erects a 'wall of separation' only between establishing a state religion and religious liberty, and was intended by Jefferson and Madison to allow for 'reasonable accommodation' of general religious principles in public life. And more. Take this book to the U.S. Supreme Court and make it required reading."

—ROBERT E. PICIRILLI, *Professor Emeritus of New Testament and Former Academic Dean, Welch College*

"This book is classic Forlines: logically incisive but enjoyable to read. In it, ordinary people and scholars alike will find one of the clearest explanations of the unique understanding of the separation of church and state set forth by the American founders. Oh, how this book is needed in our day of the encroachment of secularism on every area of life. I commend it to anyone who is concerned about the future of First Amendment liberties in this country. I've heard Professor Forlines talk about these ideas for decades. It's wonderful to have his thought on this subject made public in this important moment in American life."

—J. MATTHEW PINSON, *President, Welch College*

"This book is important and highly relevant to the subject of America as a legally secular but culturally religious society."

—GARRETT WARD SHELDON, *Author of* Political Philosophy of Thomas Jefferson *(John Hopkins University Press) and Professor Emeritus, University of Virginia* (from the Foreword)

Secularism and the American Republic

Secularism *and the* American Republic

Revisiting Thomas Jefferson *on* Church *and* State

F. LEROY FORLINES

MATTHEW STEVEN BRACEY, *EDITOR*

WELCH COLLEGE
PRESS

Secularism and the American Republic: Revisiting Thomas Jefferson on Church and State

Copyright © 2022 by F. Leroy Forlines

Published by Welch College Press
1045 Bison Trail, Gallatin, TN 37066
www.welch.edu/welchpress

Printed in the United States of America
October 2022
First Edition

All rights reserved. No part of this publication may be reproduced, stored in a retrieval system, or transmitted in any form by any means—electronic, mechanical, photocopy, recording, or otherwise—without the prior written permission of the publisher, Welch College Press, except for brief quotations, and except as provided by US copyright law.

Cover design: Studio Gearbox
Cover image: Shutterstock
Interior design and typeset: Katherine Lloyd, The DESK

Unless otherwise noted, all Scripture quotations are taken from the New King James Version (NKJV), copyright © 1979, 1980, 1982, Thomas Nelson. Used by permission. All rights reserved.

Because of the dynamic nature of the Internet, any web address or links contained in this publication may have changed since publication and may no longer be valid.

Library of Congress Control Number: 2021935397

ISBN-13: 978-0-9976087-4-8

Contents

Foreword by Garrett Sheldon ix
Acknowledgments xi
Preface xiii
Editor's Introduction by Matthew Steven Bracey xv

PART I
SECULARISM: EXPLORING THE INFLUENCE
OF SECULARISM ON THE AMERICAN FOUNDERS

ONE: The Timeline of Secularism 3
TWO: John Adams, Thomas Jefferson, and the Absence
of Secularism 15
THREE: Secularism, Thomas Jefferson, and His Interpreters 35

PART II
THE SUPREME COURT: INTRODUCING THE STRICT
SEPARATION OF CHURCH AND STATE

FOUR: Reviewing *Everson*: The First Amendment 49
FIVE: Reviewing *Everson*: Dissent 63
SIX: Reviewing *McCollum*: Religious and Secular Education 75
SEVEN: Reviewing *McCollum*: Dissent 93

PART III
THOMAS JEFFERSON: RECLAIMING JEFFERSON'S VIEW
OF RELIGIOUS FREEDOM AND THE REASONABLE
ACCOMMODATION OF CHURCH AND STATE

EIGHT: Introducing Religious Freedom: James Madison
and Thomas Jefferson 115

NINE: The First Amendment and the "Wall of Separation" 127

TEN: Report of the Commissioners for the University
of Virginia 141

ELEVEN: Report to the President and Directors
of the Literary Fund 155

TWELVE: Four Letters 167

THIRTEEN: Reviewing the Case for the Reasonable
Accommodation of Church and State 179

PART IV
CLOSING ARGUMENT: SUMMING IT UP

FOURTEEN: Reasonable Accommodation v. Strict Separation
of Church and State 191

FIFTEEN: Implications for Public Education, Secular Humanism,
and Liberty 207

APPENDICES

In Search of the Secular John Locke
by Gregory Sergent 223

Secularism and the American Experience
by Garrett Sheldon 235

Studies in Secularism: An Overview
by Matthew Steven Bracey 249

Notes 273
Bibliography 301
About the Author 311
About the Editor 312
Name Index 313
Subject Index 317

Foreword

Garrett Sheldon

I recall some years ago meeting with Professor Forlines and several other scholars and ministers to discuss his idea for a book on secularism in the United States. He outlined an intriguing and important thesis: Although the United States is formally "secular" in the sense of the legal separation of church and state, religious freedom, liberty of conscience, and the absence of an official state religion, it has still been a highly religious and predominantly Christian society, culture, and ethos—at least, historically speaking.

By examining the historical understanding of the concept of "secular" and its meaning to the founders, especially that champion of religious liberty, Thomas Jefferson, and by examining the leading Supreme Court rulings on the Constitution's First Amendment religion clauses, Professor Forlines demonstrates that these clauses were designed to make the United States a *more* religious country, in the best sense of that term. Indeed, this book is important and highly relevant to the subject of America as a legally secular but culturally religious society.

Finally, Matthew Bracey's editing is superb, and his illuminating introduction and overview of secularism studies in the appendix, which places the thesis of *Secularism and the American Republic* within decades of scholarship on the subject, are significant contributions to the subject, especially in our current times.

Garrett Ward Sheldon
Professor Emeritus
University of Virginia

Acknowledgments

I may not live to see the publication of my next two books but might be face-to-face with our Lord. As Charles Wesley's hymn says, "And clothed in righteousness Divine, Bold I approach th' eternal throne, And claim the crown, through Christ my own."

To God be all glory and praise for allowing me to spend approximately fifteen of my ninety-four years on planning, researching, and writing about how the founding fathers of the United States did not intend for secularism to characterize the legal structure of our government. Instead, our Constitution and the writings of the signers established a workable relationship between church and state.

The Lord is pleased when we give honor to whom honor is due. I wish to thank Garrett Sheldon and Gregory Sergent, who each wrote a chapter to supply pertinent background on the subject of this volume.

To aid Welch College Press in its formative years, Tim Campbell, a family friend, volunteered to launch a fundraising campaign to publish the book. Among those who responded are Gary Weeks (an attorney and family friend who taught me the proper way to research legal cases), Michael Gillock, Tim Hall, Wayne Miracle, David Potete, Barry Simpson, John Smith, Donald Southerland, Randy Stone, and anonymous donors. Regrettably, COVID-19 emerged shortly after the beginning of this campaign, which hampered more giving, and, as a result, my wife and I gave a gift of

$20,000 to speed up the publication in an attempt to have it published in my lifetime.

My thanks goes to Welch College Press for publishing this book, to the Editor-in-Chief, J. Matthew Pinson, and to the Managing Editor, Matthew Bracey, who also authored an introduction and a contributing chapter on an overview of secularism studies in the appendix. I also thank Joshua Hunter, Brandon Presley, Phillip Morgan, and Frank and Christa Thornsbury for their work in proofreading, with Josh also preparing the bibliography and indices, and Emily Vickery for assistance in the book's preparation.

A few of the many significant people in my life without whose influence and encouragement this book would not have been possible are my beloved wife, Fay, whose affection and encouragement provided continued motivation for my scholarship and ministry; my extended family; L. C. Johnson; J. P. Barrow; Charles and Laura Thigpen; Robert Picirilli; Carlisle Hanna; Earl Glenn; and Arnold Schultz.

I also wish to thank the publishers whose works I cited and/or quoted.

A last word to all the students I have taught: I learned so much from you. Please follow me to glory and to eternal Christian fellowship. "The Lord watch between me and thee, when we are absent one from another" (Genesis 31:49).

F. Leroy Forlines

Preface

My relationship with F. Leroy Forlines began in the summer of 2013 when he invited me to edit his unfinished and ever-growing manuscript on the topic of secularism. Even by that point, he had been working on the project for about a decade. Little did I know he would continue working on that manuscript for the next seven-and-a-half years until his death at the age of ninety-four on December 15, 2020. Those who talked with Mr. Forlines over the last decades of his life noted that this project filled his imagination.

Frequent were the times when he would converse with people about the origins of secularism, the significance of George Jacob Holyoake, the writings of Thomas Jefferson, the founding of the University of Virginia, the doctrine of religious liberty, or some other topic relevant to his study. Over the past seven-plus years, we spoke at length about these topics and many others. Sometimes we talked on the telephone, but often we would talk at his house in the "Florida room."

Meanwhile, while Mr. Forlines worked on his manuscript, about a dozen scholars contributed to a festschrift in his honor, entitled *The Promise of Arminian Theology: Essays in Honor of F. Leroy Forlines*.[1] In addition to co-editing the volume, I contributed a chapter entitled "Confronting Secularism," in which I summarized and analyzed the then-present state of the manuscript, which includes the material in this book, as well as that in future publications. We presented the festschrift to him in the summer of 2016. He brimmed with genuine surprise, palpable joy, and deep gratitude.

I observed urgency in Forlines's disposition over the course of his last years and months. He was, understandably, deeply concerned about the state of American culture, and he hoped that his work on secularism could contribute positively to the discussion in the public square. He believed in the significance of his work, as do I. With a final body of work in secularism studies comprising approximately 750 manuscript pages, I am proud to say that his research will result in multiple publications. This volume, which comprises about one-third of the final manuscript, is the first.

Before concluding this preface, I want to introduce readers to who Mr. Forlines was. He was a devoted Christian and ordained Free Will Baptist minister. He was an alumnus of Winterville High School, Welch College, Winona Lake Theological Seminary, Northern Baptist Theological Seminary, and Chicago School of Theology. He was Professor Emeritus in Theology at Welch College and loyal member of the Cross Timbers Free Will Baptist Church. He was, in a phrase, a man of God and of integrity.

Matthew Steven Bracey

Editor's Introduction

Matthew Steven Bracey

Leroy Forlines's contribution to the study of secularism overlaps thematically with other scholars' work. I explore this connection in some detail in an appendix entitled "Studies in Secularism: An Overview." At the same time, Forlines carves out his own niche. He demonstrates some awareness of these other studies but does not interact with them if they are beyond the specific scope of his own project.

Forlines's overarching aim concerns the introduction and influence of secularism within the American context, and he examines that question historically, culturally, sociologically, and legally. As I mentioned in the preface, Forlines's work has resulted in approximately 750 manuscript pages worth of publishable material. This particular book comprises only a portion of that work, which will result in a further publication. Still, in order to appreciate this one more fully, we will briefly consider how it fits in relation to the whole.

This book focuses on a few people and a few key documents, investigating the phenomenon of secularism in light of the American founding and the American legal tradition. The next book will focus on the cultural backdrop more generally, concentrating on the American populace and the role that American education has played in the story of secularism in the United States. Thus the overview of literature, which I review in an appendix, omits consideration of those publications that have probed the relationship between secularism and education, because they are more relevant for Forlines's next book rather than the present one.[1]

Secularism and the American Republic is divided into four parts with fifteen chapters. It also contains several appendices that include, among other things, two additional chapters by guest writers. Garrett Ward Sheldon has authored one of them in which he spends considerable time examining James Madison's background and beliefs concerning religious liberty. Sheldon is Professor Emeritus of Political Theory, Law, and Religion at the University of Virginia's College at Wise, as well as author of *The Political Philosophy of James Madison* (2001) and *The Political Philosophy of Thomas Jefferson* (1991), both published by The Johns Hopkins University Press. Greg Sergent, adjunct instructor of Religion and Politics in America also at the University of Virginia's College at Wise, has written the other chapter, in which he analyzes John Locke's doctrine of religious toleration. Each of these chapters provides additional background to the work of Forlines.

Part I. Secularism: Exploring the Influence of Secularism on the American Founders

Part one contains chapters one through three. Forlines begins chapter one by questioning whether America is legally secular and/or secularist. Numerous scholars and even Supreme Court justices contend that it is. Examples include Isaac Kramnick and R. Laurence Moore in *The Godless Constitution* and Justice William Brennan, Jr., in *Abington School District v. Schempp*. However, Forlines challenges this dominant narrative by presenting the basic

EDITOR'S INTRODUCTION

timeline of secularism. He observes that George Jacob Holyoake did not coin the term *secularism* until the mid-nineteenth century, making the supposition that the United States was founded on it an impossibility, unless people are using the term in an anachronistic and imprecise manner. Undoubtedly, other movements would have existed at the time of the American founding, such as rationalism, empiricism, and freethinking; however, those movements are not definitional equivalents to that of secularism.

In addition, Forlines examines the etymology and usage of the term *secular*, as well as its derivatives, both before and after the mid-nineteenth century. His reason for this move is to demonstrate that, though the term *secular* existed at the time of the American founding, it is distinct from *secularism*. Consequently, the two should not be conflated. As John Perry states in the *Oxford Handbook to Secularism*, "Although the Latin equivalent, *saeculum*, does have a significant history in Christian political thought, it might also create confusion if applied directly to modern governments."[2] These evidences cause Forlines to propose a chronological incompatibility to the position that America is legally secularist.

In chapter two, Forlines notes the conspicuous absence of secularist (not to be confused with secular) doctrine in the writings of two key American founders. After interacting briefly with John Adams, as well as authors who argue that he was a secularist, Forlines spends the majority of his time considering whether Thomas Jefferson was a secularist. In so doing, he investigates Jefferson's "trinity of heroes" in order to paint a fuller picture of Jefferson's influences. Part of the purpose for this focus is that Jefferson factors so prominently in Forlines's overall project. The three figures he considers are Francis Bacon, Isaac Newton, and John Locke, to whom he gives the most attention.

Forlines analyzes some of Locke's religious beliefs and his political philosophy, focusing on themes of empiricism and natural law. Forlines concludes that these figures did not influence Jefferson for the cause of secularism because they were not, strictly speaking, secularists. Sergent's chapter in the appendix, entitled "In Search of the Secular John Locke," serves as an important companion piece to this chapter. It also considers Locke's broader historical background, his concept of Christianity, and his political philosophy, emphasizing his views of personal and political liberty, church-state relations, and tolerance, and demonstrating, like Forlines, that Locke was not a secularist.

In chapter three, Forlines shifts from examining Jefferson's influences to considering his interpreters, particularly those who would identify him as a secularist, such as Susan Jacoby and Lenni Brenner. Forlines posits that Jefferson was not a secularist. In this way, Forlines agrees with law professor Noah Feldman, who argues, "Although today's secularists like to claim those framers who believed in a watchmaker God as their forebears, the eighteenth century knew no phenomenon by the name of 'secularism.'"[3] In contrast, Forlines argues that Jefferson was a religious person (even if unorthodox) who believed that religion could rightfully occupy a place in the public square and state.

Garrett Sheldon's "Secularism and the American Experience" in the appendix helpfully complements Forlines's third chapter. Although Forlines spends the majority of the chapter discussing Jefferson, he also introduces Madison, with whom he will spend considerable time in part three. Sheldon does the reverse, spending the majority of his chapter discussing Madison while also interacting some with Jefferson. In particular, he reviews Madison's Christian education and case for religious liberty, giving special attention to his Memorial and Remonstrance against

EDITOR'S INTRODUCTION

Religious Assessments, as well as Jefferson's Virginia Statute for Religious Liberty, considering their collective influence on the First Amendment. Although Forlines pivots in part two to review two key Supreme Court cases, he spends considerable time with both Jefferson and Madison, as well as with their writings, in part three, making this chapter an important foundation for the material that appears there.

Part II. The Supreme Court: Introducing the Strict Separation of Church and State

In part two, Forlines shifts gears to focus on two cases that the Supreme Court heard in the 1940s: *Everson v. Board of Education* (1947) in chapters four and five, and *McCollum v. Board of Education* (1948) in chapters six and seven. Forlines analyzes not only the majority opinions of these cases but also the concurring and dissenting opinions. They warrant the amount of attention that Forlines gives to them because of how they interpret the writings of Jefferson and Madison. For example, these cases interact with Jefferson's letter to the Danbury Baptist Association, where he wrote that the First Amendment has built a wall of separation between church and state, as well as Madison's Memorial and Remonstrance.

Justice Hugo Black, who authored these opinions, interpreted such documents to mean that American founders such as Jefferson and Madison intended the legal doctrine of strict church-state separation. Undoubtedly, these figures explicitly used the language of *separation*. However, Forlines shows that the founders did not argue for separation in the same manner that Black, and the justices who joined him, articulated it. They have fundamentally misinterpreted what these founders meant by that language, and Forlines provides compelling evidence to demonstrate his viewpoint. Although he alludes to the correct interpretation of Jefferson and Madison throughout part two, Forlines addresses it more fully in part three. The fact is that American history reveals that many localities did not follow the vision of church-state relations as Black and his colleagues explained it. However, these communities were not thereby ignoring the intentions of the founders. Rather, the justices misinterpreted the intentions of the founders and broke with the conventions that had preceded them.

Underlying Forlines's analysis of these cases is his ever-present interest in the subject of secularism. Secularists often gravitate toward these Supreme Court opinions and others like them. The reason is that they offer an interpretation of the relationship of religion and government with which they agree and then read it into the American founding and history. The crucial problem, according to Forlines, is that these cases get Jefferson and Madison wrong. In effect, then, Forlines's consideration of these cases, combined with his subsequent work in part three, forms a cohesive argument that undercuts the secularists' position.

Whereas *Everson* introduces the doctrine of strict church-state separation, *McCollum* teases it out and applies it. In chapters four and five, Forlines interacts with the majority opinion of *Everson*, as well as its two dissents. He begins by introducing the phrase that has resulted in so much dialogue through the years: Jefferson's "wall of separation." Forlines reviews the information that Black gives concerning the background to the First Amendment, concentrating on the phenomenon of religious establishment, as well as the religious coercion and persecution that followed it.

Forlines also notes Black's interaction with Patrick Henry, James Madison, and Thomas Jefferson. Henry had introduced a bill that would have established a provision for taxes to help support teachers of Christianity. Madison wrote against it in his

EDITOR'S INTRODUCTION

Memorial and Remonstrance, and, instead, Jefferson's Virginia Bill for Religious Freedom, which he had written previously, would pass into law. Next, Forlines works through *Everson's* legal incorporation of the Establishment Clause against the states. The legal doctrine of incorporation simply refers to the Court's making applicable the clauses in the Bill of Rights to the states. Prior to this decision, the Establishment Clause of the First Amendment, "Congress shall make no law respecting the establishment of religion," did not apply to state governments but only to the federal government.[4] Finally, Forlines examines Black's approach to religious establishment within the states.

In chapter five, Forlines reviews the two dissenting opinions. One is from Justice Robert H. Jackson, and the other is from Justice Wiley B. Rutledge. Generally speaking, each of them did not believe that the majority went far enough in its articulation of the principles of strict separation. Jackson goes to lengths distinguishing parochial schools from public schools and discussing them in light of the First Amendment.

Although Rutledge doubles down on the doctrine of separation, he still recognizes some challenges inherent in the discussion of church-state relations: "No one conscious of religious values can be unsympathetic toward the burden which our constitutional separation puts on parents who desire religious instruction mixed with secular for their children."[5] Forlines does not deny Rutledge's point, as well as that of the majority, that the United States Constitution has, in a manner of speaking, separated church and state. However, he interprets the meaning of that expression differently from how the Court understands it, namely that it refers to religious establishment rather than religious accommodation, which is consistent with what Jefferson and Madison held, as well as with the American tradition up to that point.

SECULARISM AND THE AMERICAN REPUBLIC

In chapters six and seven, Forlines analyzes *McCollum*. He reviews the majority opinion from Justice Black, the two concurring opinions from Justice Felix Frankfurter and Justice Jackson, and a dissenting opinion from Justice Stanley Reed. Black explores the question of religious instruction in public schools. Frankfurter offers a historical overview of education, noting the transition from sectarian to secular education and appraising various approaches to accommodation.

Although Jackson had dissented to *Everson*, he concurs in *McCollum* but nonetheless expresses some reservations about it. He questions whether the Court even has the jurisdiction to hear the case in the first place. He notes that the Court has failed to place limitations on the scope of its ruling. He also observes that the Court's commandeering of this topic has preempted the rights of localities to make laws and policies reflective of their own communities. "We must leave some flexibility to meet local conditions, some chance to progress by trial and error."[6] Jackson makes a rich observation about the place of religion in society and public education when he says:

> I think it remains to be demonstrated whether it is possible, even if desirable, to comply with such demands as plaintiff's completely to isolate and cast out of secular education all that some people may reasonably regard as religious instruction. Perhaps subjects such as mathematics, physics or chemistry are, or can be, completely secularized. But it would not seem practical to teach either practice or appreciation of the arts if we are to forbid exposure of youth to any religious influences. Music without sacred music, architecture minus the cathedral, or painting without the scriptural themes would be eccentric and incomplete, even from a secular point of

EDITOR'S INTRODUCTION

view. Yet the inspirational appeal of religion in these guises is often stronger than in forthright sermon. Even such a "science" as biology raises the issue between evolution and creation as an explanation of our presence on this planet. Certainly a course in English literature that omitted the Bible and other powerful uses of our mother tongue for religious ends would be pretty barren. And I should suppose it is a proper, if not an indispensable, part of preparation for a worldly life to know the roles that religion and religions have played in the tragic story of mankind. The fact is that, for good or for ill, nearly everything in our culture worth transmitting, everything which gives meaning to life, is saturated with religious influences, derived from paganism, Judaism, Christianity—both Catholic and Protestant—and other faiths accepted by a large part of the world's peoples. One can hardly respect a system of education that would leave the student wholly ignorant of the currents of religious thought that move the world society for a part in which he is being prepared.[7]

Whereas Jackson expresses serious reservations about the majority opinion, Reed dissents from it altogether. He interacts explicitly with Jefferson and introduces some documents that Forlines analyzes in part three, which help make sense of what Jefferson truly believed. Speaking specifically about Jefferson's statement to the Danbury Baptists that the First Amendment has built a wall of separation between church and state, Reed astutely observes, "The difference between the generality of his statements on the separation of church and state and the specificity of his conclusions on education are considerable. A rule of law should not be drawn from a figure of speech."[8]

Part III. Thomas Jefferson: Reclaiming Jefferson's View on Religious Freedom

In part three, which includes chapters eight through thirteen, Forlines's argument reaches its peak, resting on the foundation that he has laid in parts one and two. Throughout his analysis of *Everson* and *McCollum*, Forlines had given indications for why he believes that they misinterpreted Jefferson concerning church-state relations. Throughout this section, he substantiates those remarks with an appeal to the sources themselves.

In chapter eight, after presenting Henry's failed proposal attempting to establish a provision for teachers of the Christian religion, Forlines positively presents Madison's Memorial and Remonstrance against Religious Assessments and Jefferson's Virginia Statute for Religious Freedom. Referring to the Memorial and Remonstrance in particular, Forlines writes, "So significant is it that I believe it is the most important document in American history in support of religious liberty." Forlines explains that the Memorial and Remonstrance and Virginia Statute were exceedingly significant for the American articulation of church-state relations enshrined in the First Amendment. He also notes that they did not envision strict separation as *Everson* and *McCollum* interpret it but rather that they promoted religious liberty, which permits the *practice* of religion within the circumstance of private and public affairs.

In chapter nine, Forlines turns to considering the controversy surrounding the statement that Jefferson made in the letter he sent to the Danbury Baptist Association about a wall of separation. As already noted, *Everson* and *McCollum* constructed the legal doctrine of strict separation out of Jefferson's statement. In contrast, Forlines holds that Justice Black and his colleagues fundamentally misinterpreted Jefferson's meaning. Jefferson's statement referred to religious establishment rather than to religious accommodation.

In this way, Forlines is consistent with what law professor Philip Hamburger says in his book, *Separation of Church and State*. Referring to the phrase "separation between church and state," Hamburger writes: "Rather than simply forbid civil laws respecting an establishment of religion, it has more ambitiously tended to prohibit contact between religious and civil institutions." However, he notes a "disparity between separation and disestablishment."[9] In other words, they are not the same and should not be conflated. In fact, Hamburger argues boldly that "the constitutional authority for separation is without historical foundation."[10] Remarking about the impact that the application of the doctrine of strict separation has had on the American articulation of religious liberty, he writes, "Americans thereby gradually forgot the character of their older, antiestablishment religious liberty and eventually came to understand their religious freedom as a separation of church and state."[11] With these statements, Forlines would agree entirely.

Forlines also puts forth a positive case for his position. He evaluates not only the full letter that Jefferson sent to the Danbury Baptists but also the initial letter from the Baptists that prompted his reply in the first place. In addition, Forlines reviews *Reynolds v. United States*, which had inspected Jefferson's letter some seventy years prior to *Everson* and *McCollum*, to bolster his case. In the end, Forlines commends the approach of Justice Morrison Waite, author of *Reynolds*, over that of Black.

Chapters ten through thirteen may be the most exciting and important chapters in the entire book. However, to appreciate their impact fully, the reader should have read the first nine chapters, which give important background and context for Forlines's discussion. Nearly twenty years after penning his letter to the Danbury Baptists, Jefferson played an instrumental role in founding and shaping the University of Virginia, a public institution. In so doing, he made numerous remarks about the intersection of religion and government. If the majority opinions of *Everson* and *McCollum* are correct in their interpretation of Jefferson, his own example should bear out that meaning. Also, because these cases revolved around the question of church-state relations within the sphere of education, Jefferson's example is directly applicable to an honest analysis of these issues.

Significantly, the precedent that Jefferson establishes does not accord with the interpretation that Black and his colleagues asserted. Specifically, Jefferson offered a model consistent with the doctrine of reasonable *accommodation,* which is a word that he himself uses, rather than that of literal strict separation. Forlines demonstrates this claim by considering two key documents: Jefferson's Report of the Commissioners for the University of Virginia (the Rockfish Gap Report) in chapter ten and his Report to the President and Directors of the Literary Fund (President-Directors Report) in chapter eleven. Contrary to the positions of strict separation or secularism, these two documents unquestionably exemplify religious accommodation.

For example, they demonstrate that Jefferson proposed to establish a nonsectarian institution rather than a secular one, replete with an ethics professor who would teach proofs for God's existence, as well as the laws of morality, and with language professors who would teach those languages relevant to biblical and theological studies: namely Hebrew, Greek, and Latin. The documents also show that Jefferson proposed that the university build rooms that it could use for religious worship, among other activities, that it instruct in religious opinion and duty, that it teach theology alongside the other useful sciences, and that it provide for the establishment of independent divinity schools to the effect that the students of these schools and those of the university could mingle.

Writing in *The Life of Thomas Jefferson*, Henry Stephens Randall surmises, "If the proposition here made," referring to those specifically in the President-Directors Report, "to the different sects on terms so liberal had been accepted by them, the University of Virginia would now comprise the most extensive school of Theology in the world."[12] That the university did not follow all of these proposals is beside Forlines's underlying point for reviewing them. His reason for analyzing Jefferson's suggestions is that they evidence a vision on his part for the reasonable accommodation of religion in the public sphere and in public institutions. Additionally, as Forlines points out, Jefferson explicitly described these suggestions as being consistent with constitutional principles. Being that Jefferson also authored the Virginia Statute, which would influence the First Amendment, his affirmation of the constitutionality of reasonable accommodation is significant.

Forlines contends that the Rockfish Gap Report and President-Directors Report should receive much more attention than they do. In many ways, they form the crux of his overall argument, but, relative to other aspects of Jefferson's life and thought, they garner little interest from Jefferson scholars. To be fair, the Rockfish Gap Report (more so than the President-Directors Report) has received some attention, such as in Edwin Gaustad's *Sworn on the Altar of God: A Religious Biography of Thomas Jefferson*, George Marsden's *The Soul of the American University: From Protestant Established Nonbelief*, and Leonard Levy's *The Establishment Clause: Religion and the First Amendment*—all volumes with which Forlines interacts.[13]

However, Forlines would contend that these reports warrant more sustained analysis. Fortunately, several volumes have been released in recent years that indicate a hopeful trend on this front, including *The Founding of Thomas Jefferson's University* by John Ragosta, Peter Onuf, and Andrew O'Shaughnessy in 2019 and *God on the Grounds: A History of Religion at Thomas Jefferson's University* by Harry Y. Gamble in 2020.[14] The University of Virginia Press published these books after Forlines had completed his work. Had they been available to him, though, he undoubtedly would have interacted with them.

Gamble identifies "Jefferson's vision" for the University of Virginia as a "secular university."[15] Yet Gamble expresses "surprise" at the way in which religion has factored into the origins and history of this public university: "It is surprising to discover that religion even has a history at the University, let alone that religion has played an influential role in the life of the institution, and that this was true virtually from the beginning, notwithstanding Jefferson's deep misgivings about religion and his careful measures against its intrusion."[16]

Forlines would not communicate surprise in the same way that Gamble does for several reasons. First, Forlines distinguishes a *secular* university from a *secularist* university, the first referring to that which is opposite the religious cloister but not necessarily opposed to religion itself and the second referring more particularly to religion. Second, and consequently, he would recognize that a secular university might also reasonably accommodate some aspects of religion within its institution, a point for which Jefferson's reports, argues Forlines, explicitly provide.

Gamble expressly interacts with the Rockfish Gap Report and the President-Directors Report.[17] Analyzing the latter report, he remarks that it "reiterated that religion was not to be taught in the University, for that would infringe religious freedom, violate the separation of church and state, and tend to the preferential treatment of one or another denomination."[18] Forlines would articulate this differently, observing that the ethics professor's teaching proofs for God's existence and the laws of morality signifies the teaching of "religion" that nonetheless does not show preferential treatment to a given denomination, since, according to Jefferson, such proofs and laws form a basis upon which various religious sects can agree. Additionally, Forlines would argue that such a proposal does not violate separation of church and state, which is a legal doctrine that guards against the prospect of religious establishment rather than that of religious accommodation.

Working specifically through the passage in which Jefferson proposes that the University of Virginia provide for the establishment of independent divinity schools on its confines, Gamble opines, "It is not known what 'pious individuals' may have suggested this 'remedy.' The idea may have come to members of the board from outside acquaintances, or it may have originated within the board. In any event, it was certainly not Jefferson's own idea. He could accept it only with deep reluctance."[19] In addition, he characterizes it as "pure political expediency, calculated to mollify religious opposition so as not to endanger important funding requests that had been made but not yet granted."[20] Even so, he grants, "Thus the prospect of religious schools in proximity to the University was sustained, and the related enactments remained on the books," yet also adds, "But they never had any effect or application."[21]

As evidenced by Gamble's interpretation, some authors argue that Jefferson included statements about religion so that his reports would pass the muster of a given board or group but that he never intended, or else permitted, that any of those proposals would occur. Forlines argues against such notions, holding that Jefferson was genuine. Nevertheless, even if such arguments are true, even if Jefferson was playing political games, that interpretation does not affect Forlines's fundamental argument that Jefferson affirmed that reasonable church-state accommodation accords with constitutional principles.

Moving into chapter twelve, Forlines examines four additional letters, two from Jefferson and two from Madison, which give further reference for interpreting accurately Jefferson's suggestions in the Rockfish Gap Report and the President-Directors Report. Finally, Forlines, having presented a compelling yet complex case throughout part three, reviews his case for the reasonable accommodation of church-state relations in chapter thirteen. Throughout the course of the book, Forlines has slowly built his swan song, which has gained energy and momentum with each subsequent chapter. In these chapters, his argument reaches its highest notes (especially chapters ten and eleven), which he then brings to a satisfying conclusion in the final chapters, before the coda of the chapters in the appendices.

Part IV. Closing Argument: Summing It Up

Throughout the book, Forlines interacts with various cases of the Supreme Court, including *Reynolds*, *Everson*, and *McCollum*. In fact, from the beginning, Forlines conceived of his project as if it were a court case. He spoke even of calling Jefferson back to the proverbial witness stand. Clearly, separationists and secularists have invoked Jefferson's name in the publication of their viewpoint. Forlines queries what he would actually say if he were permitted to speak for himself. In many ways, part three is an exercise in pursuit of that very goal.

EDITOR'S INTRODUCTION

Forlines keeps with the legal theme in part four. Having established the basic parameters of the case in part one and presented the position of opposing counsel in part two and offered evidences for his own case in part three, he gives his closing argument in part four. Chapter fourteen functions as a summation of the overall position that Forlines has put forward throughout the book. In addition, he urges that scholars engage this subject honestly and that courts consider the weight of his argument. Finally, Forlines concludes by discussing implications of his overall argument for the areas of higher education, secular humanism, and liberty. Forlines argues that true freedom of conscience and speech requires freedom of religion, which extend beyond opinions and beyond the private sphere but also includes actions and the public sphere.

CONCLUSION

At times *Secularism and the American Republic* overlaps with the paths that other scholars have trodden. Yet Forlines charts his own course through the vast landscape of secularism studies. He examines the meanings of *secular* and *secularism*, probes into the majority opinions in *Everson* and *McCollum*, and analyzes the writings of Madison and especially Jefferson in order to understand their view of church-state relations at the founding. The sum of Forlines's argument is that the United States Constitution supports reasonable accommodation as the via media between religious establishment on the one hand and strict separation on the other. Reasonable accommodation allows for genuine religious liberty without devolving into the type of secularism that preempts the exercise of such freedom in the first place. Although consideration of these subjects may initially overwhelm some readers, Forlines explains them in a simple and straightforward manner that is simultaneously careful and responsible. What is more, *Secularism and the American Republic* is worthwhile and enjoyable.

PART I

Secularism:
Exploring the Influence of Secularism on the American Founders

CHAPTER ONE

The Timeline of Secularism

Is America Legally Secularist?

For decades secularists have made concerted efforts to remake the United States in their image. They have pressured the courts to hold that public displays of religious symbols on government property, such as a crèche or the Ten Commandments, are unconstitutional. Many scholars even hold that the founders established the United States on a secularist foundation. For example, in their book *The Godless Constitution*, Isaac Kramnick and R. Laurence Moore refer to "the intentionally secular base on which the Constitution was placed."[1] Likewise, in his book *Jefferson & Madison on Separation of Church and State*, Lenni Brenner argues that "America is culturally Protestant and legally secularist."[2]

Are the scholars who support a secularist base right? Was the United States legally founded on secularism? While secularists hold that the American founders aimed to build a secularist nation, the New England Puritans intended to build a Christian nation. As Frank Lambert affirms, the Puritans "drafted a constitution affirming their faith in God and their intention to organize a Christian Nation." The Fundamental Orders of Connecticut of

1639 signaled the same: "that their government rested on divine authority and pursued godly purposes."[3]

However, the period of the Puritans differed considerably from the period of the founding. To be sure, the United States Constitution would not invoke divine authority. "Its stated purposes," argues Lambert, "were secular, political ends."[4] He builds his case by pointing to the Treaty of Tripoli of 1797, which "assured the world that the United States was a secular state, and that its negotiations would adhere to the rule of law, not the dictates of the Christian faith."[5] Is Lambert right? Article 11 of the treaty reads:

> As the Government of the United States of America is not in any sense founded on the Christian religion; as it has in itself no character of enmity against the laws, religion, or tranquility, of Mussulmen; and, as the said States never have entered into any war or act of hostility against any Mahometan nation, it is declared by the parties, that no pretext arising from religious opinions shall ever produce an interruption of the harmony existing between the two countries.[6]

Some claim that article 11 is not authentic to the treaty. However, assuming the validity of article 11 is not tantamount to admitting that the founders built the United States on a secularist foundation. Rather, it shows that they disestablished the church from the government.

The controversy of Tripoli began because the Barbary Pirates were oppressing American ships. The pirates based their actions on a religious premise, namely that the United States was guilty for not obeying the Quran. For some time, these Muslim pirates had demanded large payoffs for safe passage of the European nations in the Mediterranean Sea. Because these nations had a church-state union, the pirates viewed them as Christian nations and required tribute. Prior to the United States' separation from Great Britain, American ships were covered by the tributes paid by Great Britain. However, when the United States declared independence, these payments no longer covered them. Circumstances forced the United States to stand on its own two feet.

American leaders tried to assuage the Muslims' concerns by distinguishing themselves from the European nations: The United States is not a Christian nation, they explained; it does not support an establishment of religion; the First Amendment requires that Congress leave all matters of religion to the states (at least before the amendment began applying also to the states in the 1940s, a point we will review in part two). Even so, the founders' attempt to pacify the Muslim nations did not work. Consequently, for some time, they sent tribute anyway. However, that would not last because, eventually, President Thomas Jefferson would send the Navy and the Marines to fight the Barbary Pirates.[7] Thus, although the founders formed an institutional separation of church and state, that does not mean that they thereby established a secularist nation.

In addition to using the Treaty of Tripoli as evidence of America's secularist base, secularists also point to other apparent proofs. Some cite the No Religious Test Clause, "No religious test shall ever be required as a qualification to any office or public trust under the United States," as well as the Establishment Clause, "Congress shall make no law respecting an establishment of religion."[8]

Another example that secularists use concerns the Supreme Court case from 1963, *Abington School District v. Schempp*, in which Justice William Brennan, Jr. stated, "It has rightly been said of the history of the Establishment Clause that 'our tradition of civil liberty rests not only on the secularism of a Thomas Jefferson but also on the fervent sectarianism . . . of a Roger Williams.'"[9] Similarly, after citing both clauses, an editorial in *Free Inquiry*, an influential publication in the secularist community, reads, "The Constitution is a wholly secular document, and our founders consciously constructed a state based on secular concerns and interests, not religious tenets. We need a campaign to recognize the secular basis of our Constitution!"[10] The *Free Inquiry* writers made this statement amid the 2008 presidential election in which both Republican and Democratic candidates were using religious rhetoric. These are just a few of many examples to which secularists point for their claim of America's secularist foundation. Are they right? What do we do with these claims?

The Timeline of Secularism

George Jacob Holyoake, Secularism, and the American Founding

Secularism derives from the Latin *saecula*, meaning "age" or "period." George Jacob Holyoake (1817–1906) first used the term *secularism* in 1846 to refer to a desire to build a human society in which religion played no part. Holyoake, an Englishman, would found the British Secular Movement in 1851–1852. "His emphasis represented a protest against the dominance and control of human life by ecclesiastical institutions," Warren Young explains. "Today secularism is the integration of life around the spirit of a specific age rather than around God. It is living as if the material order were supreme and as if God did not exist." Thus we might say that Holyoake anticipated modern secularism in some ways. Concerning the relation of secularism to atheism, Young continues, "While secularism may not indicate theoretical atheism, it certainly does represent practical atheism. . . . Secularism is man living his entire life as if there were no God."[11]

THE TIMELINE OF SECULARISM

The chronology of the birth of secularism presents a major problem for those holding that the United States rests on a secularist foundation. The Constitution was ratified in 1788. The First Amendment, which is the foundation for American church-state relations, was ratified in 1791. Yet the term *secularism* was not coined by Holyoake until 1846, much less was secularism able to inculcate American culture. A fifty-eight-year gap exists between the founders' adopting the United States Constitution and Holyoake's coining the term *secularism*. A fifty-five-year gap exists with reference to the First Amendment. This chronological discrepancy renders impossible the proposal that the United States was founded on secularism.

The Leaders of the British Secular Movement

To support my argument, I will begin by looking at the leaders of the British Secular Movement. Its major leaders were George Jacob Holyoake, Charles Bradlaugh, and Charles Watts. Holyoake, the Englishman who coined *secularism* in 1846, founded the first secularist society in 1851–1852. He displayed a moderate turn of mind, enlisting the cooperation of people who might not espouse atheism but nonetheless would limit their involvement to temporal-material concerns rather than to spiritual-eternal concerns.

Charles Bradlaugh (1833–1891) entered the scene by the mid- or late 1850s. He was an atheistic politician who, when elected to Parliament, refused to take an oath that made reference to God. His actions raised public awareness for atheism in England. Bradlaugh also established a secular society in 1866 and, unlike Holyoake, believed that atheism was essential for the success of the secularist movement. Charles Watts (1835–1906) began in England but traveled to Canada and the United States, aggressively promoting secularism. Watts also served as the vice president for the American Secular Union, an organization founded by the famous American preacher-turned-agnostic Robert Ingersoll (1833–1899), who served as the first president. Ingersoll would praise Watts for his promotion of secularism

That general period of time in the late 1800s witnessed not simply the language but also the concept of modern popular secularism. The United States founders could not have built the country on a secularist foundation. Instead, subsequent interpreters have employed anachronism and applied the ideas of secularism to the founders. At the same time, the word *secular*, which forms the root of *secularism*, did exist prior to Holyoake and the American founders. Perhaps readers would think that the etymology of the word *secular* would shed some light on these secularists' conclusions. However, as we will see, it will not provide as much as they might hope.

Secular *and Its Derivatives Before 1846*

In 1846, Holyoake coined the term *secularism*, which was derived from the term *secular*. Historically, the term *secular* and its derivatives did not hold the same meaning as *secularism*. The term *secular* referred to non-monastic church clergy rather than a religionless society. The first entry for *secular* in the *Oxford English Dictionary* (OED) reads, "Of members of the clergy: Living 'in the world' and not in monastic seclusion, as distinguished from 'regular' and 'religious.'" A "secular abbot" refers to "a person not a monk, who had the title and part of the revenues, but not the functions of an abbot."[12] The *Catholic Encyclopedia* observes the same.[13]

The secular clergy did not serve in a monastery but in a local parish; the regular clergy did not serve in a local parish but in a monastery. Thus the term *secular* made reference to one's location of service, not to one's orientation of belief. It simply contrasted with the sacred. Work that occurred in the parish was secular, whereas work that occurred in the cloister was sacred. Parish priests were secular priests. They were not godless, and they did not advocate secularism. They simply worked in the parish instead of the cloister.

Just as the term *secular*, when applied to the priest, did not mean that he was godless, the same is true when secular is applied to government. A secular government did not refer to a godless government or to a government that advocated secularism. It referred to the domain of civil or temporal government. "During the Middle Ages, no clear lines separated the religious from the secular," James Turner writes decisively. "To be sure, popes and emperors clashed over their respective powers, but both claimed spiritual as well as temporal jurisdiction; and this overlap was typical in all areas of life. The church and the world blended. Parishes provided local government, and holy days seasonal celebrations."[14]

Surprisingly few references to a secular government appear prior to the time of the American founding fathers. I have found only one. In *On Secular Authority*, Martin Luther employed the German word *weltlich*, which translates to "secular" in English. Throughout the book, he referenced secular governments, secular rulers, secular authority, and a secular sword, as distinct from spiritual governments, spiritual rulers, and so forth. Of course, Luther was not referring to governments that promote secularism. Rather he was referring to the temporal as distinguished from the eternal. He was contrasting the secular from the ecclesiastical. Harro Höpfl explains:

> In one sense, the world (*Welt*) is simply 'this life and everything connected with it and therefore includes Christians and Unchristians alike; in another sense it is 'the worldly',

as opposed to 'true Christians', the 'earth' as contrasted to 'heaven'. In the same way, the adjective *weltlich* sometimes refers neutrally to things, whether good or bad, related to this world, but it can carry a pejorative meaning of 'worldliness', or falling short of spiritual standards. In the former sense, the appropriate translation is 'secular' or 'temporal'; in the latter, it has to be rendered as 'worldly'. In some places, Luther is deliberately playing on the ambiguity of the German term; in other places, it may be that the negative connotations of the term have proved inimical to clarity of thought, especially given the generally hostile attitude towards 'secular' rulers that Luther takes in this text.[15]

Thus by *secular* Luther offered no hint whatsoever of modern secularism. This overview demonstrates that premodern usages of *secular* did not give rise to the modern notion of secularism. As such, even though these usages were around at the time of the American founding, they could not have influenced the American founders in the spirit of secularism. In addition, I have found no reference to the term *secular government* by any of America's founders.[16] In fact, the first time the term appears in a United States Supreme Court decision is in 1963 with the *Abington School District* decision.[17]

Where then do we get the modern definition of secular? The second entry for *secular* in the OED reads, "Belonging to the world and its affairs as distinguished from the church and religion; civil, lay, temporal. Chiefly used as a negative term, with the meaning non-ecclesiastical, non-religious, or non-sacred."[18] As we will see, that definition would not come until the mid-1800s. As a result, it was unavailable and hence unknown to the American founders.

Terms such as *secularist*, *secularity*, and *secularization* also offer little help in bolstering secularists' arguments that the United States was founded on a secular base. Minimal usage of the word *secularist* existed prior to Holyoake. The sole entry given by the OED occurred in 1716 by Myles Davies, who used it to refer to regular, or non-monastic, clergy: "Of the Modern Fanaticism of Seditious Priests of all the Religions in Europe, viz. . . . Of Secularists and Regularists, [etc]."[19] Thus *secularist* does not appear to conform to modern usage. The case is similar with *secularity*. The OED says that it referred to a "secular jurisdiction of power" or "the condition or quality of being secular," which concerned an "occupation with secular affairs (on the part of clergymen); secular spirit or behavior."[20] Again, these usages relate to clergy, not to a society without religion.

In several instances, the OED records the term *secularity* as referring to "worldliness" and "absence of religious principle or feeling."[21] For example, the English Puritan William Prynne used it in 1636: "Your Lordly Pompe, . . . luxury, secularity, suppression of preaching." The Anglican Edward Gee used it in 1690: "The Bishop's own Person . . . [should be far] from . . . the prophanity and secularity of others, as Hawking, Hunting, . . . and the like." George Hickes used it in 1711, referring to the "secularity of the clergy in complying with the vanities . . . of the age." Finally, *The Quarterly Christian Spectator* used it this way in 1835: "Sloth, pride, and secularity, have crept upon those [clergy] to whom mankind should look up for patterns of purity and heavenly mindedness."[22] Investigation into these usages reveals that they are occasional and pejorative.

Finally, the term *secularization* offers secularists as little help as these other derivatives. It was first used in the Peace of Westphalia of 1648, "designating the transfer of ecclesiastical property into princely hands."[23] In conclusion, the term *secular* and numerous derivatives existed at the time of the founders. However, none of them referred to the phenomenon of modern secularism.

Secular *and Its Derivatives After 1846*

When did the term *secular* and its derivatives take on a different meaning? Holyoake would prove to be an important benchmark. To summarize: In 1846, he coined the term *secularism*, and by 1851–1852, he founded the British Secular Movement. In 1854, he explained that he chose that term to express a certain positive and ethical element, which the terms 'Infidel,' 'Sceptic,' [and] 'Atheist' do not express."[24] By that point, the term gained popular usage in England and assumed a new meaning. At first the movement was mild but over the next several decades would become aggressive:

> Under the guidance of Holyoake secularism was a relatively tame movement, but with the early eighth decade of the nineteenth century its character changed under the leadership of the well-known Charles Bradlaugh and it became not only radical in politics but bitterly hostile to all forms of religion, even while adopting a sort of religious ceremonial drawn up by Bradlaugh's friend, Austin Holyoake.... In all this the more vulgar forms of secularism revealed a certain degree of affinity with Positivism, while the more cultured adherents of the movement came to prefer to term themselves as "agnostics." Since the closing decades of the nineteenth century secularism as a distinct sect seems more or less to have disappeared or to have been merged in such forms of modern anti-Christian radicalism as societies for ethical culture.[25]

By 1872, British secularists were applying the term to a non-religious education: "The Nonconformists who advocate pure Secularism in national education have in effect come down from their religious position altogether."[26] For these reasons, the

THE TIMELINE OF SECULARISM

OED defines *secularism* as the "doctrine that morality should be based solely in regard to the well-being of mankind in the present life, to the exclusion of all considerations drawn from belief in God or a future state."[27] The significant points are, first, that these developments did not occur until more than a half-century after America's founding and, second, that, when they did occur, they first occurred in England and not in the United States.

Concerning the term *secularist*, Holyoake used it as early as 1851, the same year he began organizing the secular movement in Britain: "We should use the word 'Secularist' as best indicating that province of human duty which belongs to this life."[28] Later, in 1876, William Gladstone, the British Prime Minister, stated, "The Secularist . . . does not of necessity assert anything but positive and exclusive claims of purposes, the enjoyments, and the needs, presented to us in the world of sight and experience."[29] In essence, a secularist is an "adherent of secularism."[30] As for the term *secularization*, however, it does not seem to have changed meaning as quickly as these others. Even as late as the early 1900s, it did not signify a move from a religious orientation toward a secular one. For example, *The New Schaff-Herzog Encyclopedia of Religious Knowledge*, published in 1907, displays no awareness of that meaning of the term.

America as Legally Secularist: A Chronological Incompatibility

As we have seen, Holyoake introduced the term *secularism*, and it came to refer to a worldview that had no place for the supernatural. He reintroduced the word *secularist* and redefined it as a person who advocated for secularism. The word *secularization* would also change from meaning a shift of property from ecclesiastical powers to princely powers to meaning a shift of orientation from a religious one to a religionless one. Chronologically, the introduction of these concepts and terms began in the mid-1800s and would not conclude until at least the early 1900s. In addition, their impact was primarily in England rather than in the United States. Therefore, the timeline of secularism reveals a chronological and geographical incompatibility for those claiming the United States was built on a secularist base.

Some may wonder whether I am playing a technicality game with the word *secularism*. Perhaps it was around by another name. I have considered this question, but the research has yielded no such evidence. Secularism was not around under a different name. In fact, the evidence shows that the Western world operated from a broadly Christian worldview during the founding era, even amid the popularity of Deism and Unitarianism. Although these movements were not orthodox, they were certainly not secularist.

Conclusion

If the founders did not begin with secularist assumptions about life and the world, what sort of assumptions did they begin with? To answer this question, we must examine those whose ideas influenced the world of the American founders. We will discover that they did not influence the founders in the dogma of secularism because they themselves were not secularists. In fact, we will learn that they operated from a broadly Christian view of the world. Our investigation will yield further evidence that the case for a secularist founding does not exist.

CHAPTER TWO

John Adams, Thomas Jefferson, and the Absence of Secularism

In the previous chapter, I introduced the question of whether the United States was founded on secularism. I considered the timeline of secularism, the role of George Jacob Holyoake, and the meaning of the term *secular*. In this chapter, I want to examine two major thinkers from the American founding, John Adams and Thomas Jefferson, asking if they were secularist in their outlook. Because the beliefs of Jefferson form such an important part of this book, I will give special attention to those thinkers who most influenced Jefferson. We will find that neither of these men, nor those who influenced them, were apostles of secularism.

Was John Adams a Secularist?

John Adams (1735–1826) served as the second president and first vice president of the United States, as a delegate to the First and Second Continental Congresses, and as a member of the Committee of Five that drafted the Declaration of Independence. Like other founders, he pointed explicitly to those voices that had influenced his philosophy of government. For example, writing in

1776, Adams stated, "All sober inquirers after truth, ancient and modern, pagan and Christian, have declared that the happiness of man, as well as his dignity, consists in virtue. Confucius, Zoroaster, Socrates, Mohamet, not to mention authorities, really sacred, have agreed in this."[1] By "authorities, really sacred," Adams was referring to Christian authorities.

Even with such passages, some scholars still argue that secularist voices influenced Adams and that he, in turn, similarly shaped American jurisprudence. For example, Frank Lambert, writing about Adams's view of the best structure of government, argues, "Adams appealed not to truths lodged in various documents claiming divine revelation but to 'the minds of people.' For principles of republican government, he recommended not Jesus, Saint Paul, Augustine, Luther, Calvin, Wesley, the Mathers, or Edwards, but 'Sidney, Harrington, Locke, Milton, Nedham, Neville, Burnet, and Hoadly.'" Again, Lambert states, "Though relying upon *secular authorities* to structure the Constitution, many of the Founders did believe that religion, particularly Protestant Christianity, was essential for a law abiding nation."[2] Allegedly, then, Adams viewed Jesus and company as religious authorities and Sidney and company as secular authorities.

Concerning the Constitutional Convention in particular, Lambert writes, "During four months of deliberation, those big structural and functional issues concerning the distribution and balance of power predominated. Within the context of those broader discussions, religion rarely surfaced." Then, interacting with historian John Murrin, Lambert asserts that while "the delegates were not antireligion, they were humanists determined to create a *secular state* based on sound constitutional principles, such as the separation of powers and 'checks and balances,' designed to provide a republicanism that optimally protected citizens' property and rights."³ Thus Lambert and Murrin align themselves with Kramnick and Moore, authors of *The Godless Constitution*.

I offer two points of rebuttal to this prevailing narrative of the American founding. First, Lambert contends that Adams appealed to secular rather than religious authorities. His evidence comes from Adams's thoughts on government: "The foundation of every government is some principle or passion in the minds of the people. The noblest principles and most generous affections in our nature, then, have the fairest chance to support the noblest and most generous models of government. A man must be indifferent to the sneers of modern Englishmen, to mention in their company the names of Sidney, Harrington, Locke, Milton, Nedham, Neville, Burnet, and Hoadly."⁴

Just because Adams states that the foundation of government is some principle in people's minds does not mean that he was appealing to secular authorities. After all, secularism was non-existent at the time. Instead, Lambert is employing an anachronism, importing contemporary ideas into an earlier period in which Christian ideas and ideals were part and parcel of the intellectual milieu in which these thinkers operated. The authorities that Adams mentioned, whom Lambert identifies as "secular authorities," were not secularists. They often, though not exclusively, wrote on matters other than religion; they did not write as spokesmen for the church. However, they did not write as secularists. They operated from a theistic worldview, believing that that worldview had implications for public life. Therefore, Adams, in relying on these, was not thereby relying on secularist authorities.

Second, Lambert argues that religion barely surfaced at the Constitutional Convention. However, that description paints an inaccurate picture. Article one of the Constitution explains the process of a bill becoming law. In this description, it states, "If any Bill shall not be returned by the President within ten Days (Sundays excepted) after it shall have been presented to him, the Same shall be a Law, in like Manner as if he had signed it, unless the Congress by their Adjournment prevent its Return, in which Case it shall not be a Law."[5]

The parenthetical statement is not a throwaway phrase. It indicates the respect the framers showed for the Christian holy day in the very body of the Constitution. Indeed, it illustrates the way in which their entire culture was suffused with a Christian ethos. To Lambert's point, if the topic of religion barely surfaced at the Constitutional Convention, the reason is not that it was unimportant but that it was uncontroversial. The founders exempted Sundays precisely because they were operating from a broadly Christian framework. They were not constructing a secularist nation.

Was Thomas Jefferson a Secularist? Considering His Trinity of Heroes

Scholars make similar claims about the alleged secularism of Thomas Jefferson as they do about Adams. However, as in the case of Adams, these scholars are mistaken. Thomas Jefferson (1743–1826) is one of the most important founders of the United States. To appreciate his contributions to the American founding, we will first consider three of the figures who influenced him, namely Francis Bacon, Isaac Newton, and John Locke, to whom Edwin Gaustad points as Jefferson's "noble Trinity" and "trinity of English heroes."[6] As we will see, none of these figures were apostles of secularism. In fact, each identified himself as Christian.

Francis Bacon

Francis Bacon (1561–1626) was a major figure in shaping a new direction in epistemology. His philosophical method of induction had a profound impact on early modern thought, leading Stephen Gaukroger to describe his influence as "the transformation of early-modern philosophy." Bacon initiated a move from an emphasis on syllogistic logic to induction and the scientific method.[7] As a result of Bacon's forging this new methodological path, he is frequently referred to as the father of the inductive method or the father of the scientific method. Bacon's emphases led to new ways of thinking about education, knowledge, and science. For example, rather than stressing knowledge through study of the classics, Bacon emphasized knowledge by empirical observation. He believed that the knowledge gained by empirical observation could increase man's power over nature. He held that knowledge is power. He supported a state that funds experimental science.[8]

Bacon put the subject of epistemology on center stage. Epistemology deals with the questions: "How do you know?" and "How do you know that you know?" Or to say it another way: "How do you acquire knowledge?" and "How do you test knowledge for validity?" In his theory of knowledge, Bacon rejected an a priori (lit., "from what is before") epistemology, opting instead for an a posteriori (lit., "from what comes after") epistemology. Alfred Weber observed, "The conclusion which forced itself upon English common-sense was the necessity of abandoning a priori speculation and the abused syllogism in favor of observation and induction."[9]

What is the difference between a priori logic and deductive reasoning on the one hand and a posteriori logic and inductive reasoning on the other? Why was Bacon's shift significant? In a priori thinking, the person holds a conviction about an idea before he or she examines any evidence. For instance, what follows is an a priori conviction: Johnny believes that God exists and that He is sovereign, holy, just, and fair. He holds this conviction because his parents believe it and because the church has taught it to him.

However, upon going to college, his professor convinces him that the evidence does not support his conviction, and he begins to experience serious doubts and, eventually, outright rejects the existence of God. Or perhaps he concludes that the evidence does support his conviction. Either way, Johnny was guided by an a priori conviction, holding a conviction prior to examining evidence.

Deductive reasoning, which goes hand-in-hand with a priori logic, often takes the form of a syllogism. In syllogistic reasoning, a conclusion follows as a logical necessity if we grant the truth of the major and minor premises and if the construction of the syllogism is valid:

> Major premise: All men are mortal.
> Minor premise: Socrates is a man.
> Conclusion: Therefore, Socrates is mortal.

In accepting the premises as being true, the conclusion follows logically.

Let us illustrate with another syllogism:

> Major premise: All cows are purple.
> Minor premise: Bess is a cow.
> Conclusion: Therefore, Bess is purple.

The logic of this second syllogism is as good as that of the first. However, the conclusion is absurd. Deductive reasoning is not inherently problematic. The problem with the second syllogism is not with logic itself but with its major premise.

In contrast, a posteriori logic moves in the opposite direction of a priori logic. Rather than developing an idea before examining the evidence, the person studies the evidence first and then works toward a conclusion. "[G]enuine induction, the method of modern science, does not hurry on rapidly from a few isolated and uncertain phenomena to the most general axioms," explained Weber, "but patiently and carefully studies the facts, and ascends to the laws continually and gradually."[10] When developed into a scientific investigation, inductive reasoning can be lengthy. It offers probability but not guarantee. Therefore, an element of doubt always remains present that keeps the mind open for changes and modification. Negative results are always possibilities. Hypotheses may be rejected, and new hypotheses may be developed and pursued.

Bacon favored an inductive approach over a deductive one. Although he did not invent inductive reasoning, he developed it considerably as his philosophical method, making it of central importance.[11] As Weber explained, one "must at least concede to him the honor of having raised it from the low condition to which scholastic prejudice had consigned it, and of having insured it a legal existence, so to say, by the most eloquent plea ever made in its favor."[12]

Whether we work in philosophy, science, or theology, we are in great debt to Bacon. However, through the course of time, many who followed the inductive method in their pursuit of knowledge placed too much emphasis on empirical evidence and became overcome with doubt. For that reason, secularists have felt some affinity with Bacon and have claimed him. However, Bacon's thinking does not lead invariably to secularism or atheism. Responding to the idea that knowledge leads to atheism, Bacon displayed his commitment to Christian truth, saying, "And as for the conceit that too much knowledge should incline a man to atheism, a little or superficial knowledge of philosophy may incline the mind of man to atheism, but a further proceeding therein doth bring the mind back again to religion."[13]

In addition, Bacon pointed to God's two books: (1) His Word, or the Bible; and (2) His work, or the created order. "Let no man upon a weak conceit of sobriety or an ill-applied moderation think or maintain that a man can search too far, or be too well studied in the book of God's word, or in the book of God's works; divinity or philosophy," Bacon said, "but rather let men endeavour an endless progress or proficience in both; only let men beware that they apply both to charity, and not to swelling; to use, and not to ostentation; and again, that they do not unwisely mingle or confound these learnings together."[14]

Finally, he commented on the use of reason in the study of God's Word as revealed in the Bible. He pointed, first, to "the conception and apprehension of the mysteries of God to us revealed," and, second, to "the inferring and deriving of doctrine and direction thereupon. For the obtaining of the information, it resteth upon the true and sound interpretation of the Scriptures, which are the fountains of the water of life."[15]

In conclusion, Bacon stands as a major figure in the history of thought for his emphasis on inductive reasoning. He impacted many figures of the late eighteenth century, including the founders of the United States, such as Thomas Jefferson. However, as demonstrated from his writings, he was not an apostle of secularism and thus was not a secularist influence upon Jefferson and the founders.

Isaac Newton

Isaac Newton (1642–1727) is the second figure of Jefferson's trinity. Newton's publication *Principia* (1687) represented a revolutionary turning point in human knowledge. He provided humanity with the theory of gravity, as well as an approach to the study of the universe based on precise quantitative analysis and laws of nature. Even though Albert Einstein would advance our understanding of physics, Newton's laws are still foundational for the way we understand the universe and engage in basic mechanics and engineering

Writing about gravity, Newton said, "Gravitation towards the sun is made up out of the gravitations towards the several particles of which the body of the sun is composed." At the same time, he did not attempt to explain what he could not: "But I have not been able to discover the cause of those properties of gravity from phænomena, and I frame no hypotheses; for whatever is not deduced from the phænomena is to have no place in experimental philosophy." He concluded his remarks with, "To us it is enough that gravity does really exist, and acts according to the laws which we have explained."[16]

The reason Newton did not presume to explain that which he could not is that, like Bacon, he affirmed Christian belief. In 1713 Newton added the General Scholium to his *Principia*. In it, he wrote, "This most beautiful system of the sun, planets, and comets, could only proceed from the counsel and dominion of an intelligent and powerful Being." Newton's belief in God was not deistic: "This Being governs all things, not as the soul of the world, but as Lord over all; and on account of his dominion he is wont to be called Lord God παιτοκράτωρ, or Universal Ruler."[17] With these words, Newton speaks with great conviction. He continues, explaining his thinking and feeling about God, again with deep emotion:

> God is omnipresent not virtually only, but also substantially; for virtue cannot subsist without substance. In him are all things contained and moved; yet neither affects the other. As a blind man has no idea of colours, so have we no idea of the manner by which the all-wise God perceives and understands all things. He is utterly void of all body and bodily figure,

and can therefore neither be seen, nor heard, or touched; nor ought he to be worshiped under the representation of any corporeal thing. We have ideas of his attributes, but what the real substance of any thing is we know not. In bodies, we see only their figures and colours, we hear only the sounds, we touch only their outward surfaces, we smell only the smells, and taste the savours; but their inward substances are not to be known either by our senses, or by any reflex act of our minds: much less, then, have we any idea of the substance of God. We know him only by his most wise and excellent contrivances of things, and final cause: we admire him for his perfections; but we reverence and adore him on account of his dominion: for a god without dominion, providence, and final causes, is nothing else but Fate and Nature. Blind metaphysical necessity, which is certainly the same always and everywhere, could produce no variety of things. All that diversity of natural things which we find suited to different times and places could arise from nothing but the ideas and will of a Being necessarily existing. And thus much concerning God; to discourse of whom from the appearances of things, does certainly belong to Natural Philosophy.[18]

Clearly Newton left room for God in his vocation. He was not entirely orthodox in his beliefs, rejecting the doctrine of the Trinity for example. Even so, he considered himself to be a devout Christian, writing extensively on biblical and theological issues. One issue about which we can be certain, though, is that he was not a secularist. His conviction of the Creator God prohibits it. Like Bacon, Newton predated secularism, and, as was the case with Bacon, he did not influence the American founders in the cause of secularism.

John Locke

Early in my study of this subject, an avalanche of opinions seemed to support the position that the United States Constitution was founded on secularism. Many of these same sources indicate that John Locke (1632–1704) was a secularist. I soon discovered that these claims are anachronistic. The United States was not founded on secularism, and Locke was not a secularist. Over and over again, Locke demonstrated that he was at home with Scripture, evident for example in *A Letter Concerning Toleration* (1689) and *The Two Treatises of Government* (1690). As with Newton, Locke was not orthodox in his belief, but he viewed himself as a devout Christian and a true believer.

The Sincerity of Locke's Faith: Natural Law and Political Philosophy

Nevertheless, several scholars have challenged the sincerity of Locke's Christian faith. For instance, Leo Strauss attacked Locke's articulation of natural law. Strauss claimed that Locke did not "really believe in natural law at all," since his position contains contradictions. Strauss characterized Locke as believing that "the state of nature [is] a factual description of what the earliest society is like," thereby revealing "Locke's departure from Christian teachings." Additionally, it is "contrary to the Biblical account in Genesis and evidence that Locke's teaching is similar to that of Hobbes." Alex Tuckness explains, "[O]n the Straussian account Locke's apparently Christian statements are only a façade designed to conceal his essentially anti-Christian views."[19]

Kramnick and Moore make similar points, explaining that Locke's views on government are contrary to the historic-Christian and hence classical view: "In liberal Lockean social theory the function of government is purely negative." Men will it into existence "to serve merely as an umpire in the competitive scramble for wealth and property. Government only protects life, liberty, and property. It keeps peace and order in a voluntaristic, individualistic society."[20]

In classical social theory, government performed a positive function, not merely discouraging people from harm but encouraging people to good. "Classical social ethics are positive in the sense that they insist that it is not enough to merely refrain from injuring others; moral action requires an effort to improve others, encouraging the perfection of their souls," explains Garrett Sheldon. "As Aristotle maintains that happiness comes from possessing a virtuous character, individuals are obliged to cultivate the highest goodness in others."[21]

In contrast to that view, Kramnick and Moore posit that Locke believed that government does not fulfill a positive function: "In Locke's writings government no longer seeks to promote the good or moral life. No longer does government nurture and educate its subjects in the ways of virtue, or preside over the betterment or improvement of men and society. No longer does government defend and propagate moral and religious truths."[22]

Locke did not simply avoid the classical view, they hold, but he also subverted it: "These former noble purposes of the Christian state are undermined as liberal theory assigns it the very mundane and practical role of protecting private rights, especially property rights. Two thousand years of thinking about politics in the West is overturned in Locke's writings, as the liberal state repudiates the classical and Christian vision of politics."[23] Kramnick and Moore do not provide the source material they are using to draw these conclusions. Yet they summarize Locke's view of the function of government as "purely negative," opposite the Christian view of the function of government as positive. However, they are far too unequivocal in their interpretations.

English historian Peter Laslett held a less categorical position than that of Kramnick and Moore, contending that Locke viewed the government's function as both negative and positive:

> We may look at this position in another way and say that the passage from the state of nature to the state of society and government makes possible rule by consent, which is not possible in a state of nature. This is important because it lays stress on the fact that *in Locke's theory freedom is not merely the absence of restraint, it is positive.* It is something which is enlarged by the creation of society and government, which is given substance by the existence of laws, the laws of the law courts. It can be negatively defined, therefore, as being under no other legislative power but that established by consent in the commonwealth, *and positively* as the progressive elimination of the arbitrary from political and social regulation. He is *very insistent on this positive point*, resting it originally on the right to preservation, and on the individual's inability to dispose of himself. He develops it into the denial that government can be a personal matter, a matter of will: it must always be an institutional matter, a matter of law.[24]

Laslett then illustrated his position on Locke's view of government by the concept of freedom: "Law makes men free in the political arena, just as reason makes men free in the universe as a whole. It is progressively codified by a legislative brought into being by consent, it is expressive of and in harmony with the law of nature, which continues of course in society." Then, quoting Locke, he explained that law is "*the direction of a free and intelligent Agent* to his proper Interest', and its end is '*to preserve and enlarge Freedom*.'"[25]

Locke and Modern Empiricism

Kramnick and Moore also charge that Locke represented a change from the ethics of Christianity to the ethics of modern empiricism. However, that interpretation is too simple an explanation. Locke was not responsible for the shift from a Christian ethic to a modern one; instead, that blame lies at the feet of what I call epistemological atheism. An epistemological atheist claims to believe in God but does not form his or her worldview according to that belief. As a result, he or she thinks and lives like an atheist.

Undoubtedly, the development of a popular widespread epistemological atheism was in the making. However, it did not occur with Locke, who sought to inform his views with his beliefs. Thus Locke did not influence the American founders for the cause of secularism. Although Kramnick and Moore press their case about Locke too far, their broader point that changes were afoot, particularly concerning epistemology and modern ethics, is correct.

Modern empiricism, explains Garrett Sheldon, holds that people gain knowledge solely through "individual sensory perception." Empiricism precipitated significant changes for epistemology and ethics. "For, if no unified truth can emerge from the diversity of perceptions, no one is justified in prescribing moral lessons to others; the autonomous perception and judgment of the individual must be respected. No objective standards can exist above subjective choice, given such epistemological relativism." The sole exception is "with regard to material harm and loss, or violations of individuals' rights and freedom. Therefore, liberal social ethics are confined to restraining and punishing violence and theft (the state *qua* police), but otherwise leaving individuals free to their own devices."[26]

Eugenie Scott, an avowed evolutionist, is frank in addressing the relationship of modern epistemology to supernatural explanations, "By definition, science cannot consider supernatural explanations: if there is an omnipotent deity, there is no way that a scientist can exclude or include it in research design." She refers to this position as "methodological materialism." Accordingly, by "excluding the supernatural from our scientific turf, we are eliminating the possibility of proclaiming, via epistemology of science, that there is no supernatural."[27] Conclusions about God and the supernatural are based ultimately in philosophical and not scientific evidences.

Scott illustrates the importance of modern epistemology. We cannot get far in understanding what people are saying if we do not understand where they are coming from, and we have no knowledge where they are coming from if we do not understand their approach to epistemology. To understand people, we must know something of their epistemology. Just because Enlightenment history was moving epistemology in the direction of modern empiricism does not mean that all of its figures were insincere in their supernatural beliefs. With reference to Locke, we must understand his epistemology.

We must not misconstrue Locke's common designation as the father of the Enlightenment or father of modern empiricism. Although he emphasized inductive reasoning and empirical research, he was not an absolute empiricist. Absolute empiricism is rooted in an empirical epistemology that looks only to natural causes. In contrast, Locke did not limit himself either to naturalism or to materialism. He also believed in supernatural causes. For example, in *An Essay Concerning Human Understanding*, he wrote, "We have the ideas but of three sorts of substances: 1. God. 2. Finite intelligences. 3. Bodies."[28]

Locke and Innate Knowledge

Locke is perhaps best known for his articulation of the tabula rasa or "blank slate." Although he popularized the concept, he did not formulate it. Aristotle first expressed the concept in ancient Greece, and Thomas Aquinas reintroduced it into the Western world. By *tabula rasa*, Locke meant that the human mind is empty until it is filled with external sense impressions. Alex Rosenberg characterized Locke's position by saying, "Nothing is in the mind that was not first in the senses."[29] Locke thus forthrightly denied the concept of innate knowledge. All knowledge is learned knowledge. He wrote, regarding "how we come by any knowledge, sufficient to prove it not innate,"

> It is an established opinion amongst some men, that there are in the understanding certain innate principles; some primary notions, κοιναὶ ἔννοιαι, characters, as it were stamped upon the mind of man; which the soul receives in its very first being, and brings into the world with it. It would be sufficient to convince unprejudiced readers of the falseness of this supposition, if I should only show how men, barely by the use of their natural faculties, may attain to all the knowledge they have, without the help of any innate impressions; and may arrive at certainty, without any such original notions or principles.[30]

Although Locke's wording suggests that babies are born with a blank tablet, he nevertheless suggested that the unborn baby may learn something in the womb: "Children, though they may have ideas in the womb, have none innate. Therefore I doubt not but children, by the exercise of their senses about objects that affect them in the womb, receive some few ideas before they are born."[31] Locke's observation resulted from his work as a physician.

Locke, Natural Law, and Political Philosophy

Even so, Locke believed in a divine design to nature. He believed that a natural law is woven into the fabric of reality. God designed each individual so that he or she is a moral and rational creature. As a result, people can discern some basic understanding of life by observation and experience. Locke developed much of his political philosophy from this broader belief in natural law. "Perhaps the most central concept in Locke's political philosophy," Tuckness writes, "is his theory of natural law and natural rights."[32] Natural law stands in contrast to positive law. Natural law refers to laws that are written into nature and can be discerned through reflection and common sense. Positive law refers to laws that are written by government leaders. Positive law that reflects natural law is necessary for the promotion of a healthy society.

Locke believed that humankind moves from a state of nature to a state that includes a properly organized, functioning government in which men and women surrender some of their rights to those who govern. Subjects or citizens could reassert their forfeited rights if government leaders sufficiently abuse their role. In these circumstances, the people may rise up and overthrow the government, putting those persons back into a state of nature, after which they negotiate a new government. This Lockean political philosophy encouraged the founding fathers of the United States to cast off the government of King George III, who, they judged, had become a tyrant.

Locke's View of the Certainty of Knowledge of God

In addition, Locke affirmed the certainty of the knowledge of God:

1. *We are capable of knowing certainly that there is a God.* Though God has given us no innate ideas of himself; though he

has stamped no original characters on our minds, wherein we may read his being; yet having furnished us with those faculties our minds are endowed with, he hath not left himself without witness: since we have sense, perception, and reason, and cannot want a clear proof of him, as long as we carry ourselves about us. But, though this be the most obvious truth that reason discovers, and *though its evidence be (if I mistake not) equal to mathematical certainty*: yet it requires thought and attention....

2. For man knows that he himself exists. If anyone pretends to be so sceptical as to deny his own existence, (for really to doubt of it is manifestly impossible), let him for me enjoy his beloved happiness of being nothing, until hunger or some other pain convince him of the contrary....

3. He knows also that nothing cannot produce a being; therefore something must have existed from eternity....

4. This eternal source, then, of all being must also be the source and original of all power; and so this eternal Being must be also the most powerful....

5. And most knowing. Again, a man finds in himself perception and knowledge. We have then got one step further; and we are certain now that *there is not only some being, but some knowing, intelligent being in the world*....

6. And therefore God. Thus, from the consideration of ourselves, and what we infallibly find in our own constitutions, *our reason leads us to the knowledge of this certain and evident truth,—That there is an eternal, most powerful, and most knowing Being; which whether any one will please to call God, it matters not*.[33]

Although different scholars approach the question of God's existence in different ways, the point is that Locke was neither an atheist nor a secularist. On at least one occasion in *A Letter Concerning Toleration*, Locke used the term *secular*: "In the variety and contradiction of opinions in religion, wherein the princes of the world are as much divided as in their secular interests, the narrow way would be much straitened."[34] However, Locke was obviously not promoting secularism but rather explaining that princes vary on civil or temporal concerns as much as they do over religious concerns.

Conclusion

A survey of Jefferson's trinity of heroes demonstrates that neither Bacon nor Newton nor Locke were apostles of secularism. That recognition means they did not influence Jefferson with a creed of secularism. The case is similar with respect to Adams, whose influences were not secularists either. Secularism influenced neither Adams nor Jefferson. Each of these figures played pivotal roles in the formation of the United States of America, and the claim that they established a secularist nation, or even intended to do so, rests on a weak foundation.

CHAPTER THREE

SECULARISM, THOMAS JEFFERSON, AND HIS INTERPRETERS

SUSAN JACOBY AND AMERICAN SECULARISM

As we have considered, secularism has its origin in the 1850s in Great Britain. However, discerning its origin in the United States is challenging. Although Susan Jacoby's *Freethinkers: A History of American Secularism* purports to answer the question in its subtitle, it does not. She begins her book by explaining, "Throughout this book, I have taken the liberty of using the words *secularism* and *secularist*—even though the latter was not in common usage until the second half of the nineteenth century—to denote a concept of public good based on human reason and human rights rather than divine authority."[1] The phrase above separated by dashes implies that the term *secularism* was in common usage prior to the latter half of the nineteenth century. However, as we have seen, neither the term *secularist* nor *secularism* was in common usage during this time.

Jacoby goes on to write, "The term [*secularism*] first appeared in print in 1851 and soon took on a political as well as a philosophical meaning, distinguishing the secular (a much older word than *secularist*) functions of government from the domain of religion." She then suggests a connection between the older word *civil* and the newer word *secularist*, claiming they refer to the same disposition: "In eighteenth-century political discourse, the adjective *civil* was the closest equivalent of *secularist*, and many of the founders used the word to refer to the public, nonreligious sphere of government, as distinct from the private role of religion."[2]

However, as previously established, the older terms *civil* or *secular* and the newer term *secularism* do not function in a one-to-one correspondence. Furthermore, Jacoby does not give any attention to the fact that the secularist movement did not begin in the United States but rather in Great Britain. Although the book details the history of American secularism, it should have dealt with secularism's British origins. Jacoby's approach is like writing a history of the United States but failing to mention its British and European roots.

The worldview of secularism was nonexistent in either name or spirit when the founders ratified the Constitution and Bill of Rights. Noah Feldman explains, "Although today's secularists like to claim those framers who believed in a watchmaker God as their forebears, the eighteenth century knew no phenomenon by the name of 'secularism.'"[3] With respect to Jacoby in particular, he continues, "Jacoby does not identify secularism with Darwinian influence; indeed, she does not even mention Holyoake. Her approach—anachronistic, in my view—is to identify what I have called secularism as an outgrowth of earlier American religious skepticism, thus projecting secularism backward onto Thomas Paine, Jefferson, and others of the framing generation." Her view is not only anachronistic but also hardly representative of the general populace of that time. Feldman explains, "Nonetheless, her focus is on elites, even if she does not emphasize the fact."[4]

Again, one of the most popular American founders for secularists like Jacoby is Thomas Jefferson. They claim that he was a secularist, but that is not the case. For one, his primary influences, Bacon, Newton, and Locke, failed to provide the philosophical foundations for that position. Also, Jefferson himself did not believe in or affirm secularism's teachings.

For example, in the Declaration of Independence, Jefferson made strong assertions about the laws of nature, nature's God, self-evident truths, the Creator, inalienable rights, a Supreme Judge of the world, and divine providence. After making reference to "the separate and equal station to which the Laws of Nature and of Nature's God entitle" a people dissolving the political bonds that have connected them to another, Jefferson wrote, "We hold these truths to be self-evident, that all men are created equal, that they are endowed by their Creator with certain unalienable Rights, that among these are Life, Liberty and the pursuit of Happiness." In the closing paragraph, he made appeal "to the Supreme Judge of the world for the rectitude of our intentions," and in the closing sentence, "And for the support of this Declaration, with a firm reliance on the protection of Divine Providence, we mutually pledge to each other our Lives, our Fortunes, and our Honor."[5]

Did Jefferson include this language about divinity for the sake of political expediency? Did he incorporate it because he would have been unable to get the Declaration passed without it? I believe that Jefferson made references to the divine because he believed they are true and reflect the values of the people for whom he wrote.

Lenni Brenner and the (Supposed) Secular Writings of Jefferson and Madison

Like Jacoby, Lenni Brenner makes claims about the supposed secular writings of the founders, specifically Jefferson and Madison, and the secular nature of the founding. Brenner is the editor of a volume of writings by founders Thomas Jefferson and James Madison entitled *Jefferson and Madison on Separation of Church and State: Writings on Religion and Secularism*. Even though Holyoake did not coin the term *secularism* until 1846 or found the British Secular Movement until 1851–1852, is Brenner correct? Even if Jefferson or Madison did not refer to secularism by name, perhaps they made reference to it conceptually or wrote about a secular government.

The back cover of Brenner's volume claims to include the "most complete collection of these forefathers's writings on religion and secularism."[6] However, study demonstrates that neither Jefferson nor Madison wrote about the concept of secularism. Jefferson does not use the term *secular* or any of its derivatives at any point in this collection. Madison makes but one passing reference to "secular," which regards, not secularism, but the civil government in distinction from ecclesiastical government: "Torrents of blood have been spilt in the old world, by vain attempts of the *secular arm* to extinguish Religious discord, by proscribing all difference in Religious opinions."[7] Thus, in a collection of more than four hundred pages subtitled *Writings on Religion and Secularism*, not one mention is given to anything resembling secularism.

If Not A Secularist, What Was Jefferson?

If Jefferson was not a secularist, what was he? We will begin answering this question by noting the inscriptions on the Jefferson Memorial Monument:

> Inscription under the Dome: "I have sworn upon the altar of god eternal hostility against every form of tyranny over the mind of man."

Panel One: "We hold these truths to be self-evident: that all men are created equal, that they are endowed by their Creator with certain inalienable rights, among these are life, liberty, and the pursuit of happiness, that to secure these rights governments are instituted among men. We ... solemnly publish and declare, that these colonies are and of right ought to be free and independent states.... And for the support of this declaration, with a firm reliance on the protection of divine providence, we mutually pledge our lives, our fortunes, and our sacred honor."

Panel Two: "Almighty God hath created the mind free. All attempts to influence it by temporal punishments or burthens ... are a departure from the plan of the Holy Author of our religion ... No man shall be compelled to frequent or support any religious worship or ministry or shall otherwise suffer on account of his religious opinions or belief, but all men shall be free to profess and by argument to maintain, their opinions in matters of religion. I know but one code of morality for men whether acting singly or collectively."

Panel Three: "God who gave us life gave us liberty. Can the liberties of a nation be secure when we have removed a conviction that these liberties are the gift of God? Indeed I tremble for my country when I reflect that God is just, that his justice cannot sleep forever. Commerce between master and slave is despotism. Nothing is more certainly written in the book of fate than these people are to be free. Establish the law for educating the common people. This it is the business of the state to effect and on a general plan."

Panel Four: "I am not an advocate for frequent changes in laws and constitutions, but laws and institutions must go hand in hand with progress of the human mind. As that becomes more developed, more enlightened, as new discoveries are made, new truths are discovered and manners and opinions change, with the change of circumstances, institutions must advance also to keep pace with the times. We might as well require a man to wear still the coat which fitted him when he was a boy as civilized society to remain ever under the regimen of their barbarous ancestors."[8]

However we classify Jefferson, these selections demonstrate that he was not a secularist.

If I were to rest my case here, no jury would convict Thomas Jefferson of being guilty of secularism. Throughout this book, one of my aims will be to chart Jefferson's role in the legal understanding of the relationship between church and state, or religion and government. Since many secularists have attempted to enlist Jefferson as one of their own, I will spend significant time establishing my case that Jefferson was, in no sense of the word, a secularist. I am not thereby suggesting he was an orthodox Christian; for example, he emphatically rejected the doctrine of the Trinity. My point is that neither he nor the founders were secularists and that the United States was not founded as a secularist nation.

Instead, Jefferson was a deeply religious person. Gaustad explains,

> Jefferson, like many of those whom he read as a youth, had no trouble accepting the argument for God's existence from the magnificent design evident in his creation. It was impossible, he wrote to John Adams, "for the human mind not to perceive and feel a conviction of design, consummate skill, and indefinite power in every atom of its composition." This was the case

whether one contemplated the heavens above ("the movement of the heavenly bodies, so exactly held in their course by the balance of centrifugal and centripetal forces") or the earth below ("the structure of our earth itself, with its distribution of lands, waters, and atmosphere, animal and vegetable bodies . . . insects as mere atoms of life, yet as perfectly organized as man or mammoth"). To a close observer of Nature, which Jefferson surely was, the conclusion could not be denied: we see "evident proofs of the necessity of a supernatural power to maintain the universe in its course and order."[9]

Jefferson was not only a religious person but also one of the most God-conscious presidents in United States history. Gaustad points to four evidences for this proposition: "First, Thomas Jefferson was the most self-consciously theological of all American presidents. Second, he dedicated himself more deliberately and diligently to the reform of religion than any other president." Gaustad then shifts to some external considerations: "Third, in partnership with James Madison, he did more to root liberty firmly in the American tradition than any predecessor or successor in the White House. And fourth, in succeeding centuries, no other president has been appealed to more frequently in religious matters than Jefferson."[10]

Perhaps Jefferson was a Deist or Unitarian. However, even the assumption of those theological views does not determine the answer to the question of whether a person would advocate secularism in public life, or how devoutly religious they would be. It is anachronistic to assume that either Deists or Unitarians would advocate secularism or would not be strongly religious.

Also, even if those designations are accurate in regard to Jefferson, dictionary definitions of Deism and Unitarianism do not offer a correct view of Jefferson's theology. As Gaustad reminds us, "Jefferson did not hold that God created the world and then retired from the scene: rather, he believed that God continued to create and sustain the world movement by movement." As an example of that belief, Jefferson pointed to the phenomenon of gravity, describing it as "God's law for the orderly operation of matter, one of the means by which he brought order out of chaos. And the restoration of order goes on, as Jefferson pointed out, to fill in the gaps when stars disappear or a species of animal threatens to become extinct."[11]

As another example of God's work in this world, Jefferson pointed to the discovery of self-evident truths through reason. These "required no argumentation, no Aristotelian syllogism, no Platonic presupposition, no authority whatsoever except Reason to establish their validity. And these truths, which Jefferson first referred to as 'sacred and undeniable,' came, like creation itself, fresh from the hand of God." According to Jefferson, God "built" these self-evident truths "into the very structure of the universe as surely as Newton's law of gravity was built in: they were 'inherent,' as Jefferson's draft stated. Life, liberty, and the pursuit of happiness were, therefore, beyond the reach of mere governments: these rights were decreed, sustained, and authenticated by none other than Nature's God."[12] Gaustad continues:

> Even more than the word "Reason," the word "Nature" proved adaptable, irresistible, and eminently useful. In the area of moral philosophy, for example, Jefferson advised his nephew, in brief, to forget formal instruction and consult Nature. "I think it lost time," Jefferson declared, "to attend lectures in this branch. If men and women needed a college education to know what morality was all about, what a

calamity that would be for the human race. And what "a pitiful bungler" God would be "if he had made the rules of moral conduct a matter of science." If God created human beings as social creatures, and surely he did, then of necessity he had to endow those creatures with a sense of right and wrong. "This sense is as much a part of [human] nature as the sense of hearing, seeing, feeling; it is the true foundation of morality." God gave to all persons this "moral sense, or conscience, as much a part of man as his leg or arm."

The moral sense can be strengthened through exercise, to be sure, or atrophied through disuse, just as an arm or leg can be. But the gift of conscience was not limited to an elite, to a privileged class, and certainly to moral philosophers. "State a moral case to a ploughman and a professor. The former will decide it as well, and often better than the latter, because he had not been led astray by artificial rules."[13]

Jefferson not only espoused religious views in his private life but also brought them to bear in his public life. For example, he began the Virginia Statute for Religious Freedom by saying, "Almighty God hath created the mind free." In it, he also referred to God as the "holy author of our religion" and "Lord both of body and mind."[14] Gaustad demonstrates the importance of the Virginia Statute, saying, "These words, one Republican concluded, were 'worth a thousand commentaries.'"[15] Jefferson thus placed his view of religious freedom on a theological foundation. Additionally, in his *Notes*, he wrote, "Can the liberties of a nation be thought secure, when we have removed their only firm basis, a conviction in the minds of the people, that these liberties are a gift of God?"[16]

As evident from his words, Jefferson held an exalted view of reason. Although he believed in the supernatural, he was not fond of concepts such as faith and mystery. To him, faith amounted to mystery, which was an "antonym" to reason. "The person who gave up Reason 'has no remaining guard against absurdities the most monstrous, and like a ship without rudder is the sport of every wind.' In human beings of this ilk, 'gullibility which they called faith,' wrote Jefferson in 1822, 'takes the helm from the hand of reason and the mind becomes a 'wreck.'"[17]

For Jefferson, reason is a safeguard against "propaganda": "Reason and common sense remained the tests by which to judge all things, including the propaganda coming from all the denominations and sects. And Reason tells us, as does Jesus, that we are to look at deeds more than words, at morals more than mysteries." For Jefferson, proper religion is summarized in the two great commandments: "Hear the sum of all religion 'as expressed by its best preacher,' Jefferson urged: 'fear God and love thy neighbor.' This creed contained no mystery and required no explanation—'but this won't do. It gives no scope to make dupes; priests could not live by it.'"[18]

For Jefferson, defining religion in this manner meant giving emphasis to mankind's supposed instinct for morality: "Eradicate mystery and elevate morality; dispose of any and all doctrine that would imply that men and women were not free to be moral; and recognize or, if necessary, unearth that bright gem of moral instinct." What happens if human instinct is insufficient? "If the instinct required guidance or substance, the moral code of Jesus stood ready to fill the need. Jefferson, who thought this element of religious reform to be the most significant, both socially and personally, gave it every possible emphasis."[19]

Still, even with Jefferson's hostility to faith and mystery, he was neither an atheist nor an agnostic:

He accepted, for example, the popular cosmological argument as sufficient proof of a divine being. In examining "all this design, cause and effect" evident in Nature, he wrote, one could not fail to detect "a fabricator of things from matter and motion." The Creator also regulates and preserves, and even regenerates some of the motion and matter into new forms. For as we noted earlier, Jefferson did not believe his Creator retired from the scene once the original act of creation had passed. One might well describe him as a "warm deist," or perhaps a Newtonian deist, affirming that God's molding genius was ever active, ever present. He was not in any sense an aloof, passionless deist. As Jefferson wrote in detail and even in exultation to John Adams in 1823, "it is impossible for the human mind," when contemplating the vast universe, "not to perceive and feel a conviction of design, consummate skill, and infinite power in every atom of its composition."[20]

Finally, with respect to Jefferson's views on the place of religion in public education, he "invoked the blessings of a divine providence." What about the wall of separation between church and state? We will consider this question in greater detail in subsequent chapters. For now, Gaustad's explanation is helpful: "The president had his own individual 'wall': that erected between private religion, which he would not touch in any official capacity, and public religion, which he would endorse and support." Practically, this remark means that Jefferson enthusiastically supported public religion. Thus, in the conclusion of his Second Inaugural Address (1805), he "called for 'the favor of that Being in whose hands we are, who led our fathers, as Israel of old, from their native land and planted them in a country flowing with all the necessaries and comforts of life.'"[21]

Conclusion

Those claiming that Jefferson was a secularist have not read the evidence accurately. In some cases, they have read it anachronistically. He is not a candidate for secularism. For one, he predates the timeline of secularism. However, even assuming that its forebear went under the auspices of another name, such as agnostic or atheist, that does not work either. While he was not an orthodox Christian, he nevertheless believed in the supernatural, as well as in its place in the public square.

PART II

The Supreme Court: Introducing the Strict Separation of Church and State

CHAPTER FOUR

Reviewing *Everson*: The First Amendment

In part one, I reviewed the origins of secularism and considered its influence upon the thinking of John Adams and Thomas Jefferson. George Jacob Holyoake coined the term *secularism* in 1846 and founded the British Secular Movement in 1851–1852. In the sixteenth century, Martin Luther had spoken of secular governments, secular rulers, and secular swords. In the seventeenth century, John Locke had made reference to the secular interest. However, none of these usages had anything to do with secularism. In the eighteenth century, American founders occasionally used the term as well. But, like Luther and Locke, their use of the term did not carry the meaning of secularism. Similarly, other examples of people using the term *secular* occur in the literature preceding Holyoake. However, we may distinguish the way that they employed the term, which did not refer to secularism, from subsequent usage of the term after Holyoake, which would increasingly refer to secularism.

In time some jurists would begin to interpret the founding of the United States through a secularist lens, embedding that interpretation into the constitutional structure of the nation. As we will see, though, that interpretation was not original to the founding, and it was not original to Jefferson, whose influence looms large for an American vision of the proper relationship between church and state. As we work our way into part three of this book, I will evaluate Jefferson's vision for church-state relations. But prior to doing so, I will consider, in part two, the enshrinement of a secularist reading of the founding and of Jefferson, specifically by analyzing two key Supreme Court decisions: *Everson v. Board of Education* (1947) and *McCollum v. Board of Education* (1948).

"A WALL OF SEPARATION BETWEEN CHURCH AND STATE"

Writing for the dissent in *Everson*, Justice Wiley Rutledge remarked, "This case forces us to determine squarely for the first time what was 'an establishment of religion' in the First Amendment's conception."[1] Whether or not Justice Rutledge was correct in his assessment, *Everson* stands as a case of paramount importance in a discussion of church-state relations in the United States. *Everson* was a 5–4 decision, with Justices Hugo Black, Fred M. Vinson, Stanley F. Reed, William O. Douglas, and Frank Murphy in the majority, and Justices Robert Jackson, Felix Frankfurter, Wiley B. Rutledge, and Howard Burton in the dissent. Justice Black wrote the majority opinion, and both Justices Jackson and Rutledge wrote dissenting opinions.

The background facts about this case show that a "New Jersey statute authorize[d] its local school districts to make rules and contracts for the transportation of children to and from schools." Consequently, the local school district "authorized reimbursement to parents of money expended by them for the bus transportation of their children on regular busses operated by the public transportation system," including "payment of transportation of some children in the community to Catholic parochial schools. These church schools give their students, in addition to secular education, regular religious instruction conforming to the religious tenets and modes of worship of the Catholic Faith. The superintendent of these schools is a Catholic priest." However, a New Jersey taxpayer filed a lawsuit against a school district, challenging the right of its board "to reimburse parents of parochial school students."[2]

Before tracing Black's analysis, I will consider his conclusion. By understanding where he arrived, we can better understand his path in getting there. Black sized up the heart of the case in his closing comments: "This Court has said that parents may, in the discharge of their duty under state compulsory education laws, send their children to a religious rather than a public school if the school meets *the secular educational requirements which the state has power to impose.*"[3] After explaining how New Jersey's parochial schools met the state's requirements, Black concluded the case with these famous words: "The First Amendment has erected a wall between church and state. That wall must be kept high and impregnable. We could not approve the slightest breach. New Jersey has not breached it here."[4]

We do not see the full impact of this case in the decision. *Everson* represented a victory for the township of Ewing's board of education to reimburse bus fare money to parents who used public transportation to send their children to Catholic parochial schools. However, it also represented a significant clue into the Supreme Court's interpretation of the First Amendment. Regarding the relationship between the church and state, Black drew a definite line: "We could not approve the slightest breach." Black's phrase demonstrates that the Court was heading toward a separationist interpretation of the First Amendment. The

Court's direction did not bode well for the more historic reading of church-state accommodation, which is more reflective of the intentions of the founders and of Jefferson.

Background to the First Amendment: Religious Establishment, Coercion, and Persecution (Justice Black)

Justice Black does not disregard the early history of the United States in *Everson*, although he paints only part of the picture. However, this chapter will not consider that part of the story he does not present, because its aim is to introduce readers specifically to *Everson* in order to present contemporary orthodoxy concerning church-state relations before considering the historic approach to the question in subsequent chapters. Additionally, owing to the significance of this case, we will consider its very words to a much greater degree than we might otherwise would have.

Black begins the story by introducing the early settlers, the establishment of religion, and the persecution that resulted from the failure to follow the state-sanctioned church: "A large proportion of the early settlers of this country came here from Europe to escape the bondage of laws which compelled them to support and attend government favored churches." By "government favored churches," he is referring to state-sponsored churches, namely the establishment of religion. Black then mentions the religious wars that occurred throughout Europe, saying, "The centuries immediately before and contemporaneous with the colonization of America had been filled with turmoil, civil strife, and persecutions, generated in large part by established sects determined to maintain their absolute political and religious supremacy."[5]

Religious establishment and persecution was not limited to any one place or to any one religious group but, regrettably, characterized any number of groups: "With the power of government supporting them, at various times and places, Catholics had persecuted Protestants, Protestants had persecuted Catholics, Protestant sects had persecuted other Protestant sects, Catholics of one shade of belief had persecuted Catholics of another shade of belief, and all of these had from time to time persecuted Jews."[6] In other words, these governments compelled religious exercise rather than encouraging its free exercise; they promoted religious coercion rather than religious liberty.

Next, Black turns to specific examples of the types of persecution that these groups employed against those who would not follow the religious establishment: "In efforts to force loyalty to whatever religious group happened to be on top and in league with the government of a particular time and place, men and women had been fined, cast in jail, cruelly tortured, and killed." He also indicates examples of the offenses that garnered these types of punishments, explaining: "Among the offenses for which these punishments had been inflicted were such things as speaking disrespectfully of the views of ministers of government-established churches, nonattendance at those churches, expressions of non-belief in their doctrines, and failure to pay taxes and tithes to support them."[7]

Regrettably, the early settlers to the colonies brought these norms with them: "These practices of the old world were transplanted to and began to thrive in the soil of the new America." Notwithstanding the fact that they had suffered as a result of these policies, they established similar policies in the colonies: "The very charters granted by the English Crown to the individuals and companies designated to make the laws which would control the destinies of the colonials authorized these individuals and companies to erect religious establishments which all, whether believers or non-believers, would be required to support and attend."[8]

The early settlers not only followed suit with regard to establishment but also did the same with regard to persecutions: "An exercise of this authority was accompanied by a repetition of many of the old world practices and persecutions," especially toward Roman Catholics, Quakers, and Baptists: "[M]en and women of varied faiths who happened to be in a minority in a particular locality were persecuted because they steadfastly persisted in worshipping God only as their own consciences dictated."[9]

Regardless, Black paints a grim picture of religious establishment and religious coercion. He explains that states imposed taxes on dissenters "to support government-sponsored churches," specifically "to pay ministers' salaries and to build and maintain churches and church property," which "aroused" the "indignation" of "freedom-loving colonials." He then says that these ministers "preached inflammatory sermons designed to strengthen and consolidate the established faith by generating a burning hatred against dissenters" and that these commonplace practices "shock[ed] the freedom-loving colonials into a feeling of abhorrence."[10] Black's tone and verbiage, particularly his characterization of *indignation, inflammatory sermons, burning hatred,* and *abhorrence,* signal his eventual articulation of the strict separation of church and state, as opposed to the reasonable accommodation of church and state.

Further Background to the First Amendment: Henry, Madison, and Jefferson

In order to provide support for the claim that the state taxed dissenters to support religious establishment, Justice Black cites Patrick Henry's Bill Establishing a Provision for Teachers of the Christian Religion (1784). The bill proposed that taxes help support teachers of Christianity. Henry's bill would serve as a foil for three other key documents with which the majority and dissenting opinions of *Everson* would interact: (1) Memorial and Remonstrance against Religious Assessments (1785) by James Madison; (2) Virginia Statute for Establishing Religious Freedom (1786) by Thomas Jefferson; and (3) Letter to the Danbury Baptist Association of Connecticut (1802) by Thomas Jefferson. Practically no one disagrees about these documents' relative importance, but, as we will see, much disagreement emerges regarding their relative meanings.

The discussion that would emerge from these documents during the period of the founding precipitated the ratification of the First Amendment and significantly shaped the American understanding of church-state relations. In part three of this book, I will consider these documents in greater detail. However, I mention them now because, as we will see, *Everson* interacts with them. The point, though, is that *Everson's* interpretation of these documents differs considerably from the historic understanding. Whereas *Everson* interpreted them to stand for the strict separation of church and state, which accords with a secularist interpretation of the American founding, the founders promoted a vision of the reasonable accommodation of church and state.

Black continues, explaining that this background of religious establishment, coercion, and persecution set the stage for the ratification of the First Amendment, which reads, "Congress shall make no law respecting the establishment of religion, or prohibiting the free exercise thereof."[11] He points to the wide support at the founding for non-establishment and free exercise, saying, "No one locality and no one group throughout the Colonies can rightly be given entire credit for having aroused the sentiment that culminated in adoption of the Bill of Rights' provisions embracing religious liberty."[12]

Still, Black highlights the importance of Virginia: "The people there, as elsewhere, reached the conviction that individual religious liberty could be achieved best under a government which was stripped of all power to tax, to support, or otherwise to assist any or all religions, or to interfere with the beliefs of any religious individual or group." Of particular significance from Virginia were Madison and Jefferson; these men, says Black, "led the fight" against the Virginia legislature's attempting "to renew Virginia's tax levy for the support of the established church."[13]

In the Remonstrance, Madison argued against provisions that would tax the population to support religious establishment. Black summarizes Madison's argument with four points: "In it, he eloquently argued [1] that a true religion did not need the support of law; [2] that no person, either believer or non-believer, should be taxed to support a religious institution of any kind; [3] that the best interest of a society required that the minds of men always be wholly free; and [4] that cruel persecutions were the inevitable result of government-established religions."[14]

Similarly, Jefferson argued against tax levies for religious establishment in his Virginia Statute for Religious Freedom, which reads:

> *Almighty God hath created the mind free*; that all attempts to influence it by temporal punishments, or burthens, or by civil incapacitations, tend only to beget habits of hypocrisy and meanness, and are a departure from the plan of the *Holy author of our religion who being Lord both of body and mind*, yet chose not to propagate it by coercions on either . . . ; that to compel a man to furnish contributions of money for the propagation of opinions which he disbelieves, is sinful and tyrannical; that even the forcing him to support this or that teacher of his own

religious persuasion, is depriving him of the comfortable liberty of giving his contributions to the particular pastor, whose morals he would make his pattern. . . . That no man shall be compelled to frequent or support any religious worship, place, or ministry whatsoever, nor shall be enforced, restrained, molested, or burthened, in his body or goods, nor shall otherwise suffer on account of his religious opinions or belief.[15]

Jefferson had first written this bill in 1777. The Virginia General Assembly debated its ratification in 1779 but did not adopt it at that time, partly because of Patrick Henry's strong opposition to it. Madison then reintroduced Jefferson's bill to the Assembly in 1785, which ratified it in 1786; at the time, Jefferson served as Minister Plenipotentiary in France.

In later chapters, I will analyze Jefferson's Virginia Statute at length, as well as Madison's Remonstrance, investigating their original meanings to see whether they comport with a secularist interpretation. For the time being, I have wanted to introduce some of its language to the reader.

The reason that Black spent such a considerable amount of time with these documents in his majority opinion in *Everson* is the great significance they hold in the background to the ratification of the First Amendment: "This Court has previously recognized that the provisions of the First Amendment, in the drafting and adoption of which Madison and Jefferson played such leading roles, had the same objective and were intended to provide the same protection against governmental intrusion on religious liberty as the Virginia statute."[16] Although Black was correct in his assessment of these documents' importance, he was incorrect in his interpretation. As we will see, Black interpreted these documents, as well as the First Amendment, according to an understanding of the strict separation of church and state. However, historical analysis will demonstrate that reasonable accommodation better fits the vision of the founders.

Incorporating the First Amendment Against the States

The background material to the First Amendment demonstrates that its Establishment Clause stands against the proposition of tax-supported religious establishments. However, readers will notice that the First Amendment, on its face, applies only to the federal government, not to state governments. It begins with "Congress shall," not "State governments shall." Readers may, therefore, question what relevance *Everson*, which regards a state statute (New Jersey), has for the First Amendment.

From the founding until the mid-twentieth century, the First Amendment, including its religion clauses, as well as the Bill of Rights, applied only to the federal government and not to state governments. To illustrate, in *Permoli v. Municipality No. 1 of City of New Orleans* (1845), Justice John Catron made the following observation: "The Constitution makes no provision for protecting the citizens of the respective states in their religious liberties; this is left to the state constitutions and laws: nor is there any inhibition imposed by the Constitution of the United States in this respect on the states."[17]

However, the historic orthodoxy began to change with the adoption of the Fourteenth Amendment in 1868, which reads, "No State shall make or enforce any law which shall abridge the privileges or immunities of citizens of the United States; nor shall any State deprive any person of life, liberty, or property, without due process of law; nor deny to any person within its jurisdiction the equal protection of the laws."[18] These clauses have given rise to the legal doctrine of incorporation, which means that the Supreme Court began to incorporate, or to apply, these clauses to the states as they had to the federal government. As Black explained in *Everson*, "Prior to the adoption of the Fourteenth Amendment, the First Amendment did not apply as a restraint against the states. Most of them did soon provide similar constitutional protections for religious liberty. But some states persisted for about half a century in imposing restraints upon the free exercise of religion and in discriminating against particular religious groups."[19]

Notwithstanding the question of whether those who ratified the Fourteenth Amendment intended the incorporation of the Bill of Rights against the states, the fact remains that this interpretation has fundamentally altered the balance of federalism in the United States. Specifically, the Court began selectively incorporating the clauses in the Bill of Rights against the states, shifting power away from the states but also extending greater protection against religious establishment. Concerning the religion clauses in the First Amendment, then, the Court incorporated the Free Exercise Clause ("Congress shall make no law ... prohibiting the free exercise thereof") against the states in *Cantwell v. Connecticut* (1940), and it incorporated the Establishment Clause ("Congress shall make no law respecting an establishment of religion") against the states in *Everson* (1947).[20] Thus the doctrine of incorporation explains the relevance of the First Amendment in the *Everson* decision.

Religious Establishment and the Strict Separation of Church and State

"In recent years," writes Justice Hugo Black, "the question has most frequently arisen in connection with proposed state aid to church schools and efforts to carry on religious teachings in the public schools in accordance with the tenets of a particular sect." Because these types of cases regarded state laws, they were considered by state courts, which generally ruled in accord with the spirit of non-establishment. Nevertheless, different scenarios have demonstrated certain challenges: "Their decisions," writes Black, "show the difficulty in drawing the line between tax legislation which provides funds for the welfare of the general public and that which is designed to support institutions which teach religion."[21] Rather than working through these challenges in a manner that promoted the reasonable accommodation between church and state, the Supreme Court, in its majority opinion, used these difficulties to articulate the legal doctrine of the strict separation between church and state.

Black pointed to the First Amendment's Establishment Clause as his justification for strict separation, not only in the federal government but also in state governments:

> The "establishment of religion" clause of the First Amendment means at least this: neither a state nor the Federal Government can set up a church. Neither can pass laws which aid one religion, aid all religions, or prefer one religion over another. Neither can force nor influence a person to go to or to remain away from church against his will or force him to profess a belief or disbelief in any religion. No person can be punished for entertaining or professing religious beliefs or disbeliefs, for church attendance or non-attendance. No tax in any amount, large or small, can be levied to support any religious activities or institutions, whatever they may be called, or whatever from they may adopt to teach or practice religion. Neither a state nor the Federal Government can, openly or secretly, participate in the affairs of any religious

organizations or groups and vice versa. In the words of Jefferson, the clause against establishment of religion by law was intended to erect "a wall of separation between church and State."[22]

In mentioning a "wall of separation," Black is referring to a letter that Jefferson wrote to the Danbury Baptist Association. As with Madison's Memorial and Remonstrance against Religious Assessments, as well as with Jefferson's Virginia Statute for Religious Freedom, I will give a detailed analysis of that document in part three. Black continues his interpretation of the First Amendment, saying that it "requires the state to be neutral in its relations with groups of religious believers and non-believers; it does not require the state to be their adversary. State power is no more to be used so as to handicap religions, than it is to favor them."[23]

Thus Black interprets the First Amendment's Establishment Clause to mean that it requires the strict separation of church and state. His language demonstrates that he applied this principle to religious establishment and religious preference, opting instead for religious neutrality. Undoubtedly, the First Amendment stands against religious establishment, as well as religious coercion and persecution. But, as we will see in later chapters, non-establishment does not necessarily preempt religious preference, nor does it require religious neutrality.

Nonetheless, Black concludes *Everson* with these famous words: "The First Amendment has erected a wall between church and state. That wall must be kept high and impregnable. We could not approve the slightest breach."[24] Throughout the majority opinion, Black referenced three documents to inform his understanding of the meaning of the First Amendment, and he interpreted them to promote the strict separation of church and state. Contrary to

Black, I will argue that they promote—and, consequently, that the First Amendment promotes—not the strict separation of church and state but rather the reasonable accommodation of them.

Conclusion

Black, in his opinion, has reviewed a history of religious establishment, coercion, and persecution. He has also given some background to those documents that would inform the meaning of the First Amendment, namely Madison's Memorial and Remonstrance and Jefferson's Virginia Statute. Additionally, he has referred to the legal doctrine of incorporation to demonstrate the First Amendment's relevance for the case at hand, as well as the Court's approach to religious establishment within states, distinction between parochial schools and public schools, and its articulation of the legal doctrine of strict separation. Although he did not finally find that the facts of this case required the application of strict separation—"New Jersey has not breached it here"—the opinion is nonetheless significant because it gives expression to the doctrine, which the Court would apply in *McCollum* just one year later. However, before considering that case, we will review the two dissenting opinions of *Everson*.

CHAPTER FIVE

REVIEWING *EVERSON*: DISSENT

In the previous chapter, I introduced *Everson v. Board of Education*, as well as its interpretation of the "wall of separation between church and state," a phrase that it borrowed from Thomas Jefferson's letter to the Danbury Baptist Association. As we will consider in part three, I do not believe that the historical evidence supports the Supreme Court's interpretation of Jefferson's letter. Additionally, I analyzed the Court's overview of certain background information to the religious clauses of the First Amendment, as well as its incorporation of the Establishment Clause against the states and an overview of its suggested approach to religious establishment within the state. This chapter will continue analyzing *Everson*, focusing particularly on its understanding of the legal doctrine of the strict separation of church and state.

DISTINGUISHING PAROCHIAL SCHOOLS AND PUBLIC SCHOOLS IN LIGHT OF SEPARATION (JUSTICE JACKSON)

Four other justices joined Justice Black's majority opinion, which affirmed the legality of the Board of Education's action in reimbursing the parents of Catholic children for bus fare to attend

Catholic parochial schools. However, in addition to this majority opinion, two minority opinions also emerged from the four dissenting justices. Since only the majority ruling has any legal authority, some may wonder why anyone would bother to write a minority opinion. Dissenting justices write minority opinions so that they become part of the context of the legal opinion. Like majority opinions, minority opinions are entered into the records of a court. Though they are not legally binding, they may influence opinions that come before that court at a later date. In this case, all of those who voted against the majority ruling were even more rigid in their separationist opinion than the majority. Nonetheless, they make some insightful points.

I was twenty years old when the Supreme Court heard this case. At the time I was not in an academic atmosphere. I also remember a strong opposition to giving any kind of support to Roman Catholic schools in the culture of eastern North Carolina. I recall a fear of what might occur if Catholics gained more influence in matters of government. The dissenters in *Everson* expressed similar concerns, namely that the New Jersey statute applied only to the parents of children at Catholic schools. It made no reference to other private schools or to for-profit schools. Perhaps the reason the law dealt only with Catholics is that only Catholic parents requested the reimbursement. However, for their part, most parents from other private and parochial schools objected to the state's offering aid to parents whose children attended Catholic parochial schools.

Although parochial schools were attached to local church parishes, they also belonged to a much larger body, owing to the ecclesial structure of the Roman Catholic Church. "The function of the Church school," writes Justice Jackson, who authored one of the dissenting opinions in *Everson*, "shows only that the schools are under superintendence of a priest and that 'religion is taught as part of the curriculum.' But we know that such schools are parochial only in name—they, in fact, represent a worldwide and age-old policy of the Roman Catholic Church."[1] Jackson then quotes from several canons regarding education from the Canon Law of the Church. These canons explain that Catholic schools will teach the Catholic faith and morality, including instruction in doctrine and piety. They also hold that Catholic children should attend only Catholic schools and that the Church has the rights of authority and inspection of a school's religious curriculum.

Accordingly, the school policy of the Catholic Church "does not leave the individual to pick up religion by chance. It relies on early and indelible indoctrination in the faith and order of the Church by the word and example of persons consecrated to the task."[2] Jackson does not mince words in his rhetoric regarding indoctrination. However, traditionally, *indoctrination* referred simply to the act of teaching or instructing someone; to that extent, all education is indoctrination. Contemporarily, it refers to the uncritical instruction of someone; to that extent, Jackson is not demonstrating charity in his characterization of Catholic education, and Catholic educators—and, for that matter, non-Catholic educators—would take issue with the characterization as neither analytical nor careful.

Nevertheless, Jackson then contrasts the public school system, which he describes as having greater consistency with Protestantism, from the Catholic approach: "Our public school, if not a product of Protestantism, at least is more consistent with it than with the Catholic culture and scheme of values. It is a relatively recent development dating from about 1840."[3] Having dated the public school system to the mid-nineteenth century, prior to the appearance of George Jacob Holyoake and the introduction of secularism, Jackson then claims the following: "It [public school] is organized on the premise that secular education can be isolated from all religious teaching so that the school can inculcate all needed temporal knowledge and also maintain a strict and lofty neutrality as to religion. The assumption is that after the individual has been instructed in worldly wisdom he will be better fitted to choose his religion."[4]

Jackson's usage of the term *secular* refers to secularism, which aims to separate religion from the state (separation). But in the period that he is discussing, the timeline of secularism (see chapter one) demonstrates that *secular* did not refer to the absence of religion but rather simply to the temporal in contrast to the eternal. To be sure, Jackson uses the term *temporal*. However, his usage does not align with a non-secularist, non-separationist meaning of the term because, in that case, he would have contrasted temporal knowledge from eternal knowledge (he does not). In addition, he would have recognized that students could simultaneously receive an education regarding temporal (secular) and eternal matters. Instead, Jackson contrasts temporal knowledge with religious knowledge, and he argues that the public school system isolates, or separates, secular instruction from religious instruction (separation).

Because secularism did not emerge until after the point in time that Jackson has in mind, Jackson makes the same error of chronology that the secularists have made. Public schools may give secular instruction, but that does not preempt religious instruction because the secular traditionally referred to the temporal. This deficient understanding of notions like religious establishment and secularism leads Jackson to state: "Catholic education is the rock on which the whole structure [of the Roman Catholic Church] rests, and to render tax aid to its Church school is indistinguishable to me from rendering the same aid to the Church itself."[5] But, of course, he bases this statement on an understanding of the strict separation of church and state rather than on their reasonable accommodation.

Jackson continues with a discussion of the two religion clauses in the First Amendment saying, "They [religious groups] all are quick to invoke its protections [for free exercise]; they all are irked when they feel its restraints [against establishment]." Then, picking up on the point about non-establishment, interpreted through a separationist lens, he writes, "taxation may not be pursued by a state in a way that even indirectly will interfere with religious proselyting."[6] But Jackson's comment about religious proselytizing reveals a misunderstanding in his mind about the nature of free exercise, or what we also call religious liberty.

The term *proselytize* tends to evoke a negative connotation in people's minds. We tend to think of those who proselytize for their cause as those who resort to objectionable or unacceptable means in promoting their cause. Nevertheless, strictly speaking, the term refers simply to a person who is trying to win converts to his way of thinking and acting. In that sense of the word, the right of free exercise cannot manifest itself without the right of proselytizing; the right of religious liberty requires that people have the right for people to reason together. However, Jackson seems to see them as mutually exclusive. If the state would presume to limit religious liberty to what occurs in the privacy of a person's mind, then it does not protect religious liberty. Religious liberty does not refer simply to what goes on in the privacy of a person's mind but also to what manifests itself in a person's actions.

Applying an interpretation of strict church-state separation to the religion clauses of the First Amendment, Jackson continues, "We cannot have it both ways. Religious teaching cannot be a private affair when the state seeks to impose regulations which infringe on it indirectly, and a public affair when it comes to taxing citizens of one faith to aid another, or those of no faith to aid all." Whereas the Establishment Clause may create restraints, the Free Exercise Clause gives opportunity: "If these principles seem harsh in prohibiting aid to Catholic education, it must not be forgotten that it is the same Constitution that alone assures Catholics the right to maintain these schools at all when predominant local sentiment would forbid them."[7] So just as Jefferson and Madison stood against Henry's bill that provided for tax-supported religious instruction, so also Jackson stands against a tax for religious instruction. However, we will find that Jefferson and Madison objected to religious aid in an accommodationist manner, whereas Jackson objected to it in a separationist one.

Jackson then writes, "If the state may aid these religious schools, it may therefore regulate them. Many groups have sought aid from tax funds only to find that it carried political controls with it. Indeed this Court has declared that 'It is hardly lack of due process for the Government to regulate that which it subsidizes.' . . ."[8] Whereas Jackson would have seen church-state accommodation as tantamount to establishment, Jefferson and Madison did not.

Doubling Down on the Separation of Church and State (Justice Rutledge)

In addition to Jackson's writing a dissenting opinion, Justice Rutledge also wrote a dissenting opinion. As with the majority opinion of Black and the dissenting opinion of Jackson, I have also selected material from Rutledge's opinion that will be significant going forward for our understanding of the Court's thinking in relation to church-state relations. Generally speaking, the dissenting opinions interpreted the doctrine of church-state separation even more strongly than the majority opinion.

Still, Rutledge demonstrated some compassion, writing, "No one conscious of religious values can be unsympathetic toward the burden which our constitutional separation puts on parents who desire religious instruction mixed with secular for their children." He then points out two reasons for sympathy: "[1] They pay taxes for others' children's education, at the same time the added cost of instruction for their own. [2] Nor can one happily see benefits denied to children which others receive, because in conscience they or their parents for them desire a different kind of training others do not demand.... Hardship in fact there is which none can blink."[9]

Despite his words of compassion, Rutledge does not believe that they can extend constitutionally to policies of compassion because he, like Black and Jackson, applies a separationist interpretation to the First Amendment: "But if those feelings should prevail, there would be an end to our historic constitutional policy and command."[10] However, Rutledge bases his understanding of historic constitutional policy on a misreading of the meaning of the religion clauses in the First Amendment, as well as those foundational documents by Jefferson and Madison informing its meaning.

Rutledge continues by clarifying that religious children have the right to attend public schools but that they pass it by so that they may receive religious instruction: "The child attending the religious school has the same right as any other to attend the public school. But he foregoes exercising it because the same guaranty which assures this freedom forbids the public school or any agency of the state to give or aid him in securing the religious instruction he seeks."[11]

Rutledge then explains that difficulties would accompany religious instruction in the context of public education and points to secular instruction as the solution forward: "Were he to accept the common school, he would be the first to protest the teaching there of any creed or faith not his own. And it is precisely for the reason that their atmosphere is wholly secular that children are not sent to public schools under the *Pierce* doctrine."[12] As was the case with Jackson, Rutledge employs a particular usage of the term *secular*. For him a secular education is mutually exclusive from a religious education. However, that was not the historic meaning of the term *secular*. Historically, the student could simultaneously receive religious and secular instruction; that is, the student could receive an education about eternal and temporal things at the same time.

Consequently, Rutledge does not interpret the *Pierce* decision through a clear lens. *Pierce v. Society of Sisters* (1925) is an especially significant case regarding religious matters and the separation of church and state. In November of 1922 Oregon voters passed a referendum (Oregon's Compulsory Education Act) requiring that all children between the ages of eight and sixteen attend public schools until they had received an eighth-grade education. They had intended that this bill would curtail the influence of parochial schools.

However, in a unanimous vote, the Supreme Court overturned this law with Justice James McReynolds writing, "The child is not the mere creature of the state; those who nurture him and direct his destiny have the right, coupled with the high duty, to recognize and prepare him for additional obligations."[13] Readers will note that, in *Everson*, Rutledge interprets *Pierce* to stand for the proposition that public schools are "wholly secular." However, the majority *Pierce* opinion recognizes the historic understanding of the term *secular* when it characterizes the Society of Sisters as "devot[ing] its property and effort to the secular and religious education and care of children."[14]

Rutledge then turns to constitutional and historical grounds for his separatist interpretation, pointing specifically to the

Constitution, Madison's Remonstrance, and even the apostle Paul's doctrine of religious liberty. However, as with his reading of *Pierce*, his reading of these grounds is deficient. He writes, "But that is a constitutional necessity, because we have staked the very existence of our country on the faith that complete separation between the state and religion is best for the state and best for religion. Remonstrance, Par. 8, 12."[15] As I have remarked already, historical precedent does not support Rutledge's claim that "constitutional necessity" leads to "complete" church-state separation. He makes specific reference to Madison's Remonstrance and the United States Constitution. However, as we will investigate in part three in great detail, these documents, as well as historical precedent, support the reasonable accommodation of church and state rather than the strict separation of them.

Referring back to Madison's Remonstrance, Rutledge continues, writing, "That policy necessarily entails hardship upon persons who forego the right to educational advantages the state can supply in order to secure others it is precluded from giving. Indeed this may hamper the parent and the child forced by conscience to that choice. But it does not make the state unneutral to withhold what the Constitution forbids it to give."[16]

Rutledge thus refers to the hardship that church-state separation causes for those who decline to attend public schools. However, neither Jefferson nor Madison intended any such hardships, which are not in keeping with their beliefs and their words. In other words, such hardships do not result from the intention of the reasonable accommodation of church and state. Instead, they result from interpreting the First Amendment as requiring the separation of church and state. However, that interpretation rests on a foundation of secularism, which does not emerge until more than a half-century after the founding of the United States.

Additionally, readers will note Rutledge's use of the term "forbid." Contrary to his claim, the Constitution does not "forbid" the state's aiding of religion; it forbids the state's establishment of religion, but aid and establishment are not the same thing.

Picking up with his point about neutrality, Rutledge explains, "It is only by observing the prohibition rigidly that the state can maintain its neutrality and avoid partisanship in the dissensions inevitable when sect opposes sect over demands for public moneys to further religious education, teaching or training in any form or degree, directly or indirectly."[17] However, no entity—least of all the state—is truly neutral. The state's propping up of secularist instruction in place of religious instruction as neutral is a myth. A strictly secularist instruction gives preference to one religion (e.g., secular humanism) over others. As we will see in later chapters, that is not in keeping with the vision of either Jefferson or Madison. In addition, both the words and the actions of Jefferson particularly demonstrate his commitment to reasonable church-state accommodation rather than their strict separation.

Finally, Rutledge makes an argument from the apostle Paul: "Like St. Paul's freedom, religious liberty with a great price must be bought. And for those who exercise it most fully, by insisting upon religious education for their children mixed with secular, by the terms of our Constitution the price is greater than for others."[18] In a final irony, Rutledge appeals to a religious authority in an opinion in which he is arguing for a secularist result. Apparently, what is appropriate for an opinion of the Supreme Court is somehow inappropriate for the pedagogy of public education.

Rutledge is right that civilizations buy religious liberty at a great price. Additionally, religious liberty is in keeping with the teachings of Scripture. However, Rutledge misunderstands the doctrine of religious liberty, believing that it exists most fully in a secularist society with church-state separation rather than in a society with church-state accommodation. But that would relegate expressions of religious belief and practice to private affairs. As we will consider later, the implications of religious liberty permit people to live their lives in society, including in education, in light of their religious beliefs.

Conclusion

Everson v. Board of Education is important because, in the words of Justice Rutledge, it "forces us to determine squarely for the first time what was 'an establishment of religion' in the First Amendment's conception."[19] We have seen that the majority justices in *Everson* articulated the legal doctrine of strict separation based partly on their interpretation of Jefferson's "wall of separation between church and state." However, the justices misappropriated Jefferson, who did not seek strict separation in the way that these justices viewed it; as we will see in part three, he interpreted establishment narrowly and sought the reasonable accommodation of church and state. I have also noted that *Everson* extended its view of religious establishment, not just to the federal government but also to state governments. On its face the First Amendment applies to Congress, not to the states. Nevertheless, the Supreme Court applied the doctrine of incorporation to the religion clauses so that they would apply also to the states.

The *Everson* opinions introduced numerous items that help us better understand the background issues of religious liberty. For example, Justice Black reviewed the background of religious persecution and coercion, which occurred both in Europe and the Colonies and both by Roman Catholics and Protestants. Similarly, they introduced four key documents that factored into the American founders' discussions regarding religious liberty during the founding era. Henry proposed A Bill Establishing a Provision for Teachers of the Christian Religion, which would support Christian instruction specifically through taxation.

However, Madison's Remonstrance successfully defeated Henry's bill. To be sure, the United States is better off as a nation that Virginia did not enact the bill and that the nation did not follow that path. And for his part, Madison handled the situation brilliantly; in fact, I consider it one of the greatest moments in our history. Similarly, Jefferson penned the Virginia Statute for Religious Freedom, which also offers a helpful vision for these issues. The importance of these documents lies in their forming the background of the religion clauses in the First Amendment.

As we have seen, *Everson* interpreted Jefferson and Madison in relation to Henry for the proposition of the strict separation of church and state. Even so, the justices did not ultimately find that the facts of this case warranted the application of the doctrine. *Everson* also alluded to Jefferson's Letter to the Danbury Baptist Association of Connecticut in its case for strict separation. However, when we study these documents more closely, we will note that the *Everson* Court misinterpreted Jefferson and Madison.

In considering this topic, I have judged it worthwhile not to limit our knowledge to a few excerpts but rather to give close scrutiny to its passages to inform our comprehension of the subject. I will take a similar approach in the next chapter as we work our way through another significant case, *McCollum v. Board of Education* (1948). Like *Everson*, *McCollum* will shed light on the justices' understandings of Jefferson's and Madison's views of the relationship between the church and state. Then, I will assess the justices' views of these figures and documents to see whether their interpretations comport with Jefferson's and Madison's intentions.

CHAPTER SIX

REVIEWING MCCOLLUM: RELIGIOUS AND SECULAR EDUCATION

In chapters four and five, I reviewed *Everson v. Board of Education* (1947), specifically noting the ways in which the justices interpreted the religion clauses of the First Amendment. I also considered how they justified their position of the strict separation of church and state on founders such as Thomas Jefferson and James Madison. In this chapter, I will begin analyzing these justices' conclusions regarding the vision of the American founders for church-state relations, finding that their view of strict separation rests on a faulty foundation because they misappropriated the founders. In this chapter, I will also continue to uncover the Supreme Court's position in the mid-twentieth century concerning the strict separation of church and state by investigating a second case of significance, *McCollum v. Board of Education* (1948).

As with *Everson*, Justice Hugo Black delivered the Court's majority opinion. In addition, I will give close scrutiny to the various opinions of the Court. These include a majority opinion authored by Justice Black, a concurring opinion written by Justice Felix Frankfurter, a second concurring opinion authored by Justice

Robert H. Jackson, and, finally, a dissenting opinion by Justice Stanley F. Reed. Justices will often add concurring opinions if they would like to make a point that they believe the majority has failed to make and dissenting opinions if they disagree with the majority.

I will first work my way through Black's majority opinion. I will then examine the comments from the concurring opinions from Justice Frankfurt and Justice Jackson. Finally, I will review Justice Reed's dissenting opinion. Among other things, I will note the justices' reviews of the development of public schools in the United States, their understandings of secularism, and the way in which they rely on Thomas Jefferson to inform their thinking concerning the important issue of church-state relations in the United States.

Religious Instruction in Public Schools (Justice Black)

Writing for the majority opinion, Justice Black tells us what is at the heart and core of this case: "This case relates to the power of a state to utilize its tax-supported public school system in aid of religious instruction insofar as that power may be restricted by the First and Fourteenth Amendments to the Federal Constitution."[1] Whereas *Everson* concerned transportation, *McCollum* regards religious instruction. Even though the Bill of Rights references only the federal government on its face, the Supreme Court nonetheless applied the Establishment Clause of the First Amendment ("Congress shall make no law respecting an establishment of religion") to the state of Illinois vis-à-vis the Fourteenth Amendment through the legal doctrine of incorporation, which I considered in chapter four.[2]

The facts of *McCollum* reveal that the Champaign Board of Education in the state of Illinois permitted religious teachers from external religious groups "to come weekly into the school buildings during the regular hours set apart for secular teaching, and then and there for a period of thirty minutes substitute their religious teaching for the secular education provided under the compulsory education law." Illinois's compulsory education law "requires parents to send their children, aged seven to sixteen, to its tax-supported public schools where the children are to remain in attendance during the hours when the schools are regularly in session . . . unless the children attend private or parochial schools which meet educational standards fixed by the State."[3]

Vashti McCollum, the mother of a student in the district, as well as a resident and taxpayer in Champaign County, objected to the Board of Education's allowance of this practice and filed suit. However, the Circuit Court of Champaign County did not rule in favor of McCollum. On appeal the Illinois Supreme Court affirmed the lower court's ruling in favor of the school district. Finally, McCollum appealed to the United States Supreme Court, which would reverse and remand the case back to the lower courts.

Specifically, McCollum "charged that this joint public-school religious-group program violated the First and Fourteenth Amendments to the United States Constitution," explained Justice Black. "The prayer of her petition was that the Board of Education be ordered to 'adopt and enforce rules and regulations prohibiting all instruction in and teaching of all religious education in all public schools in Champaign District Number 71, . . . and in all public school houses and buildings in said district when occupied by public schools.'"[4]

Justice Black gives context for the school district's decision to permit religious teaching on school property during school hours: "In 1940 interested members of the Jewish, Roman Catholic, and a few of the Protestant faiths formed a voluntary association called the Champaign Council on Religious Education." The Board of Education then authorized them to "offer classes in religious instruction to public school pupils in grades four to nine, inclusive."[5] The classes lasted thirty to forty-five minutes per week. Religious teachers taught them "at no expense to the school authorities, but the instructors were subject to the approval and supervision of the superintendent of schools."[6]

Schools did not force students to attend these classes in religious studies. Instead, they permitted students to attend only after receiving signatures from their parents specifying that they could. For students not opting to attend classes in religious studies, schools provided other spaces for them to pursue "secular studies."[7] The facts of the case are interesting in themselves. But, for my purpose, I am most interested in how Black developed his case against the Champaign Board of Education and, in particular, his interpretation of church-state relations and Thomas Jefferson.

Black identifies what he believed is a key problem with the background of this case: "the use of tax-supported property for religious instruction and the close cooperation between the school authorities and the religious council in promoting religious education." As practiced by the Champaign Board of Education, "The operation of the state's compulsory education system thus assists and is integrated with the program of religious instruction carried on by separate religious sects." Far from practicing the strict separation of church and state, the school district "integrates" them. Additionally problematic, Black finds that these classes in religious instruction potentially "release" students from their "legal duty" to receive "secular education."[8] For Black this arrangement is altogether untenable.

Our study of Black's interpretation of church-state relations in *Everson* should signal to us how he would judge the facts in

McCollum. He does not appeal to the historic reading of the Establishment Clause of the First Amendment, which allowed for the reasonable accommodation of church and state (I will consider that historic reading in part three). Instead, Black argues strongly for strict church-state separation, and he finds that the facts of *McCollum* violate that ideal: "This is beyond all question a utilization of the tax-established and tax-supported public school system to aid religious groups to spread their faith. And it falls squarely under the ban of the First Amendment (made applicable to the States by the Fourteenth)."[9]

In order to build his case against the school district, Black begins with what the Court had previously established in *Everson*. In that case the Court had interpreted the First Amendment to mean that neither federal nor state governments could establish, aid, or give preference to any one religion; neither could they force, influence, or punish a person toward or away from any one religion. Additionally, "neither a state nor the Federal Government can, openly or secretly, participate in the affairs of any religious organizations or groups, and vice versa."[10]

From such principles Black invoked Jefferson's name to argue for "a wall of separation between church and state." Black also pointed out that the majority and dissenting opinions of *Everson* "agreed that the First Amendment's language, properly interpreted, had erected a wall of separation between Church and State," even if they disagreed about its particular application to the facts.[11] But, as we will see, Black and his colleagues misinterpreted Jefferson's meaning. With these principles in place, Black moves to the present case.

Relying on the law established in *Everson*, the respondents argue that the First Amendment forbids "government preference of one religion over another," effectively barring the Illinois program. Of course, the First Amendment, on its face, does no such thing; it forbids only the establishment of religion on the federal level. Additionally, the respondents asked the Court to "distinguish or overrule our holding in the *Everson* case that the Fourteenth Amendment made the 'establishment of religion' clause of the First Amendment applicable as a prohibition against the States." In other words, they were asking the Court to reverse its decision to incorporate the Establishment Clause against the states. However, the Court declined this request: "After giving full consideration to the arguments presented we are unable to accept either of these contentions."[12] Black argues that the First and Fourteenth Amendments require this result. Yet, incidentally, the Court had established that connection only a year prior.

Black denies that his interpretation of these principles "manifest[s] a governmental hostility to religion or religious teachings." He makes this denial by identifying America's "national tradition as embodied in the First Amendment's guaranty of the free exercise of religion." He argues, "The First Amendment rests upon the premise that both religion and government can best work to achieve their lofty aims if each is left free from the other within its respective sphere."[13]

Regardless of what Black believed, and regardless even of whether he was right, it was not what the American founders believed, and it is not what the First Amendment means. Numerous quotations from the founders about the bedrock of morality and religion for American government demonstrate this point. To give just one example from John Adams, "Our Constitution was made only for a moral and religious people. It is wholly inadequate to the government of any other."[14] In other words, Adams did not believe, like Black, that religion and government work best when they leave one another alone.

Nonetheless, Black specifies two facts that indicate apparent constitutional malfeasance: (1) "The State's tax-supported public school buildings [are] used for the dissemination of religious doctrines"; and (2) "the State also affords sectarian groups an invaluable aid in that it helps to provide pupils for their religious classes through use of the state's compulsory public school machinery." He concludes with these words, "This is not separation of Church and State."[15] But, of course, the First Amendment does not say anything about church-state separation; instead, it allows for church-state accommodation. And, as we will see, it was accommodation, not separation, that Jefferson supported.

Historical Overview of Education (Justice Frankfurter)

In addition to its majority opinion, *McCollum* produced two concurring opinions, as well as a dissenting opinion. Justice Frankfurter delivered one of the concurring opinions, which Justices Jackson, Rutledge, and Burton joined. Frankfurter affirmed the Supreme Court's decision but also argued that it had not concluded its responsibility on the matter of church-state relations. For one thing, he points out that working through the implications of church-state relations requires more than a single case.

With regard to *McCollum* particularly, he begins by aiming to understand the Champaign Board of Education's program "as a conscientious attempt to *accommodate* the allowable functions of Government and the special concerns of the Church within the framework of our Constitution and with due regard to the kind of society for which it was designed."[16] We note then that the school district followed a trajectory of accommodating church and state. Additionally, as we will note, they were not acting in a vacuum but rather were following the pattern that they had received. In the end, Frankfurter would issue a concurring opinion rather than a dissenting one, but the fact remains that church-state accommodation demonstrated the convention while church-state separation represented innovation.

In order to accomplish his aim, Frankfurter looks to history, tracing the history of education in the West from Europe to the American Colonies and the United States. "Traditionally, organized education in the Western world was Church education. It could hardly be otherwise when the education of children was primarily study of the Word and the ways of God." This order held true in Protestant and Roman Catholic countries alike, in countries with less and more church-state identification. "The basis of education was largely the Bible," explains Frankfurter, "and its chief purpose inculcation of piety." Adams's point about a moral and religious people illustrates this latter point. "To the extent that the State intervened," Frankfurter continues, "it used its authority to further aims of the Church."[17]

Shifting specifically to the United States, Frankfurter explains that the aim of education has evolved throughout different periods of its history. "The evolution of colonial education, largely in the service of religion, into the public school system of today is the story of changing conceptions regarding the American democratic society, of the functions of State-maintained education in such a society, and of the role therein of the free exercise of religion by the people."[18] In other words, although education in the West has historically found its basis in religion, its foundation would evolve over time to a secular base, culminating with the holdings of *Everson* and *McCollum*.

However, Frankfurter, as well as the Court's majority, identifies this shift in focus as occurring at the American founding. Specifically, they point to documents such as James Madison's Memorial and Remonstrance against Religious Assessments (1785) and Jefferson's Virginia Statute for Religious Freedom (1786), which each give important context for the First Amendment's Establishment Clause and Free Exercise Clause. Additionally, they identify Jefferson's letter to the Danbury Baptist Association of Connecticut (1802), which references a "wall of separation between church and state," as explaining the meaning of the First Amendment. We will see that they fundamentally misinterpreted these documents.

Interpreting the history of education in the West in light of the American founding, Frankfurter writes, "The modern public school derived from a philosophy of freedom reflected in the First Amendment." He then recalls Madison's Remonstrance, which I introduced in chapter four and will analyze further in chapter six. Frankfurter interprets the Remonstrance as challenging "a proposal which involved support to religious education."[19] To be sure, Frankfurter is correct in his assessment that Madison's Remonstrance challenged Patrick Henry's Bill Establishing a Provision for Teachers of the Christian Religion. While that particular situation emerged in the Commonwealth of Virginia, a similar drama played out in other states with other figures challenging similar bills. However, as we will see, the proposals of Madison, Jefferson, and others like them did not amount to the strict church-state separation touted by *McCollum*.

Instead, these cases solidified that interpretation. Nevertheless, it was not what the tradition, which had sought church-state accommodation, had bequeathed to them. The Champaign Board of Education's exercise in accommodation illustrates this basic point. As we saw in our review of *Everson*, accommodation morphed, in many of these governments, into religious establishment, which created problems of religious coercion and persecution. Still, strict separation presents serious problems too, such as denying people the full extent of their religious liberty. Consequently, the American founders promoted reasonable church-state accommodation that set up safeguards against the dangers associated with religious establishment while also protecting citizens' right of free exercise: "Congress shall make no law respecting the establishment of religion, or prohibiting the free exercise thereof."[20]

From Sectarian Education to Secular Education

Regardless, Justice Frankfurter believed that the states had become increasingly secular in their approaches to public education prior to the enactment of the Fourteenth Amendment and certainly prior to its incorporation of the First Amendment. Pointing to the Commonwealth of Massachusetts as an example, he writes, "In Massachusetts, largely through the efforts of Horace Mann, all sectarian teachings were barred from the common school to save it from being rent by denominational conflict."[21] However, the barring of sectarian teachings is not tantamount to the barring of religious teachings. *Sectarian teaching* refers to the differences of individual sects and not to religious teachings per se. Consequently, Frankfurter's example is weak evidence for his proposition.

Moving to discuss the Fourteenth Amendment and the doctrine of incorporation, Frankfurter writes, "The upshot of these controversies, often long and fierce, is fairly summarized by saying that long before the Fourteenth Amendment subjected the States to new limitations, the prohibition of furtherance by the State of religious instruction became the guiding principle, in law and feeling, of the American people."[22] However, as I alluded to in the previous chapter, the Fourteenth Amendment's Privileges and Immunities Clause, Due Process Clause, and Equal Protection Clause do not prohibit religious instruction in a state, according to its plain meaning. It reads, "No State shall make or enforce any law which shall abridge the privileges or immunities of citizens of the United States; nor shall any State deprive any person of life, liberty, or property, without due process of law; nor deny to any person within its jurisdiction the equal protection of the laws."[23]

The amendment makes reference to the states, as well as to the application and denial of their laws, but it does not identify specifically what those laws are, much less that they concern religious instruction. Instead, it seems to leave the content of those laws largely to the states themselves. Additionally, for the sake of argument, assume that the states were moving in the direction of secular education anyway, such that the incorporation of the Fourteenth Amendment against the states did not force secular education on unwilling states. Still, the fact remains that it was the prerogative of state governments to make that decision for themselves and not the federal government to impose a decision on them. Besides, the facts of *McCollum* demonstrate the opposite because they signify a school district that apparently was not moving in a secular direction. What is more, the Champaign Board of Education's posture was not an isolated incident.

As a result, Frankfurter's statement, "The prohibition of furtherance by the State of religious instruction became the guiding principle, in law and feeling, of the American people," is misleading.[24] It may have represented the beliefs of some Americans, but it did not represent the beliefs of "the American people," which implies its totality. Even those for whom the statement is true did not (successfully) redress their concerns through legislative processes. In fact, the ideal of federalism attempts to address a diversity of opinion among a given population; the United States as a federation aims to divide power between a federal government and state governments, as well as between numerous localities within the given states. However, rulings such as those in *Everson* and *McCollum* chip away at that ideal in favor of an unnatural uniformity of belief and practice.

In developing his case, Frankfurter remarks, "It is pertinent to remind that the establishment of this principle of separation in the field of education was not due to any decline in the religious beliefs of the people." He then illustrates that claim by pointing to Mann and Madison: "Horace Mann was a devout Christian, and the deep religious feeling of James Madison is stamped upon the Remonstrance."[25] However, Frankfurter's point that people were still religious, while interesting, is irrelevant. At issue is a proper reading of the First Amendment. In addition, neither Madison nor Mann supported the "principle of separation" as Frankfurter and the majority construed it. I will consider Madison in the next chapter. The evidence Frankfurter offers about Mann mentions only sectarian teaching particularly and not religious teaching more generally, which is what strict church-state separation refers to.

Based on these premises, Frankfurter shifts to talk specifically about the "secular public school." He begins by explaining, "The secular public school did not imply indifference to the basic role of religion in the life of the people, nor rejection of religious education as a means of fostering it. The claims of religion were not minimized by refusing to make the public schools agencies for their assertion." He then gives us a clue into how he is thinking of the term *sectarian*, which I considered above: "The non-sectarian or secular public school was the means of reconciling freedom in general with religious freedom."[26]

For someone like Mann, as well as Jefferson, whom I will consider later, *sectarian* referred most often to differences in particular confessions and/or denominations rather than to religion generally. For them nonsectarian instruction could exist simultaneously with religious instruction and still demonstrate consistency with the First Amendment. However, Frankfurter understood the term *sectarian* in much broader terms: religion more generally. For this reason, he associates the nonsectarian school with the secular school, which he associates with secularism rather than with its historic meaning of temporal. Concerning his statement concerning indifference, I repeat what I stated above: It is interesting but ultimately irrelevant.

Frankfurter then appeals to the spirit undergirding the principle of democracy and to the prospect of religious coercion. "The sharp confinement of the public schools to secular education," he says, "was a recognition of the need of a democratic society to educate its children, insofar as the State undertook to do so, in an atmosphere free from pressures in a realm in which pressures are most resisted and where conflicts are most easily and most bitterly engendered."[27]

However, a democratic society does not require such a sharp confinement. The expression of the democratic spirit within public education may manifest itself in any number of ways that accord with reasonable church-state accommodation and offend neither non-establishment nor free exercise. Insofar as the state undertakes to pursue the path that Frankfurter puts forward, it may do that; however, it was not the federal government's prerogative to do so, least of all the Supreme Court's, at least under the laws that were at its disposal at the time. Additionally, strict church-state separation is not the only way to protect against the prospect of religious coercion. Genuine religious liberty may exist alongside an order that upholds an accommodation of church and state.

Frankfurter continues, explaining that the ideal of the public school "promot[es] cohesion among a heterogeneous democratic people," for which reason it "must keep scrupulously free from entanglement in the strife of sects."[28] But, again, a society can promote freedom from entanglement with sects, whether interpreted to mean a given confession or religion more generally, while also promoting cohesion. In other words, people within the United States have not historically believed that societal cohesion requires the strict separation of church and state.

However, Frankfurter doubles down on his language of confinement. Having already used the phrase *sharp confinement*, he also uses *strict confinement*: "The preservation of the community from divisive conflicts, of Government from irreconcilable pressures by religious groups, of religion from censorship and coercion however subtly exercised, requires strict confinement of the State to instruction other than religious, leaving to the individual's church and home, indoctrination in the faith of his choice."[29] Frankfurter appears to interpret any church-state entanglement as necessarily "divisive" with "irreconcilable pressures" and "censorship and coercion." His view rests upon an either-or interpretation of the facts: either confinement or division, either separation or coercion.

However, the First Amendment has historically charted a middle path between confinement on one hand and coercion on the other. That path is reasonable church-state accommodation that avoids establishment but also permits the free exercise of religion in all of life, including in education. Frankfurter's model also discriminates against a "religious" indoctrination but otherwise favors a secular indoctrination. As I considered in chapter four, indoctrination refers simply to the act of teaching or instructing someone.

Next, Frankfurter argues that the ideal of the secular public school did not arise overnight; instead, it was hard-fought and hard-won. "This development of the public school as a symbol of our secular unity was not a sudden achievement nor attained without violent conflict," he writes. "While in small communities of comparatively homogeneous religious beliefs, the need for separation presented no urgencies, elsewhere the growth of the secular school encountered the resistance of feeling strongly engaged against it."[30] As I have argued, the principle of federalism embedded within American government gives different localities the freedom to attend to these community-specific differences.

Frankfurter continues, "But the inevitability of such attempts is the very reason for Constitutional provisions primarily concerned with the protection of minority groups."[31] Undoubtedly, the Constitution contains numerous provisions in protection of minority groups. Yet, depending on the provision in mind, the Constitution extends protection of those groups to certain governmental bodies. For example, those provisions in the Bill of Rights applied initially only to the federal government prior to the Court's incorporating them against the states. Many states chose to extend similar protections to their respective citizens as those contained in the Bill of Rights, but the point is that that was their legislative prerogative.

Throughout his concurring opinion, Frankfurter draws on the founding era to bolster his case for the strict separation of church and state. For example, as we have seen, he appeals to Madison's Remonstrance as well as the First Amendment. But he admits, "We are dealing not with a full-blown principle, nor one having the definiteness of a surveyor's metes and bounds."[32] He then pivots to the year of 1875 in which President Ulysses S. Grant made a speech to the Convention of the Army of Tennessee.

While introducing Grant's remarks, he writes, "By 1875 the separation of public education from Church entanglements, of the State from the teaching of religion, was firmly established in the consciousness of the nation."[33] Frankfurter says that, but the facts demonstrate otherwise. The fact that cases such as *Everson* and *McCollum* rose to the Court's attention in the first case illustrates that the doctrine of strict church-state separation was not as established as Frankfurter imagines—not even in the mid-to-late 1940s, much less in the 1870s. What is more, *Everson* and *McCollum* are not isolated incidents but are representative of other cases like them. In Frankfurter's own words, "We are dealing not with a full-blown principle."

Still, Frankfurter appeals to Grant's speech:

> Encourage free schools and resolve that not one dollar appropriated for their support shall be appropriated for the support of any sectarian schools. Resolve that neither the state nor the nation, nor both combined, shall support institutions of learning other than those sufficient to afford every child growing up in the land the opportunity of a good common school education, *unmixed with sectarian, pagan, or atheistical dogmas.* Leave the matter of religion to the family altar, the church, and the private school, supported entirely by private contributions. Keep the church and state forever separated.[34]

Grant's use of the term *sectarian* is fairly problematic for the proposal of reasonable church-state accommodation. He distinguishes sectarian schools from free schools with a "good common school education," which he says is "unmixed with sectarian, pagan, or atheistical dogmas." He then unequivocally states to leave the matter of religion to other entities and to "keep the church and state forever separated."

What are we to make of Grant's remarks? Recalling the timeline of secularism, by the point of Grant's speech, secularism was a fledgling yet existent movement. Additionally, people's use of the term *sectarian* was shifting to refer more broadly to varying religious groups in addition to denominational confessions. Grant seems to conflate the two because he distinguishes the sectarian from the pagan and the atheistic, but also he seems to associate these three "dogmas" with "sectarian schools" more broadly. Nonetheless, even he presents a moderate vision relative to those later atheistic secularists who want to stamp out religious expression, not simply from public education, but also from society more generally.

Regardless, Grant is just one man. He may offer a vision, but the President cannot pronounce by fiat what will occur. The constitutional order of the United States leaves the legal conventions of given localities to particular legislative bodies. For his part, Frankfurter interprets Grant by saying, "President Grant urged that there be written into the United States Constitution particular elaborations including a specific prohibition against the use of public funds for sectarian education, such as had been written into many State constitutions."[35] Frankfurter is alluding to the failed Blaine Amendment, which would have nationally legalized Grant's vision.

However, Grant was unsuccessful in his efforts to realize his newfangled ideas. The controversy surrounding Grant's speech and the Blaine Amendment demonstrates that the principle of strict church-state separation had not taken root across the nation by this point, much less in the antebellum period or the founding era. Additionally, Grant speaks in the heyday of modernity when many people believed that students of diverse backgrounds could rally around a common, neutral body of knowledge that is taught objectively by unbiased teachers. For that reason, Grant can refer to "a good common school education, unmixed with sectarian, pagan, or atheistical dogmas." However, within just a few short decades, the progressive educational philosophy of John Dewey et al. would dash even that vision with people increasingly recognizing man's situated-ness.

Additionally, if the failure of modernity and the ascendency of postmodernity have taught us anything, they have taught us that education is necessarily tied to the teacher's philosophies of life, whether implicit or explicit. They have also taught us that the student's educational experience is necessarily value-laden—whether in what it teaches (curriculum) or what it does not teach (null curriculum). In other words, an educational institution cannot ultimately demonstrate a posture of religious neutrality, whether sectarian, pagan, or atheistic.

Conclusion

In this chapter I have examined the majority opinion of Justice Black, who considered the phenomenon of religious instruction in public schools, as well as part of the concurring opinion of Justice Frankfurter, noting his historical overview of education, including a shift from sectarian education to secular education. In the next chapter, I will conclude my analysis of Frankfurter's opinion, in addition to reviewing Justice Jackson's reservations about the majority opinion and Justice Reed's dissenting from the majority opinion.

CHAPTER SEVEN

REVIEWING MCCOLLUM: DISSENT

In chapter six I analyzed Justice Hugo Black's majority opinion, as well as half of Justice Felix Frankfurter's concurrence. In particular, I focused on Black's understanding of religious instruction in public schools and Frankfurter's historical overview of education, including the shift from sectarian to secular education. In this chapter I will conclude my analysis of Frankfurter's opinion, looking specifically to his overview of various approaches to church-state accommodation. After that I will turn to Justice Robert H. Jackson's concurrence in which he expresses some reservations about the majority's decision. Finally, I will conclude with Justice Stanley F. Reed's dissent.

APPROACHES TO ACCOMMODATION (JUSTICE FRANKFURTER)

Continuing his concurrence, Justice Frankfurter admits, "Prohibition of the commingling of sectarian and secular instruction in the public school is of course only half the story." The other half of the story, he argues, concerns the rights of religious people to pursue a religious education: "A religious people was naturally concerned about the part of the child's education entrusted 'to the family altar, the church, and the private school.'" Frankfurter manifests a genuine concern for the challenges that this vision for public education creates for "religious people." That concern leads him to discuss religious education, first summarizing it and then identifying numerous challenges that emerged. Although "religious education took many forms," a primary form that it assumed was through denominational initiation. Religious schools attempted to teach their students both about temporal and eternal matters. However, they "were often beset by serious handicaps, financial and otherwise."[1]

Speaking specifically of finances, Frankfurter remarks, "Laboring under financial difficulties and exercising only persuasive authority, various denominations felt handicapped in their task of religious education." After all, a given population subsidizes public schools through taxation; however, they do not similarly subsidize religious schools. As a result, many attempted "to obtain public funds for religious schools" but were unsuccessful, owing to the "principle of Separation by the establishment of church schools privately supported."[2] The prospect of a government using tax dollars to support religious schools directly is similar to that of Patrick Henry's bill establishing a provision for Christian teachers specifically. However, we can distinguish between those kinds of fact scenarios (which I will consider in greater detail in part three) relative to those informing the backgrounds of *Everson* and *McCollum*.

Additionally, my present purpose is not to pronounce judgment on these holdings per se. Instead, I aim to demonstrate the ways in which these justices applied the Constitution and the First Amendment to the cases before them and how the path they charted was not altogether congruent with what had preceded them. In later chapters, I will argue that the First Amendment, as well as Thomas Jefferson and James Madison, support a vision of church-state accommodation, which is the via media between the extremes of church-state establishment and strict church-state separation. For now, though, we are trying to understand all we can about the reasons for the current order of church-state separation.

In addition to financial difficulties, the leadership of religious schools also faced challenges about how best to integrate temporal and eternal subjects into the curriculum. "There were experiments with vacation schools, with Saturday as well as Sunday schools. They all fell short of their purpose," explains Frankfurter. "It was urged that by appearing to make religion a one-day-a-week matter, the Sunday school, which acquired national acceptance, tended to relegate the child's religious education, and thereby his religion, to a minor role not unlike the enforced piano lesson."[3]

With time these disagreements evolved into a "week-day church school," which occurred "on one or more afternoons a week after the close of the public school." Yet even that solution was not ideal, because "children continued to be children; they wanted to play when school was out, particularly when other children were free to do so." The reality of that challenge led church leaders to reassert the prospect of an earlier approach: "Church leaders decided that if the week-day church school was to succeed, a way had to be found to give the child his religious education during what the child conceived to be his 'business hours.'"[4] Frankfurter explains that, as a result, George U. Wenner made a proposal at the Interfaith Conference on Federation in New York City in 1905. Underlying the proposal was the assumption that "the public school unduly monopolized the child's time and that the churches were entitled to their share of it. This, the schools should 'release.'"[5]

Citing the example of the Third Republic of France, the Federation proposed, essentially, that public schools treat one afternoon per week as an opportunity to pursue elective options. In that scenario, some students could elect to receive religious instruction, while others could elect otherwise: "Upon the request of their parents children [could] be excused from public school on Wednesday afternoon, so that the churches could provide 'Sunday school on Wednesday,'" which they "carried out on church premises under church authority. Those not desiring to attend church schools would continue their normal classes."[6]

Frankfurter then explains that religious leaders requested a non-compete agreement: "Lest these public school classes unfairly compete with the church education, it was requested that the school authorities refrain from scheduling courses or activities of compelling interest or importance." Notwithstanding the difficulties that religious leaders were already facing, their proposal was not met with universal acceptance: "The proposal aroused considerable opposition." However, with time the proposal worked its way into the public school system: "It took another decade for a 'released time' scheme to become part of a public school system. Gary, Indiana, inaugurated the movement."[7]

Frankfurter then outlines what this proposal looked like in practice:

> The religious teaching was held on church premises and the public schools had no hand in the conduct of these church schools. They did not supervise the choice of instructors or the subject matter taught. Nor did they assume responsibility for the attendance, conduct or achievement of the child in a church school; and he received no credit for it. The period of attendance in the religious schools would otherwise have

been a play period for the child, with the result that the arrangement did not cut into public school instruction or truly affect the activities or feelings of the children who did not attend the church schools.[8]

In the face of a burgeoning secular elite, the Federation's proposal elicited suspicion and even resistance. However, this resistance was by no means even close to universal; in fact, it may not even have been mainstream.

"From such a beginning 'released time' has attained substantial proportions," Frankfurter details. "In 1914–15, under the Gary program, 619 pupils left the public schools for the church schools during one period a week. According to responsible figures almost 2,000,000 in some 2,200 communities participated in 'released time' programs during 1947."[9] That is a substantial number. The fact that the Federation's proposal manifested in so many public school systems demonstrates that viewpoints regarding church-state relations were certainly not fixed but rather were in flux. It also demonstrates a general expectation that the leaders of given localities had for church-state accommodation and that church-state separation signified a shift from that expectation.

Frankfurter offers this historical background presumably to make a case that these developments represented a diversion from the apparent ideal of church-state separation. However, as I demonstrate, his case rests on partial information and raises more questions than it answers. Regardless, he shifts from that backdrop to the case before him concerning the Champaign Board of Education in Illinois: "If it were merely a question of enabling a child to obtain religious instruction with a receptive mind the thirty or forty-five minutes could readily be found on Saturday or Sunday."[10] Notwithstanding his suggestion, the background that he has already provided demonstrates that such attempts were not generally successful.

Frankfurter continues, "If that were all, Champaign might have drawn upon the French system, known in its American manifestation as 'dismissed time,' whereby one school day is shortened to allow all children to go where they please, leaving those who so desire to go to a religious school."[11] Although Frankfurter suggests here that the Champaign school district might have adopted some version of "dismissed time," he has already demonstrated in his opinion that even that proposal met with opposition. So his suggestion hardly puts the question to rest.

Besides, Frankfurter then proceeds to criticize the proposal of "dismissed time" by seeing it in terms of favoring one option over another instead of seeing it as attempting to accommodate various aims: "The momentum of the whole school atmosphere and school planning is presumably put behind religious instruction, as given in Champaign, precisely in order to secure for the religious instruction such momentum and planning."[12] He then, again, equivocates somewhat by speaking in generalities about hypotheticals that do not characterize the Champaign school district:

> We do not consider, as indeed we could not, school programs not before us which, though colloquially characterized as 'released time,' present situations differing in aspects that may well be constitutionally crucial. Different forms which 'released time' has taken during more than thirty years of growth include programs which, like that before us, could not withstand the test of the Constitution; others may be found unexceptionable. We do not now attempt to weigh in the Constitutional scale every separate detail or various combination of factors which may establish a valid 'released time' program.

Nonetheless, Frankfurter makes his position clear with respect to these types of cases, saying, "We find that *the basic Constitutional principle of absolute separation* was violated when the State of Illinois, speaking through its Supreme Court, sustained the school authorities of Champaign in sponsoring and effectively furthering religious beliefs by its educational arrangement."[13] So, even though Frankfurter speculates about whether the Champaign school district might have pursued other paths, his conjecture changes his conclusions. For while he shows some sympathy toward those who would be disappointed with his opinion, his position is ultimately one of absolute church-state separation.

Frankfurter bases his concurring opinion partly on his interpretation of Jefferson's views. He writes, "Separation means separation, not something less. Jefferson's metaphor in describing the relation between Church and State speaks of a 'wall of separation,' not of a fine line easily overstepped."[14] By "wall of separation," Frankfurter is referring to a statement in Jefferson's letter to the Danbury Baptist Association of Connecticut. Suffice it to say that he views attempts to accommodate church and state as violating the Constitution. To be sure, they violate Frankfurter's vision for church-state relations, but they do not, in fact, violate Jefferson's views of church-state relations because, as we will see in following chapters, he misunderstood Jefferson's meaning.

Frankfurter then turns to a particular vision of public education, writing, "The public school is at once the symbol of our democracy and the most pervasive means for promoting our common destiny. In no activity of the State is it more vital to keep out divisive forces than in its schools, to avoid confusing, not to say fusing, what the Constitution sought to keep strictly apart."[15] Frankfurter's reference to democracy implies some input of the *demos*, the people. As his analysis has borne out, myriad localities pursued an approach to church-state relations of accommodation. Yet, unlike his claim that the Constitution sought to keep them strictly apart, I will argue that the First Amendment supports a vision of accommodation—perhaps not every approach to accommodation but accommodation nonetheless.

Additionally, Frankfurter's ideal of keeping division out of Americans' "common" education is noble. Nevertheless, amid a nation of so many people, that ideal, even according to the standards of his day, is unrealistic. For that reason the founders' ideal of federalism, wherein localities within a given federation make policies that best fit their populace, is a better approach than Frankfurter's one-size-fits-all approach.

Undoubtedly, Frankfurter believes that the Supreme Court's pursuit of strict church-state separation accords with the Constitution as well as the health of the nation: "'The great American principle of eternal separation'—Elihu Root's phrase bears repetition—is one of the vital reliances of our Constitutional system for assuring unities among our people stronger than our diversities." He remarks that the Court has the "duty to enforce this principle in its full integrity."[16] He then quotes from *Everson*, writing, "We renew our conviction that 'we have staked the very existence of our country on the faith that complete separation between the state and religion is best for the state and best for religion.'" He concludes his opinion by quoting Robert Frost: "If nowhere else, in the relation between Church and State, 'good fences make good neighbors.'"[17]

Phrases that Frankfurter uses throughout his concurrence, such as "absolute separation," "eternal separation," and "complete separation," are rather strong terms. Still, as we have seen, he shows more sympathy than these phrases convey. Nevertheless, they do not characterize the visions of Jefferson and Madison, on whom these justices rely. Additionally, they do not characterize the approach of church-state accommodation—again, not to be confused with religious establishment—that many localities had pursued through the course of United States history.

Reservations about the Majority Opinion (Justice Jackson)

Although Justice Jackson joined Justice Frankfurter's concurrence, Jackson felt disposed to give attention to additional points. Whereas Frankfurter gave an overview of education in Europe, the Colonies, and the United States, including shifting opinions from a sectarian education to a secular one and their implications for the relationship of church and state, Jackson focused on several reservations that he held about the majority opinion. These include concerns about whether the Supreme Court had jurisdiction to hear the case, the Court's failure to put sufficient limitations on the scope of its holding, the rights of local communities and states to make laws and policies that reflect their respective demographics, and others.

To begin, Jackson questions whether the Court had jurisdiction to hear the *McCollum* case in the first place: "I think it is doubtful whether the facts of this case establish jurisdiction in this Court." Nonetheless, Jackson affirms that the Court "should place some bounds on the demands for interference with local schools that we are empowered or willing to entertain." Yet he also expresses various concerns about the Court's involvement. First, "I make these reservations a matter of record in view of the number of litigations likely to be started as a result of this decision."[18]

Jackson's concession that he doubts that the Court had jurisdiction even to hear the case demonstrates that these issues were generally reserved to state courts to rule on in accordance with the unique demographic make-up of the people of that state. That approach recognized distinctions within the larger national body, which is a characteristic for which federations allow. Even though Jackson doubted the Court's jurisdiction, he also indicated his belief that the Court should rule on the subject of church-state relations anyway. Among other things, this judgment indicates an activist Court going beyond its proper charge—again, because these issues were generally left to states. Finally, Jackson observes that much litigation will result from the Court's majority holding. More specifically, the reasons that litigation would follow were at least twofold: first, because the Court was stepping beyond its proper delegation and, second, because the Court's holding of strict church-state separation would indicate a shift away from attempts at reasonable church-state accommodation.

Jackson also expresses concern for potential embarrassment or humiliation of the child: "When others join and he does not, it sets him apart as a dissenter, which is humiliating."[19] Even so, Jackson continues, it is not a sufficient constitutional consideration: "Even admitting this to be true, it may be doubted whether the Constitution which, of course, protects the right to dissent, can be construed also to protect one from the embarrassment that always attends nonconformity, whether in religion, politics, behavior or dress."[20] Whether Jackson would say the same in the contemporary United States is an interesting question to consider. Nonetheless, while we can appreciate Jackson's concern, his constitutional point is accurate.

Jackson then returns to his concerns about the Court's jurisdiction, as well as to the importance of placing limitations on the Court's authority. In order to make that point, he focuses on Vashti McCollum and her requests to the Court. "The plaintiff, as she has every right to be, is an avowed atheist," Jackson explains.[21]

Undoubtedly, he is right, and McCollum's religious commitments are in keeping with the First Amendment. He then shifts to McCollum's specific requests:

> What she has asked of the courts is that they not only end the 'released time' plan but also ban every form of teaching which suggests or recognizes that there is a God. She would ban all teaching of the Scriptures. She especially mentions as an example of invasion of her rights "having pupils learn and recite such statements as, 'The Lord is my Shepherd, I shall not want.'" And she objects to teaching that the King James version of the Bible "is called the Christian's Guide Book, the Holy Writ and the Word of God," and many other similar matters.[22]

In essence, McCollum requested the strict separation of church and state, which the Court's majority upheld. She seems to have failed to recognize that the beliefs she promoted favor the accommodation of one type of religious belief, namely that of the atheistic variety, to the exclusion of others. Nonetheless, the Court failed to practice judicial restraint but, instead, sustained McCollum's complaint and directed the Illinois courts to comply with its ruling, notwithstanding the fact that, as Jackson correctly argued, it lacked the jurisdiction to do so.

With these points in place, Jackson then expresses grave concern about the Court's failure to establish responsible bounds for its decision and its implications for education. Justice Black issued the majority opinion "without laying down any standards to define the limits of the effect of our decision." He proceeds to use the language of *danger* and *warning*, saying, "To me, the sweep and detail of these complaints is a danger signal which warns of the kind of local controversy we will be required to arbitrate if we do not place appropriate limitation on our decision and exact strict compliance with jurisdictional requirements."[23] Additionally, local communities are generally in the best position to determine what is best for their respective communities.

Jackson continues his concerns by talking about people's sensitivities: "If we are to eliminate everything that is objectionable to any of these warring sects or inconsistent with any of their doctrines, we will leave public education in shreds. Nothing but educational confusion and a discrediting of the public school system can result from subjecting it to constant law suits."[24] As the course of American legal history since that late 1940s has demonstrated, Jackson's concerns have proven prescient. In fact, matters have worsened considerably.

Even against his prior admission that the Court's jurisdiction in this case is "doubtful," he writes, "We may and should end such formal and explicit instruction as the Champaign plan, and can at all times prohibit teaching of creed and catechism and ceremonial, and can forbid forthright proselyting in the schools." Yet Jackson goes on to point out additional complications resulting from the plaintiff's requests, as well as the Court's agreeing with her requests: "I think it remains to be demonstrated whether it is possible, even if desirable, to comply with such demands as plaintiff's completely to isolate and cast out of secular education all that some people may reasonably regard as religious instruction."[25]

As I have argued, Jackson's point is entirely correct. A truly secular education is impossible because all instruction makes implicit assumptions and claims, if not explicit declarations, about questions of divinity, morality, and so forth, whether through its formal curriculum or its null curriculum. Jackson proposes, "Perhaps subjects such as mathematics, physics or chemistry are, or can be, completely secularized."[26] I would disagree with that claim insofar as the presentation and interpretation of all subjects are value-laden, not to mention that the philosophy undergirding one's understanding of these subjects are also laden with values. Still, we can recognize that these subjects are distinct from the others that Jackson gets into.

"But it would not seem practical to teach either practice or appreciation of the arts if we are to forbid exposure of youth to any religious influences. Music without sacred music, architecture minus the cathedral, or painting without the scriptural themes would be eccentric and incomplete, even from a secular point of view."[27] Again, Jackson is entirely on point. The logical conclusion of McCollum's request would result in difficulties for those educators attempting to demonstrate integrity toward their subject. The fact is that our views of the world undergird all that we do. Whether they are "sectarian, pagan, or atheistical"—to use the Court's language—they demonstrate a religious viewpoint.

"Yet the inspirational appeal of religion in these guises is often stronger than in forthright sermon," Jackson continues. "Even such a 'science' as biology raises the issue between evolution and creation as an explanation of our presence on this planet. Certainly a course in English literature that omitted the Bible and other powerful uses of our mother tongue for religious ends would be pretty barren." Jackson concludes his remarks on this point by talking about the inevitability of religion, a point that I introduced above:

> The fact is that, for good or for ill, *nearly everything in our culture worth transmitting, everything which gives meaning to life, is saturated with religious influences*, derived from paganism, Judaism, Christianity—both Catholic and Protestant—and other faiths accepted by a large part of the world's peoples. One can

hardly respect a system of education that would leave the student wholly ignorant of the currents of religious thought that move the world society for a part in which he is being prepared. But how one can teach, with satisfaction or even with justice to all faiths, such subjects as the story of the Reformation, the Inquisition, or even the New England effort to found "a Church without a Bishop and a State without a King," is more than I know. It is too much to expect that mortals will teach subjects about which their contemporaries have passionate controversies with the detachment they may summon to teaching about remote subjects such as Confucius or Mohammed.[28]

Next, Jackson expresses reservations about the Court making pronouncements that will affect local communities and states when the fact is that they are in the better positions to set policy for the people within their communities and states. I mentioned this same basic point above; customs and conventions will vary among different groups and subgroups of people. "Neighborhoods differ in racial, religious and cultural compositions," he writes. "It must be expected that they will adopt different customs which will give emphasis to different values and will induce different experiments. And it must be expected that, no matter what practice prevails, there will be many discontented and possibly belligerent minorities."[29]

In any society of people, we will find those with whom we disagree. We have to learn how to live with people who have different viewpoints from ours rather than acting as if those viewpoints do not exist by functionally exiling those viewpoints outside the bounds of society. Such approaches do not keep with the human experience. Consequently, says Jackson, "We must leave some flexibility to meet local conditions, some chance to progress by trial and error."[30]

Jackson then renews his objection about the complaint's demands, not to the mention the Court's obliging those demands, exceeding proper bounds, as well as issues related to the Court's failure to give helpful guidelines and limitations to states: "While I agree that the religious classes involved here go beyond permissible limits, I also think the complaint demands more than plaintiff is entitled to have granted. So far as I can see, this Court does not tell the State court where it may stop, nor does it set up any standards by which the State court may determine that question for itself." Jackson also recognizes that the Court's doctrine of strict church-state separation is easier said than done. The task of education is an exceedingly complex one: "The task of separating the secular from the religious in education is one of magnitude, intricacy and delicacy."[31]

Even though Jackson issues a concurring opinion, he acknowledges the difficulties of a one-size-fits all approach to this question of the relationship between church and state. "To lay down a sweeping constitutional doctrine as demanded by complainant and apparently approved by the Court, applicable alike to all school boards of the nation, 'to immediately adopt and enforce rules and regulations prohibiting all instruction in and teaching to religious education in all public schools,'" Jackson writes, "is to decree a uniform, rigid and, if we are consistent, an unchanging standard for countless school boards representing and serving highly localized groups which not only differ from each other but which themselves from time to time change attitudes."[32]

Jackson then remarks that the Court's holding demonstrates that it is acting more like a board of education than a court of law: To impose this decree is "to allow zeal for our own ideas of what is good in public instruction to induce us to accept the role of a super board of education for every school district in the nation."[33] Jackson thus recognizes that localities differ one from another and, consequently, require different approaches. The Court's approach also preempts creative, localized trouble-shooting that responds to the contingencies of that locality, and it oversteps prudential considerations.

In addition to passing over sensible prudential bounds, the Court exceeds constitutional and legal authority. Jackson explains: "It is idle to pretend that this task is one for which we can find in the Constitution one word to help us as judges to decide where the secular ends and the sectarian begins in education. Nor can we find guidance in any other legal source. It is a matter on which we can find no law but our own prepossessions."[34]

Thus notwithstanding the majority opinion, in which Justice Black presumed to appeal to numerous legal and historical sources, Jackson argues to the contrary, that neither American constitutional nor legal history offers any legitimate reference point. Additionally, Jackson's remark that it "is a matter on which we can find no law but our own prepossessions," suggests that the majority's appeal to various legal bases indicates pretext rather than precedent. In this way, Jackson and I make similar arguments.

Jackson then explains that the Court has only begun to hear complaints if, indeed, it is going to begin deciding cases such as *McCollum*. "If with no surer legal guidance we are to take up and decide every variation of this controversy, raised by persons not subject to penalty or tax but who are dissatisfied with the way schools are dealing with the problem, we are likely to have much business of the sort," he writes, before concluding with these words: "And, more importantly, we are likely to make the legal 'wall of separation between church and state' as winding as the famous serpentine wall designed by Mr. Jefferson for the University he founded."³⁵ It is fitting that he would end his concurrence with a reference to the Jefferson and the University of Virginia because, as I will consider, his vision for the university comprises key evidence for the reasonable accommodation of church and state.

Dissenting from the Majority Opinion (Justice Reed)

Justice Reed had previously voted with the majority in the *Everson v. Board of Education* but produced the sole dissent in *McCollum*. "As I am convinced that this [majority] interpretation of the First Amendment is erroneous, I feel impelled to express the reasons for my disagreement."³⁶ He establishes the difficulty of identifying a specific example of unconstitutional behavior: "I find it difficult to extract from the opinions any conclusion as to what it is in the Champaign plan that is unconstitutional."³⁷ After reviewing several possibilities, he writes, "I can only deduce that religious instruction of public school children during school hours is prohibited," but then he adds: "The history of American education is against such an interpretation of the First Amendment."³⁸

Rather, Reed explains that, over time, justices of the Court have extended the meaning of religious establishment beyond what the previous generations, including the founders, had envisioned. Specifically, religious establishment had applied to the legal establishment of a church. However, "never until today," writes Reed, "has this Court widened its interpretation to any such degree as holding that recognition of the interest of our nation in religion, through the granting, to qualified representatives of the principal faiths, of opportunity to present religion as an optional, extracurricular subject during released school time in public school buildings, was equivalent to an establishment of religion."³⁹

So much of this question goes back to one's understanding of Jefferson's view of the church-state relationship. A key aim of this book is to reach an understanding of what Jefferson believed about these matters because it has implication for a proper understanding of the First Amendment. I have already considered how Justices Black (majority) and Frankfurter (concurrence) interpret Jefferson. However, Reed takes a different approach, introducing into the Court's record some very important information about Jefferson.

Reed sets the scene, saying, "Mr. Jefferson, as one of the founders of the University of Virginia, a school which from its establishment in 1819 has been wholly governed, managed and controlled by the State of Virginia, was faced with the same problem that is before this Court today: the question of the constitutional limitation upon religious education in public schools."[40] Reed then introduces the annual report that Jefferson delivered to the President and Directors of the Literary Fund on October 7, 1822. As we will see, he supports reasonable accommodation rather than strict separation.

The Visitors (what today we might call a board) of the University, which included James Madison, approved Jefferson's report. That Madison comprised this group is significant because his views are such an important focus in the *Everson* and *McCollum* opinions. By assenting to Jefferson's report, Madison assented to its content. Additionally, if we find that the majority and concurring opinions interpreted Jefferson incorrectly—that, instead, Reed interprets him correctly—then we can expect the same with respect to Madison.

The substance of Jefferson's report was adopted into the Regulations of the University, providing: "Should the religious sects of this State, or any of them, according to the invitation held out to them, establish within, or adjacent to, the precincts of the

University, schools for instruction in the religion of their sect, the students of the University will be free, and expected to attend religious worship at the establishment of their respective sects, in the morning, and in time to meet their school in the University at its stated hour."[41] I will investigate Jefferson's report at some length in chapter eleven, but Reed's dissent serves as an appropriate introduction to the document.

Notwithstanding the contrary interpretations of Black et al., Jefferson did not interpret the Establishment Clause as broadly as they would. Neither did he pursue the strict separation of church and state. "Thus, the 'wall of separation between church and State' that Mr. Jefferson built at the University which he founded did not exclude religious education from that school," explains Reed. "The difference between the generality of his statements on the separation of church and state and the specificity of his conclusions on education are considerable. A rule of law should not be drawn from a figure of speech."[42]

Concerning Madison, Reed explains that his Memorial and Remonstrance against Religious Assessments lacks relevance for *McCollum*.[43] Just as I will consider Jefferson's letter to the Danbury Baptist Association, as well as his Report of the Commissioners for the University of Virginia at some length in part three, I will likewise consider Madison's Remonstrance. Suffice it to say for now: Throughout the Remonstrance, Madison refers to "establishment." Additionally, the historical setting of the document demonstrates that the Remonstrance signified a protest against an effort by Virginia to support Christian sects by taxation.

By contrast, circumstances surrounding the accommodation of religion at the University of Virginia, as well as the Champaign school district in *McCollum*, were quite distinct. As we have seen, Madison assented to Jefferson's vision, which offers a clearer indication of his views of church-state accommodation within the sphere of public education than his general statements on a different subject. The majority opinions of *Everson* and *McCollum* focused on Madison's Remonstrance, as well as Jefferson's letter to the Danbury Baptist Association. However, Black not only misinterpreted Madison and Jefferson but also failed to deal sufficiently with Jefferson's report to the commissioners, which should have carried much more weight than it did.

In order to guard against the wrong impression, Reed finds much in the majority and dissenting opinions with which he agrees. For example, he explains, "I agree, as there stated, that none of our governmental entities can 'set up a church.' I agree that they cannot 'aid' all or any religions or prefer one 'over another.' . . . I agree that pupils cannot 'be released in part from their legal duty' of school attendance upon condition that they attend religious classes." Again, alluding to Madison's Remonstrance, he writes, "Of course, no tax can be levied to support organizations intended 'to teach or practice religion.' I agree too that the state cannot influence one toward religion against his will or punish him for his beliefs." Reed identifies his primary difference from his fellow justices: "Champaign's religious education course does none of these things."[44]

Conclusion

Throughout part two I have reviewed *Everson v. Board of Education* and *McCollum v. Board of Education*. These cases introduced key documents, especially from Jefferson and Madison. I have argued that the justices largely misinterpreted these documents, except for Reed in *McCollum*. In part three I will turn our attention particularly to these documents in order to discern the intentions of Jefferson and Madison with the hope that they will provide a better way forward than the view of strict separation that we have inherited from these cases.

PART III

Thomas Jefferson: Reclaiming Jefferson's View of Religious Freedom and the Reasonable Accommodation of Church and State

CHAPTER EIGHT

Introducing Religious Freedom: James Madison and Thomas Jefferson

In part two we examined two Supreme Court cases of considerable importance for our discussion: *Everson v. Board of Education* (1947) and *McCollum v. Board of Education* (1948). In their opinions of these cases, the justices discussed several major documents, authored by James Madison and Thomas Jefferson, which have exerted critical influence on the contemporary legal interpretation of how the church and state should relate in society. Throughout part three of this book, we will work our way through these documents, as well as through other relevant records, to help us understand their view of the proper relationship of church and state, or religion and government.

As I made plain previously, we will find that the majority and concurring opinions of *Everson* and *McCollum* misinterpreted these documents, setting the United States on the wrong path. Undoubtedly, Madison and Jefferson both emerge as major players from the founding era who shape the nation's thinking concerning church-state relations, but my main aim is to get at the heart of Jefferson's views on this relationship.

SECULARISM AND THE AMERICAN REPUBLIC

Patrick Henry's Failed Proposal

In order to clarify Jefferson's approach to religious freedom, we must first provide some context by giving attention to the contributions of Madison. He objected strongly to a bill that Patrick Henry proposed in 1784, entitled A Bill Establishing a Provision for Teachers of the Christian Religion. Its aim was to raise taxes in support of Christian teachers promoting Christian morals. He also proposed that the state permit taxpayers to choose which teachers they would support by their taxes. If not for Madison's intervention, Henry's bill likely would have passed the Virginia legislature.

Madison did not believe that the Commonwealth of Virginia should be involved in any way in raising taxes to support religion. He thus led in a move to delay any action until the next meeting of the legislature and published his Memorial and Remonstrance against Religious Assessments in 1785. Madison recalls these details in a letter from November 24, 1826, to Marquis De La Fayette: "In the year 1785, a bill was introduced under the auspices of Mr. Henry, imposing a general tax for support of 'Teachers of the Christian Religion.' It made progress, threatening a majority in its favor. As an expedient to defeat it, we proposed that it should be postponed to another session, and printed in the meantime for public consideration."[1]

Madison went on to explain how his strategies succeeded to quash Henry's bill, as well as how, instead, Jefferson's Virginia bill passed into law, becoming the Virginia Statute for Religious Freedom. "The experiment succeeded," wrote Madison. "The memorial was so extensively signed by the various religious sects, including a considerable portion of the old hierarchy, that the projected innovation was crushed, and under the influence of the popular sentiment thus called forth, the well-known Bill prepared by Mr. Jefferson, for 'Establishing Religious freedom,' passed into a law, as it now stands in our code of statutes."[2] As we have seen, today's Supreme Court agreed with Jefferson and Madison and applied this philosophy to their constitutional interpretation. Therefore, we can rightly say that they should consider as unconstitutional any bill with the same purpose as Henry's: namely, to raise taxes to support teachers of the Christian religion.

JAMES MADISON'S MEMORIAL AND REMONSTRANCE

Madison wrote the Memorial out of a deep conviction that Henry's bill would precipitate a wrong direction for the Commonwealth of Virginia. This document presents the most thorough treatment of the matter of church-state relations that a founding father set forth. So significant is it that I believe it is the most important document in American history in support of religious liberty. As a result, we are going to analyze it with some detail before shifting to consider Jefferson's bill.

Through the course of the document, Madison presented fifteen reasons for his remonstrance (or protest). While we will not review all of them, we will consider ten quotations from them and analyze them. (1) "We hold it for a fundamental and undeniable truth, 'that religion or the duty which we owe to our Creator and the manner of discharging it, can be directed only by reason and conviction, not by force or violence.'"[3] Any fair reading of Madison's Remonstrance will demonstrate that he clearly rests his case on theological foundations. He identifies religion as the duty that we owe to our Creator.

In his concurrence in *McCollum*, Justice Felix Frankfurter correctly observed that "the deep religious feeling of James Madison is stamped upon the Remonstrance."[4] Madison offered a vision of religious freedom that is consistent with a Christian view, holding that the states should not coerce religious belief. People have the freedom to choose or to reject Christianity, as well as religion more generally. The principles that Madison establishes are in the best interest of all people, whether Christian, pagan, secularist, or other.

(2) "It is the duty of every man to render to the Creator such homage and such only as he believes to be acceptable to him." Madison refers to the classical virtue of duty, as well as restating his point against religious coercion, which Justice Hugo Black also established in *Everson*. He also points out that all people owe the duty of honor to their Creator, which precedes any obligation that they have to civil society. He continues, "This duty is precedent, both in order of time and degree of obligation, to the claims of Civil Society. Before any man can be considered as a member of Civil Society, he must be considered as a subject of the Governor of the Universe: And if a member of Civil Society, do it with a saving of his allegiance to the Universal Sovereign."[5]

As we established in part one, the phenomenon of secularism did not exist as such at this time. Madison certainly does not give any indication of its existence. Instead, he points to the importance of believing in a deity. And yet, in his vision of religious freedom, he will not suggest religious establishment in the context of state-supported education either. At the same time, had secularism entered onto the scene by that point, the principles Madison establishes demonstrates that he would not have recommended turning state-supported educational institutions over to secularists. Again, restating his point about religious coercion, Madison writes, "We maintain therefore that in matters of Religion, no man's right is abridged by the institution of Civil Society and that Religion is wholly exempt from its cognizance."[6]

(3) "Who does not see that the same authority which can establish Christianity, in exclusion of all other Religions, may establish with the same ease any particular sect of Christians, in exclusion of all other Sects?" By this question, Madison points out that governments with the power to exclude other religions may also exclude Christianity. For this reason (among others), Christians should support the doctrine of religious liberty. Particularizing the question to Henry's bill, to which Madison is responding, he asks, "That the same authority which can force a citizen to contribute three pence only of his property for the support of any one establishment, may force him to conform to any other establishment in all cases whatsoever?"[7]

(4) "If 'all men are by nature equally free and independent,' all men are to be considered as entering into Society on equal conditions; as relinquishing no more, and therefore retaining no less, one than another, of their natural rights." Note how Madison applies his principle to religion. He identifies religious freedom as a "natural right." The Creator has embedded this right in nature. Thus civil authority does not *give* this right, although it may choose to recognize it. If civil government gave natural rights, then it could also take them away. Appealing again to non-coercion, as well as conscience, Madison writes, "Above all are they to be considered as retaining an '*equal* title to the free exercise of Religion according to the dictates of Conscience.'"[8]

(5) "Whilst we assert for ourselves a freedom to embrace, to profess and to observe the Religion which we believe to be of divine origin, we cannot deny an equal freedom to those whose minds have not yet yielded to the evidence which has convinced us."[9] By *religion* Madison is referring to Christianity. Thus the personal pronouns that follow indicate that he is appealing to Christians and that he identifies himself among them—at least in some

broad sense. At the time of the American founding, atheism was almost non-existent, although Deism and Unitarianism enjoyed some success. Even so, the population at large operated within a Christian frame of reference, within the context of Christianity's moral ideals. Noah Feldman gives an excellent depiction of the United States at the time of the founding, explaining:

> In the framers' America, almost everybody was a Protestant of some kind, and atheism as a publicly acknowledged stance was essentially unknown. The remaining orthodox Calvinists still adhered to the doctrine of the predestined salvation of only the elect, while moral liberal Protestants increasingly opened the doors of possible salvation much wider, and deists like Jefferson rejected the very idea of a personal God. But these different ideas swam in a sea of Protestant assumptions, and the framers' generation argued politics in the light of the ideals connected to their common Protestant legacy. Rather than insisting anachronistically on "Judeo-Christian values," it would be more accurate to say that the framers assumed a whole set of principles that grew out of Protestant Christianity as interpreted by English liberals such as John Locke.[10]

From one angle, when we examine a culture, we are looking at the way people live. From another angle, we are considering the way they think they ought to live in their most noble aspirations and ideals. Invariably, we discover a gap between the way people live and the way they propose that they should live. At certain points in our history, this gap has been bigger than at other times. However, at the time of our founding fathers, a gap certainly existed. Still, Christianity's moral ideals were deeply embedded in the psyche of the culture. With these things in mind, Madison then mentions human transgression and divine judgment, writing, "If this freedom be abused, it is an offence against God, not against man: To God, therefore, not to man, must an account of it be rendered."[11]

(6) Having appealed to the notions of duty, non-coercion, natural rights, and conscience, Madison turns to history and then to experience. Referring to Henry's bill, Madison explains, "The establishment proposed by the Bill is not requisite for the support of the Christian Religion. To say that it is, is a contradiction to the Christian Religion itself," he continues, pointing to Christian history, "for every page of it disavows a dependence on the powers of this world: it is a contradiction to fact; for it is known that this Religion both existed and flourished, not only without the support of human laws, but in spite of every opposition from them, and not only during the period of miraculous aid, but long after it had been left to its own evidence and the ordinary care of Providence."[12]

Note Madison's theological astuteness from that quotation. His mentioning the "period of miraculous aid" refers to the time following the death and resurrection of Jesus Christ; it refers to that period of the Book of Acts in which the apostles performed miracles. During His own ministry, Jesus had performed many miracles, which evidenced God's stamp of approval on Jesus and His claims. His disciples continued to perform miracles—hence the "period of miraculous aid"—but only for a time, after which they began to cease. Yet Christianity still flourished, Madison observes, even after the period of miraculous aid had elapsed and despite the opposition that met it in time prior to the reign of Constantine.

(7) Having appealed to the notions of duty, non-coercion, natural rights, conscience, and history, Madison turns to experience. "Experience witnesseth that ecclesiastical establishments, instead of maintaining the purity and efficacy of Religion, have had a contrary operation." Referring from the time of Constantine to the present

day, Madison continues, "During almost fifteen centuries has the legal establishment of Christianity been on trial. What have been its fruits? More or less in all places, pride and indolence in the Clergy, ignorance and servility in the laity, in both, superstition, bigotry and persecution." In other words, history and experience demonstrate that the marriage of church and state, or religious establishment, has had a negative effect on Christianity rather than a positive one. "Enquire of the Teachers of Christianity for the ages in which it appeared in its greatest luster; those of every sect, point to the ages prior to its incorporation with Civil policy."[13] That is to say, they point to that age prior to Constantine. Christianity does not require the support of the civil government for its welfare.

(8) "Torrents of blood have been spilt in the old world, by vain attempts of the secular arm, to extinguish Religious discord, by proscribing all difference in Religious opinion."[14] I include this quotation for two reasons. First, his appeal to religious coercion and the religious warfare that followed advances Madison's argument for religious freedom. Second, his usage of a "secular arm" has no reference to the movement of secularism, which would not emerge for another sixty-plus years. Instead, it has more in common with that older usage, meaning something akin to temporal in contrast to eternal. I would also mention that Madison's reference to *secular* evidences the only time that I have discovered where he used that term or any of its derivatives.

(9) "The policy of the Bill is adverse to the diffusion of the light of Christianity. The first wish of those who enjoy this precious gift ought to be that it may be imparted to the whole race of mankind."[15] Evidently, Madison affirms the "light of Christianity," which he refers to as a "precious gift." However, Henry's bill, owing to its coercive nature, would violate the principle of religious freedom and harm the prospect of Christian witness.

INTRODUCING RELIGIOUS FREEDOM

(10) "Compare the number of those who have as yet received it [the precious gift] with the number still remaining under the dominion of false Religions; and how small is the former! Does the policy of the Bill tend to lessen the disproportion?" Madison asks. "No," he answers emphatically, "it at once discourages those who are strangers to the light of revelation from coming into the Region of it; and countenances by example the nations who continue in darkness, in shutting out those who might convey it to them."[16] *Strangers* refer to those who have not received the light of revelation. *Revelation* refers to the revealing of God, whom Madison has referred to as Creator, Governor of the Universe, Universal Sovereign, and Providence. The *darkness* refers to the state of those who do not walk with the light of God's revelation.

Madison returns to Henry's bill, saying it would do more harm than good: "Instead of Leveling as far as possible, every obstacle to the victorious progress of Truth, the Bill with an ignoble and unchristian timidity would circumscribe it with a wall of defense against the encroachments of error."[17] Governments that would forbid religious freedom by decree to those who may belong to other religions demonstrate an "unchristian timidity."

In the twenty-first century, many consider it great bigotry for anyone to claim that his religion is true and that another's is false. However, for his part, Madison did not hesitate to state that some religions are false. At the same time, he believed strongly in the doctrine of religious freedom, even for those who profess false religions. In the same way, they may believe their religion true and other religions false. Whatever the case, the marketplace of ideas serves as the superior platform upon which to reason out these disagreements rather than coerced belief, which, as Madison has said, begets bigotry, persecution, and other poisonous fruits.

THOMAS JEFFERSON'S VIRGINIA STATUTE FOR RELIGIOUS FREEDOM

Having reviewed Henry's failed bill and Madison's Remonstrance, we turn now to Jefferson's bill, which would become the Virginia Statute for Religious Freedom. Understanding Jefferson's views on this topic is important for several reasons. For one, the Supreme Court invoked them in its articulation of the strict separation of church and state. As we will see, the justices fundamentally misinterpreted him. Second, like Madison, he would significantly shape the American vision of church-state relations from the founding. Jefferson drafted a bill for establishing religious freedom in 1777, the year after he had written the Declaration of Independence. In 1779 he tried to get it passed into law in Virginia but failed. The time was not yet ripe.

However, with Henry's attempting to pass a bill that would raise taxes to support Christian teachers in 1784 and Madison's strong opposition to it in his Remonstrance in 1785, Jefferson's bill was reintroduced, becoming law in 1786. Incidentally, Jefferson was in France at the time, serving as Minister Plenipotentiary. These three documents (Henry's bill, Madison's Remonstrance, and Jefferson's bill) furnish the context for understanding the religion clauses in the First Amendment. In fact, Justice Black wrote the following in *Everson*: "The provisions of the First Amendment, in the drafting and adoption of which Madison and Jefferson played such leading roles, had the same objective and were intended to provide the same protection against governmental intrusion on religious liberty as the Virginia statute."[18]

Jefferson's bill reads in part:

> Almighty God hath created the mind free; that all attempts to influence it by temporal punishments, or burthens, or by

civil incapacitations, tend only to beget habits of hypocrisy and meanness, and are a departure from the plan of the holy author of our religion, who being Lord both of body and mind, yet chose not to propagate it by coercions on either, as was in his Almighty power to do. . . . We are free to declare, and do declare, that the rights hereby asserted are of the natural rights of mankind, and that if any act shall be hereafter passed to repeal the present or to narrow its operation, such act will be an infringement of natural right.[19]

As we saw in part one, secularism as such would not make its debut until the mid-1800s. George Jacob Holyoake would not even coin the term *secularism* until 1846, and the British Secular Movement would not form until five years later. Consequently, by no stretch of the imagination could we consider Jefferson a secularist. Similarly, he was not an agnostic; Thomas H. Huxley would not even coin the term until approximately fifty years after Jefferson's death. Yet neither was Jefferson an orthodox Christian, rejecting, as he did, the doctrine of the Trinity.[20] Nevertheless, Jefferson was one of the most God-conscious presidents in United States history, and he affirmed the doctrine of religious freedom. Although he was not a secularist, he undoubtedly would have afforded this freedom to its advocates also.

Several of the themes in this quoted portion bear similarities to those in Madison's Remonstrance: among them a theological foundation, non-coercion, and natural rights. Jefferson identifies a deity as Almighty God and Lord. He also explains that civil authorities should guarantee to people the religious freedom to follow their own convictions. To make that point, Jefferson appeals to natural rights, by which he means those rights that God has woven into the very fabric of nature. Recognizing the possibility that future governments would nullify the bill, he also states that restrictions on religious freedom would violate man's natural rights.

Conclusion

The 1780s were an important decade for religious liberty. Through the course of this chapter, we reviewed Madison's Memorial and Remonstrance against Religious Assessments at some length. We also introduced Jefferson's Virginia Statute for Religious Freedom, although we did not spend as much time with it as we did with Madison's Remonstrance because it is considerably shorter and because we will spend considerable time with Jefferson in the subsequent chapters. However, both documents, the Remonstrance and the Virginia Statute, signify a vision of religious liberty that stood at odds with Henry's bill and that would manifest itself in the religion clauses in the First Amendment, which we will consider in the next chapter.

CHAPTER NINE

THE FIRST AMENDMENT AND THE "WALL OF SEPARATION"

The Bill of Rights of the Constitution of the United States begins with the First Amendment. This amendment, as we have discussed, was important in the Supreme Court's understanding of the relationship between church and state, or religion and government. However, before considering it, we will survey the ratification process of the Constitution and the Bill of Rights, as well as the involvement of James Madison and Thomas Jefferson. From May until September in 1787, the Constitutional Convention met in Philadelphia. The final draft of the Constitution was presented on September 17, 1787, and it was ratified within a year. At the time, Jefferson served as the Minister Plenipotentiary to France. As a result, he was physically absent and could not participate in the give-and-take of hammering out the details of the Constitution.

Nevertheless, he exerted some influence on its content owing to his close relationship with Madison, the "Father of the Constitution."[1] In fact, Jefferson received a draft of the Constitution in November of 1787. Although he generally approved of it, he urged adding a Bill of Rights. Madison initially disagreed with Jefferson's view, not thinking that it was necessary. However, as debate ensued, Madison began to champion a Bill of Rights. By June 8, 1789, he submitted seventeen amendments; in the process of debate, they were reduced to twelve. By September 24, 1789, the House of Representatives and Senate had approved the Bill of Rights and sent them to the states for ratification. By 1791 the states adopted ten amendments, which became the Bill of Rights.[2]

For our purposes, the most important amendment is the First Amendment, particularly the Establishment Clause and the Free Exercise Clause: "Congress shall make no law respecting an establishment of religion, or prohibiting the free exercise thereof."[3] How should we interpret these clauses? A series of letters between the Danbury Baptist Association of Connecticut and Jefferson will help answer this question.

THOMAS JEFFERSON AND THE DANBURY BAPTIST ASSOCIATION

On October 7, 1801, the Danbury Baptist Association sent Jefferson a letter, expressing concerns about the prospect of religious coercion. By this time, Jefferson was the third president of the United States. He replied a few months later, referring to "a wall of separation between church and state." As we noted in part two, that phrase would exert a major influence on the legal interpretation of the First Amendment nearly 150 years later in *Everson v. Board of Education* and *McCollum v. Board of Education* in which the majority opinion argued that it demonstrated Jefferson's vision for the strict separation of church and state. In the words of Justice Hugo Black, "The First Amendment has erected a wall between church and state. That wall must be kept high and impregnable. We could not approve the slightest breach."[4] However, as we will see, the full context of this interchange does not justify that interpretation.

THE "WALL OF SEPARATION"

The Danbury Baptists give rise to the issues at hand; Jefferson responds with an appeal to the First Amendment. Because the interchange between Jefferson and the Danbury Baptists serves as a critical ground on which discussions of church-state relations occur, I will include the entire letter that the Danbury Baptists sent to Jefferson, as well as the entire letter that he sent back to them:

> Among the many millions in America and Europe who rejoice in your Election to office; we embrace the first opportunity which we have enjoyed in our collective capacity, since your Inauguration, to express our great satisfaction, in your appointment to the chief Magistracy in the United States: And though our mode of expression may be less courtly and pompous than what many others clothe their addresses with, we beg you, Sir to believe, that none are more sincere.
>
> Our Sentiments are uniformly on the side of Religious Liberty—That Religion is at all times and places a matter between God and Individuals—That no man ought to suffer in Name, person or effects on account of his religious Opinions—That the legitimate Power of civil Government extends no further than to punish the man who *works ill to his neighbor*: But Sir, our constitution of government is not specific. Our ancient charter, together with the Laws made coincident therewith, were adopted as the Basis of our government, At the time of our revolution; and such had been our Laws & usages, and such still are; that Religion is considered as the first object of Legislation; & therefore what religious privileges we enjoy (as a minor part of the State) we enjoy as favors granted, and not as inalienable rights: and these favors we receive at the expense of such degrading acknowledgements, as are inconsistent with the rights

of freemen. It is not to be wondered at therefore; if those, who seek after *power & gain* under the pretense of *government & Religion* should reproach their fellow men—should reproach their chief Magistrate, as an enemy of religion Law & good order because he will not, dare not assume the prerogatives of Jehovah and make Laws to govern the Kingdom of Christ.

Sir, we are sensible that the President of the united States, is not the national Legislator, & also sensible that the national government cannot destroy the Laws of each State; but our hopes are strong that the sentiments of our beloved President, which have had such genial affect already, like the radiant beams of the Sun, will shine & prevail through all these States and all the world till Hierarchy and tyranny be destroyed from the Earth. Sir, when we reflect on your past services, and see a glow of philanthropy and good will shining forth in a course of more than thirty years we have reason to believe that America's God has raised you up to fill the chair of State out of that good will which he bears to the Millions which you preside over. May God strengthen you for the arduous task which providence & the voice of the people have called you to sustain and support you in your Administration against all the predetermined opposition of those who wish to rise to wealth & importance on the poverty and subjection of the people——————

And may the Lord preserve you safe from every evil and bring you at last to his Heavenly Kingdom through Jesus Christ our Glorious Mediator.[5]

The Danbury Baptists begin by expressing gratitude for Jefferson's election to the presidency and ensuring the sincerity of their sentiments. They explain that they support the doctrine of religious liberty, commenting on themes we considered in the last

THE "WALL OF SEPARATION"

chapter, including non-coercion and natural rights. When they say, "Our constitution of government is not specific," they are referring to the State of Connecticut's constitution. They then express concern that the civil government might view religion as "favors granted" rather than an "inalienable right" and, consequently, might even view it as a proper "object of legislation." That concern summarizes well the essence of their complaint.

Such a prospect could preempt free religious expression and lead to religious coercion. If the government views religious expression as something it grants, then it will also view it as something it can take away. Undoubtedly, that vision goes against the principles that Madison established in the Memorial and Remonstrance against Religious Assessments and that Jefferson established in the Virginia Statute for Religious Freedom. The Danbury Baptists then express confidence and hope in Jefferson that he can promote a vision of religious liberty against the prospect of religious "tyranny." Still, they recognize the division of powers among the branches of government, as well as between state and federal governments. They then end their letter with a prayer on Jefferson's behalf.

Jefferson responded approximately three months later on January 1, 1802, with what Daniel Dreisbach describes as "meticulous care and planned effect":[6]

> The affectionate sentiments of esteem and approbation which you are so good as to express towards me, on behalf of the Danbury Baptist Association, give me the highest satisfaction. My duties dictate a faithful and zealous pursuit of the interests of my constituents, and in proportion as they are persuaded of my fidelity to those duties, the discharge of them becomes more and more pleasing.

Believing with you that religion is a matter which lies solely between man and his God, that he owes account to none other for his faith or his worship, that the legislative powers of government reach actions only, and not opinions, *I contemplate with sovereign reverence that act of the whole American people which declared that their legislature should "make no law respecting an establishment of religion, or prohibiting the free exercise thereof," thus building a wall of separation between Church and State.* Adhering to this expression of the supreme will of the nation in behalf of the rights of conscience, I shall see with sincere satisfaction the progress of those sentiments which tend to restore to man all his natural rights, convinced he has no natural right in opposition to his social duties.

I reciprocate your kind prayers for the protection and blessing of the common Father and Creator of man, and tender you for yourselves and your religious association, assurances of my high respect and esteem.[7]

Jefferson begins by expressing thanks for the compliments of Danbury Baptists on his behalf. He informs them that he works toward the interests of his constituents, which, presumably, include them. He then repeats some of the themes concerning religious liberty that we have considered heretofore. Next, he appeals explicitly to the Establishment Clause and Free Exercise Clause of the First Amendment, interpreting them as "building a wall of separation between church and state." He also describes these clauses as an "act of the whole American people" and an "expression of the supreme will of the nation in behalf of the rights of conscience," which are reflective of man's "natural rights." Jefferson concludes the letter with additional thanksgiving for the Danbury Baptists' prayers for him.

THE "WALL OF SEPARATION"

As we established in part two, Jefferson's reply to the Danbury Baptists, especially the italicized portion, has been subject to considerable discussion in the Supreme Court. Justice Wiley B. Rutledge, who authored a dissent in *Everson*, wrote, "This case forces us to determine squarely for the first time what was 'an establishment of religion' in the First Amendment's conception."[8] As we have seen, the majority, using Jefferson's phrase that there is "a wall of separation between church and state," interpreted religious establishment to include a public school district's reimbursing parents for money they expended to transport their children to parochial schools.

Additionally, in *McCollum*, it would interpret establishment to include a public school's offering non-compulsory classes in religious instruction to its students. In light of the broader context of the letter from the Danbury Baptists, Jefferson wrote with the prospect in mind of state-sponsored religious coercion. He responded against a background of constituents that were concerned about the violation of their inalienable right of religious liberty. Neither the fact pattern of *Everson* nor of *McCollum* describes what Jefferson had in mind.

REYNOLDS V. UNITED STATES

One of the cases to which both *Everson* and *McCollum* make reference is *Reynolds v. United States* (1878). It also made reference to Jefferson's usage of the "wall of separation." In fact, it is the first case of the Supreme Court that introduced the correspondence between Jefferson and the Danbury Baptists. The background of *Reynolds* reveals that a grand jury indicted George Reynolds for the crime of bigamy. President Abraham Lincoln had signed the Morrill Anti-Bigamy Act into law in 1862. Reynolds was a member of the Church of Jesus Christ of Latter-day Saints, not to mention a secretary to Brigham

Young, the second president of the LDS. At the time, Utah was still a territory rather than a state. After making its way through the federal court system, the case was heard by the Supreme Court.

Reynolds appealed to the concept of religious liberty to make his case, arguing that the First Amendment allowed him to practice his religion freely, which included bigamy. The Supreme Court ultimately confirmed the lower courts' conviction of Reynolds. Chief Justice Morrison Waite delivered the Court's majority opinion, and it would serve as a model for *Everson* and *McCollum*. As we work our way through the case, we will give attention to those portions that appertain to our primary concern—namely the correct interpretation of the First Amendment—which is informed by Jefferson's Virginia Statute and his response to the Danbury Baptists. Additionally, the interpretation of Jefferson's letter presented in *Reynolds* will shed light on his understanding of the First Amendment.

After reviewing Patrick Henry's attempt to pass his bill and Madison's strong opposition to it, Waite turns to consideration of the Virginia Statute. Quoting from Jefferson, he says: "To suffer the civil magistrate to intrude his powers into the field of opinion, and to restrain the profession or propagation of principles on supposition of their ill tendency is a dangerous fallacy which at once destroys all religious liberty." In other words, government officials should not exceed their proper delegation by intruding into the "field of opinion," specifically religious opinion. Additionally, they should not restrain religious "profession or propagation" just because they believe that such professions are wrong-headed. Jefferson describes these prospects as a "dangerous fallacy" that is contrary to "religious liberty."[9]

However, these principles are not carte blanche for people to do anything they please. That would destroy true religious liberty. Liberty is not license; license destroys liberty. Jefferson explains in the Virginia Statute: "It is time enough for the rightful purposes of civil government for its officers to interfere when principles break out into overt acts against peace and good order." Having quoted these two portions from Jefferson's bill, Waite writes, "In these two sentences is found the true distinction between what properly belongs to the church and what to the State."[10] Specifically, the state has some interest in religious principles when they "break out into overt acts against peace and good order."

We previously established the connection between Jefferson's bill and the First Amendment, even providing a quotation from Justice Black in *Everson* to that effect.[11] Waite also places the two in context. "In a little more than a year after the passage of this statute, the convention met which prepared the Constitution of the United States. Of this convention, Mr. Jefferson was not a member, he being then absent as minister to France." However, he was able to keep abreast of the proceedings. "As soon as he saw the draft of the Constitution proposed for adoption, he, in a letter to a friend, expressed his disappointment at the absence of an express declaration insuring the freedom of religion."[12]

Nevertheless, Jefferson "was willing to accept it as it was, trusting that the good sense and honest intentions of the people would bring about the necessary alterations."[13] Then, as Jefferson predicted, during the ratification process of the Constitution, several states, Virginia among them, "included in one form or another a declaration of religious freedom in the changes they desired to have made." Accordingly, Madison, with others, proposed the First Amendment "at the first session of the first Congress. . . . It met the views of the advocates of religious freedom, and was adopted."[14] These developments provide the context that Waite establishes from which he turns immediately to consider Jefferson's remarks to the Danbury Baptists.

Waite quotes at length from the second paragraph of Jefferson's letter that I presented above, including the portion about "a wall of separation." Waite then remarks, "Coming as this does from an acknowledged leader of the advocates of the measure," namely Jefferson, "it may be accepted almost as *an authoritative declaration of the scope and effect of the amendment thus secured.* Congress was deprived of all legislative power over *mere opinion*, but was left free to reach *actions* which were in violation of social duties or subversive of good order."[15] By so stating, Waite is referring to that part of Jefferson's letter where he writes, "The legislative powers of government reach actions only, and not opinions."[16]

Consequently, the Court, judging the facts of *Reynolds* in light of Congress's legislative act, lacks the authority to forbid religious opinions, as well as religious actions that accord with social duty or good order. In the event that religious actions cause social unrest but are nonetheless consonant with social duties or good order, a government lacks the proper authority to quash those actions precisely because those actions are right. However, if people commit actions in the name of religion that violate social duties or subvert good order, thereby posing a genuine threat to a civil society, then a government may regulate those actions. This distinction demonstrates the importance of Jefferson's remarks in his letter to the Danbury Baptists about a government's authority. The case of practiced bigamy exceeds mere opinion and, instead, demonstrates religious action that does not accord with social duty and subverts good order. Therefore, the language of Jefferson's letter supports the Court's conclusion.

Additionally, Waite argues that Jefferson's statements in his letter to the Danbury Baptists are consistent with the principles he had established previously in the Virginia Statute. To support this claim, Waite points to an episode in which the very issues of bigamy and polygamy arose shortly after the passing of Jefferson's bill. Specifically, he explains that the "legislature of that State [Virginia] substantially enacted the statute of James I., death penalty included," on December 8, 1788, "because, as recited in the preamble, 'it hath been doubted whether bigamy or poligamy be punishable by the laws of this Commonwealth.'"[17]

Waite observes that they passed this statute "after the passage of the act establishing religious freedom," namely Jefferson's Virginia Statute, "and after the convention of Virginia had recommended as an amendment to the Constitution of the United States the declaration in a bill of rights that 'all men have an equal, natural, and unalienable right to the free exercise of religion, according to the dictates of conscience.'" That the Virginia legislature passed this law against bigamy and polygamy *after* these two developments constitutes a "significant fact" because it signifies that that this kind of legal prohibition was consistent with their understanding of religious liberty.[18]

Waite goes on to explain that the understanding of religious liberty from the founding era had not changed over the course of a century, as the *Reynolds* case demonstrates: "From that day to this, we think it may safely be said there never has been a time in any State of the Union when polygamy has not been an offence against society, cognizable by the civil courts and punishable with more or less severity." As a result, the application of religious liberty is not inconsistent with the legal prohibition of improper expressions of marriage. "In the face of all this evidence, it is impossible to believe that the constitutional guaranty of religious freedom was intended to prohibit legislation in respect to this most important feature of social life."[19]

Again, Jefferson, the legislature of Virginia, and the majority justices in *Reynolds* did not interpret the doctrine of religious freedom to mean that anything goes. Waite offers two examples: "Suppose one believed that human sacrifices were a necessary part of religious worship; would it be seriously contended that the civil government under which he lived could not interfere to prevent a sacrifice?" Again, "Or if a wife religiously believed it was her duty to burn herself upon the funeral pile of her dead husband; would it be beyond the power of the civil government to prevent her carrying her belief into practice?"[20] No, right morals undergird the true expression and protection of religious freedom.

The case of marriage, the bedrock of stable society, is a case in point: "Marriage, while from its very nature a sacred obligation, is nevertheless, in most civilized nations, a civil contract, and usually regulated by law. Upon it society may be said to be built, and out of its fruits spring social relations and social obligations and duties with which government is necessarily required to deal."[21] Marriage is not simply a matter of opinion; it concerns the health of civil society. "In fact, according as monogamous or polygamous marriages are allowed, do we find the principles on which the government of the people, to a greater or less extent, rests."[22]

Owing to these considerations, Waite explains, "The statute immediately under consideration is within the legislative power of Congress," which is "constitutional and valid as prescribing a *rule of action*. . . . Laws are made for the government of actions, and while they cannot interfere with *mere religious belief and opinions*, they may with *practices*."[23] Although the civil government cannot make laws against religious opinions, it may interfere with religious actions that would undermine the development of a civilized society, that would violate social duties and subvert good order. Waite's language indicates that he is basing his opinion specifically

THE "WALL OF SEPARATION"

on the distinction that Jefferson had introduced in his letter to the Danbury Baptists, in addition to establishing consistency with Jefferson's Virginia Statute.

INTERPRETING *EVERSON*

Fast-forward to *Everson* and Justice Black writes, "In the words of Jefferson, the clause against establishment of religion by law was intended to erect 'a wall of separation between church and State.'"[24] As we established in part two, Black interprets the Establishment Clause by virtue of Jefferson's phrase in his letter to the Danbury Baptists. However, the careful reader of Black's opinion will note that he does not refer specifically to Jefferson's letter. Instead, he cites *Reynolds*, which we have just reviewed, for authority.

With all due respect to Black, I have given a careful reading to Waite's opinion, and summarized and analyzed it at some length. Nowhere does he make any interpretive comments concerning Jefferson's phrase about a "wall of separation." In fact, the only time that the phrase even appears in *Reynolds* is when Waite quotes the letter. This fact would indicate that Black relied on *Reynolds* only in form. Although his opinion has the appearance of historical precedent, it lacks real substance.

As we have seen, Waite's analysis primarily concerns Jefferson's distinction between opinions and actions. If we are looking for a proper understanding of the doctrine of religious liberty, neither *Everson* nor *McCollum* have it right. Instead, we will find it in the State of Virginia in the 1780s with Madison's Memorial and Remonstrance and Jefferson's Virginia Statute, which influenced the religion clauses in the First Amendment, as well as Jefferson's interpretation of those clauses in his letter to the Danbury Baptists. Thus, despite Black's interpretation of Jefferson's "wall of separation" in his majority opinion in *Everson*, the interpretive leap he makes is not clear either from a plain reading of Jefferson or from *Reynolds*, both of which we have considered.

CONCLUSION

Black's approach of reading Jefferson's phrase back into the First Amendment has produced an interpretation that was contrary to Jefferson's meaning. Instead, we should adopt Waite's approach, seeking to understand the First Amendment in light of the events of the 1780s, which we have done. That context gives us the clues we need to interpret Jefferson's "wall of separation" phrase properly. However, it does not give us our only clues. In the following chapters, we will review further documents from Jefferson that shed light on his view of religious liberty and the appropriate intersection of religion and government. What we will find is that he supported the reasonable accommodation of church and state rather than the strict separation of the two.

CHAPTER TEN

Report of the Commissioners for the University of Virginia

We have previously analyzed two documents from Thomas Jefferson that inform a proper understanding of the First Amendment: the Virginia Statute for Establishing Religious Freedom and his letter to the Danbury Baptist Association. We turn now to consider his Report of the Commissioners for the University of Virginia (dated August 4, 1818), which I view as the most significant discovery that I made through course of research for this book. If you are like me, the chances are high that you have never heard of this report—until now—and I do not believe it has received nearly the scholarly attention that it warrants.[1]

The Report of the Commissioners for the University of Virginia, also called the Rockfish Gap Report, will shed further light on Jefferson's understanding, interpretation, and application of the First Amendment. As I have argued, his vision was not inspired by secularism. Additionally, it does not prompt the strict separation of church and state. Instead, the Rockfish Gap Report demonstrates that Jefferson supported reasonable church-state accommodation, specifically within the realm of public education.

SECULARISM AND THE AMERICAN REPUBLIC

An Overview of the Founding of the University of Virginia

To set the stage, we turn to the year 1814. It was then that Jefferson was elected to the board of trustees for Albemarle Academy. This school did not have any students, but it was in the early stages of its development. By February 14, 1816, Albemarle Academy's name was changed to Central College, and the governor appointed "a board of six visitors," which "could appoint professors and other officers."[2] Edwin Gaustad explains that the governor's appointment gave "the institution (if and when students did show up) more than local significance."[3]

With a new name came all new board members, except for Jefferson, who was the "only one of the old academy board who was re-appointed." New appointees included James Madison, James Monroe, Joseph C. Cabell, David Watson, and J. H. Cocke. Herbert Baxter Adams explains the significance of these developments: "In the new corporation were vested all the rights and privileges of the old board, which handed over the records of Albemarle Academy. The records of Central College extend from May 5, 1817, to May 11, 1818. They are interesting for the light they throw upon the gradual evolution of the University of Virginia from a local seminary."[4]

By February 21, 1818, the Virginia General Assembly approved of funds for a public school, and the governor appointed a group to find a location for the school. Ultimately, this group would choose the site of Central College (formerly Albemarle Academy) for this school, namely the University of Virginia. "At the session of 1818–1819, the Legislature located the University at the Central College, and sanctioned the plan recommended by the University Commissioners."[5] It was after this meeting that Jefferson wrote A

Bill for the Establishment of an University (1818), which would finally open its door to students on March 7, 1825.

The Presidential Triumvirate of the University of Virginia

The founding of the University of Virginia stands alone in having multiple United States presidents involved: Thomas Jefferson, James Madison, and James Monroe. Numerous scholars have commented on the significance of this point. For example, Herbert Adams writes, "Probably no institution of learning in the United States ever had so many presidential trustees."[6]

Similarly, Gaustad observes, "When these three distinguished Americans gathered at Charlottesville for a meeting of the board in May 1817, a curious public might have concluded that momentous happenings were afoot. From such a triumvirate as this, John Adams wrote that same month, 'the world will expect something very great and very new.'" However, Adams tempered his hope with caution: "But perhaps it should not be too new, Adams tactfully suggested, for, 'prejudices are too deeply rooted to suffer it to last long.' He then sensibly cautioned that Jefferson's grand scheme 'will not always have three such colossal reputations to support it.'"[7] As we will see, Jefferson's report strikes a balance to this tension.

Jefferson's Rockfish Gap Report laid the foundation for this august institution of learning. It presents a vision for the reasonable accommodation of church and state at a public educational institution. In addition, significantly, Jefferson developed it in the company of founding fathers such as Madison, Monroe, and others. Consequently, it offers something of a representative look at these figures' views concerning the topics at hand: religious liberty, church-state relations, and public education. We will find that it reveals a much different approach from those presented in *Everson v. Board of Education* and *McCollum v. Board of Education*.

Report of the Commissioners for the University of Virginia

Although Jefferson's Report of the Commissioners for the University of Virginia comprises approximately six thousand words, we will give attention only to those portions that concern our topic. We will find that it contains passages against religious establishment and in favor of religious liberty. We will also find that Jefferson envisioned a public school that was not sectarian or secularist or hostile to religion. Instead, his approach makes room for the reasonable accommodation of church and state; it is not the secularist proposal of strict separation. To begin, we will consider a selection in which Jefferson criticizes religious establishment after which we will spend the majority of our time discussing those passages regarding accommodation.

To give some context to this first one, Jefferson extols the role of education in the advancement of a civilization before denouncing the tendency of some groups to remain stuck in a state of "barbarism and wretchedness." Jefferson applies this principle to the phenomenon of religious establishment: "This doctrine is the genuine fruit of the alliance between Church and State." He then argues that proponents of religious establishment are concerned, at bottom, with money, power, and comfort: "the tenants of which, finding themselves but too well in their present condition, oppose all advances which might unmask their usurpations, and monopolies of honors, wealth, and power, and fear every change, as endangering the comforts they now hold."[8] Jefferson's remarks about the champions of religious establishment notwithstanding, he stands resolutely against the doctrine itself. Yet he also supported reasonable church-state accommodation within the context of public education.

Some paragraphs later Jefferson turns to the application of religious liberty at the University of Virginia. His articulation of these principles demonstrates that Jefferson cared deeply about giving people advantages in *moral* education, and so did the University Commission. Gaustad explains, "The group agreed with the author of the Rockfish Gap Report 'that advantages of well directed education, moral, political, & economical are truly above all estimate.'" The Rockfish Gap Report gave Jefferson "the opportunity to ring the changes on some of his favorite themes," including that "education promoted the love of virtue."[9] To demonstrate these claims, we will analyze the passage in which Jefferson addresses them, breaking it down into three sections.

(1) *Conformity with Constitutional Principles*

Jefferson begins, "In conformity with the principles of our Constitution, which places all sects of religion on an equal footing, with the jealousies of the different sects in guarding that equality from encroachment and surprise, and with the sentiments of the Legislature in favor of freedom of religion, manifested on former occasions, we have proposed no professor of divinity."[10] We might think that Jefferson is referring to the Constitution of the United States, but, in fact, he is referring to the Constitution of Virginia. The year was 1818, and the Supreme Court of the United States would not begin incorporating the Bill of Rights against the states until the twentieth century, which we considered in part two. Thus Jefferson is explaining that Virginia's Constitution treated all religious sects equally.

However, as we observed previously, the intent of the religion clauses in the First Amendment of the federal constitution is the same as that which appears in the Virginia Constitution. Recall that Virginia served as a significant touchpoint for the dispute about religious liberty. Thus the difference is one of application rather than of meaning. Although the word *sect* often signals heterodox or even heretical forms of Christianity in our day, it meant something different in Jefferson's day. It meant something akin to denomination. So Jefferson likely had in mind the various denominations of Christianity. Even so, I believe that he would have also given the same freedom to non-Christian groups.

Jefferson then explains that they have not proposed a professor of divinity at the University of Virginia. That is the primary clause in this particular passage. Divinity professors are sectarian. Because they set forth a particular theology, they would necessarily give an advantage to the confession of their conviction. Thus, in order to achieve the goal of putting all sects (or denominations) on equal footing, Jefferson proposes that the university not appoint a professor of divinity.

"In Jefferson's principal blueprint for the University, the Rockfish Gap Report of 1818," George Marsden explains, "he and his associates . . . had stated that at a state school a professor of divinity would be constitutionally inappropriate, since that would be inevitably sectarian."[11] Thus, significantly, he is not hostile to divinity professors per se; he is simply attempting to avoid sectarianism. And yet he does not want to exclude religious instruction in basic theology and morals more generally from the university, as the next passage demonstrates.

(2) *Proofs for the Existence of God and the Laws of Morality*

Jefferson writes, "The proofs of the being of a God, the creator, preserver and supreme ruler of the universe, the author of all the relations of morality, and of the laws and obligations these infer, will be within the province of the professor of ethics to which adding the developments of these moral obligations, of those in which all sects agree, with a knowledge of the languages, Hebrew, Greek, and Latin, a basis will be formed common to all sects."[12]

Rather than a professor of divinity teaching the theology of a particular sect (or denomination), Jefferson proposes that the professor of ethics teach that upon which all sects agree. Specifically, he mentions proofs for God's existence and the laws of morality that result therefrom, which Gaustad identifies as "the essentials of religion."[13] Jefferson designates God as "the creator, preserver and supreme ruler of the universe," as well as the "the author of all the relations of morality, and of the laws and obligations these infer."

Also, he identifies knowledge of the Hebrew, Greek, and Latin languages as being an additional subject upon which sects can agree. These three languages serve important roles for biblical studies because they correspond to the Old Testament (written in Hebrew), the New Testament (written in Greek), the Vulgate (a Latin translation of both testaments), and much theological literature through the ages. As Jefferson would later describe them in his Report to the President and Directors of the Literary Fund, they are "the depositories of the originals, and of the earliest and most respected authorities of the faith of every sect."[14] Undoubtedly, Greek and Latin would have also served students for the purposes of classical and historical literature. But very few, if any, would have had an interest in Hebrew apart from the Old Testament. Thus this passage demonstrates Jefferson's proposal of the reasonable accommodation of church and state.

The implications of Jefferson's proposal are significant; they are not consistent with the strict church-state separation of *Everson* and *McCollum*. Yet those cases based their holdings partly on the authority of Jefferson and the expression from his letter to the Danbury Baptist Association that the First Amendment has built a "wall of separation between Church and State."[15] But, as I have argued, Jefferson, when he used that phrase, was referring to the phenomenon of religious establishment—nothing more. His pitch for the reasonable accommodation of church and state at the University of Virginia, which I have just reviewed, demonstrates that the Supreme Court misinterpreted Jefferson's meaning in his letter. He could not have meant the strict separation of church and state because that was not what he pursued in his own practice.

The interpretation I have put forward is based on a plain reading of the text. Jefferson founded a university that was unique in its mission to provide an educational atmosphere that would avoid religious establishment while also upholding students' religious liberties. For that reason, Jefferson proposed that an ethics professor, rather than a divinity professor, teach proofs for God's existence and the laws of morality. The culture in which Jefferson carried out this project manifested a great variety of opinion among Christians. Nonetheless, Christian thinking was embedded in its collective psyche.

Some skeptics have argued that Jefferson wrote the report in such a precise manner so as to ensure its approval, after which he would disregard the parts about religion. In short, this argument accuses Jefferson of duplicity, of his saying one thing but meaning another. It suggests, accordingly, that Jefferson did not really mean what he said with respect to the ethics professor teaching proofs for God's existence and the laws of morality. However, the evidence, which we are considering throughout part three of this book, conclusively demonstrates the opposite of the skeptics' arguments; the evidence shows that Jefferson was sincere.

However, whether he was sincere or not, the fact remains that Jefferson expressly identifies the proposal he sets forth as being "in conformity with the principles of our Constitution." This means that he believed that it is consistent with constitutional principles. The reason he mentions the Virginia Constitution is that it was the highest authority that applied at the time. Again, the First Amendment would not have applied to Virginia at this point. But had it applied, he would have appealed also to it.

Still others have argued that Jefferson intended to open a "seminary for atheists." Herbert Baxter Adams, Associate Professor of History at Johns Hopkins University in the late nineteenth century, interacted with that very argument, but he dismissed it for numerous reasons. The first concerns the broader religious context. In the decades leading up to the period presently under consideration, skeptics were attacking traditional religion and morals: "French thought seems to have played an important part in strengthening the general opposition to religion . . . in the form of indifference."[16]

However, religious revivals "here and there" kept the influence of skepticism at bay, such as that of Devereux Jarratt (1733–1801) in Virginia. The impact of these revivals lasted for decades, well into the historical period in which Jefferson was working. "It is not my intention to describe the manner in which the revival was conducted," Adams writes, but "by 1825," the year that the University of Virginia would open its doors to students, "its effects were very manifest." Thus Adams explains that he could not believe the argument that Jefferson intended to establish a seminary for atheists: "That Mr. Jefferson was foolish enough to believe that he could establish, in the face of this reaction [the religious revivals] (to say nothing of the total inutility of the project), a university to be concluded on atheistical principles, I, at least, can never be brought to believe."[17]

In other words, the idea of establishing a seminary for atheists would have been pointless within the cultural context. For Jefferson to have attempted it would mean that he was foolish. However, Adams argues, Jefferson was far from foolish. Consequently, he would not have even attempted to establish a seminary for atheists. Besides all of that, Jefferson was not an atheist. No (substantial) movement of atheists had even organized by this point in American culture. Deists and Unitarians had organized movements but not atheists. Even one of the most well-known skeptics during this period of American history, Thomas Paine, was not an atheist but rather a Deist who believed in one God and in life after death.[18]

Undoubtedly, some of Jefferson's religious views were incompatible with orthodox Christianity, but he supported people's freedom to follow their own reason and conscience. Thus Adams offered the same interpretation that I have argued, namely that Jefferson followed the "principle of holding an even balance between the sects (and the same is true to a less degree of parties) [which] has liberalized Southern thought to a most gratifying extent."[19] By the term *liberalized*, Adams means that the principle of non-sectarianism had *freed* Southern thought. But again, non-sectarianism is not atheism.

The second reason that Adams rejected the argument that Jefferson intended to found a seminary for atheists concerns the data resulting from the career paths of alumni, in particular the clergy, seminarians, and missionaries. Recognizing that his "information on this point is not exhaustive," he points to some representative examples. Remarking on the clergy, he writes, "If regard be had to the clergy, the statistics would not seem to prove that the University has served as a nursery for atheists.... Of those who entered the ministry, five have become bishops, viz, Bishops Lay, Galleher, Peterkin, Dudley, and Doggett."[20]

Of the seminarians, he says: "To the various theological seminaries the University has furnished such men as John A. Broadus, R. L. Dabney, and F. S. Sampson, of Virginia, Charles A. Briggs of New York, and William H. Whitsitt, of South Carolina. Prof. Crawford H. Toy, of Harvard University, may be mentioned as one of the most distinguished of the masters of arts." Of the missionaries, he says: "A large number of alumni have entered on missionary work; indeed, Colonel Venable says: 'Wipe out the foreign missionaries of the Southern Presbyterian Church who are University men and you almost destroy the enterprise.'"[21] In other words, if Jefferson aimed to create a seminary for atheists, he did a poor job at it. But, of course, that is just the point: That was not his vision.

Jefferson did not intend to found a seminary for atheists but rather a nonsectarian public university that would reasonably accommodate students from diverse sects, as well as religious nonsectarian ideals and morals. That said, I believe, based upon the principles that Jefferson outlines in the Rockfish Gap Report, that the university would have accepted both atheists and secularists into the institution. But the point remains that Jefferson established a nonsectarian public school. For these reasons, Adams rightly rejects the notion that Jefferson intended to open a seminary for atheists. "The opinion that the new institution was to be a seminary for atheists has left its evil fruits, as everything that is false must do," he writes. "It has not even yet wholly died out; but sensible people are at last becoming a little ashamed to express it."[22]

We have considered Jefferson's very words from the Rockfish Gap Report, which establish, clearly, that he aimed to found a nonsectarian institution. Besides, at bottom, the crucial issue is whether Jefferson believed that the principle of non-sectarianism is consistent with constitutional concerns of religious freedom. The evidence indicates that he did. What better proof do we need of the constitutionality of the reasonable accommodation of church and state than the sanction of the author of the Virginia Statute of Religious Freedom? What is more, James Madison and a large number of Virginian luminaries signed onto his plan. Thus the interpretation that Justice Hugo Black and company adopted in *Everson* and *McCollum* concerning the strict separation of church and state stands in error.

(3) Peculiar Tenets

Jefferson concludes this train of thought with these words: "Proceeding thus far without offence to the Constitution, we have thought it proper at this point to leave every sect to provide, as they think fittest, the means of further instruction in their own peculiar tenets."[23] Jefferson finishes by reiterating the point that his proposal does not offend constitutional principles. Then, having identified those subjects on which the sects should agree—namely proofs for the existence of God and the laws of morality—Jefferson explains that individual sects can instruct in those subjects upon which they do not agree. For example, divinity professors at sectarian institutions may teach theology and doctrine as they see fit.

The language from Jefferson's report indicates that he expressed interest in maintaining a cordial relationship with different religious sects, which, at the time of his work, were primarily a variety of Christian sects. In fact it was something he worked hard at. While Jefferson criticized certain sects and certain clergy at times, he did not criticize religion per se but rather honored it. We see this last point demonstrated throughout his writings: e.g., in the introductory and concluding material of Jefferson's letter to the Danbury Baptist Association, in the passages that we have analyzed from the Rockfish Gap Report, and in additional writings that we will review in the following chapter.

REPORT OF THE COMMISSIONERS

Reception of the Rockfish Gap Report

Jefferson's report met with enthusiasm. In a letter to his daughter, Martha Jefferson Randolph, Jefferson describes the congeniality of the Rockfish Gap Meeting, "I have never seen business done with so much order, & harmony, nor an abler nor pleasanter society."[24] In addition to Jefferson's signature, twenty others affixed their names to the report, "signed and certified by the members present, each in his proper hand-writing, this 4th day of August, 1818," including: Hugh Holmes, Creed Taylor, Phil. C. Pendleton, Peter Randolph, Spencer Roane, Wm. Brockenbrough, John M. C. Taylor, Arch'd Rutherford, J. G. Jackson, Arch'd Stuart, Phil. Slaughter, James Breckenridge, Wm. H. Cabell, Henry E. Watkins, Nat. H. Claiborne, James Madison, Wm. A. C. Dade, A. T. Mason, William Jones, and Thomas Wilson.[25]

Jefferson was not the only one to believe that a nonsectarian model of reasonable church-state accommodation within the context of public education is consistent with constitutional principles. So did these other luminaries, practically all of which were lawyers, judges, and/or politicians. Significantly, James Madison also signed it, meaning that the author of the Memorial and Remonstrance against Religious Assessments believed that Jefferson's model was consistent with his own understanding of the application of religious freedom. We cannot brush aside or explain away what these leaders joined together to promote. The vision of Jefferson, Madison, and these luminaries of the reasonable accommodation of church and state stands in distinct contrast to that of Justice Black and the secularists who believe in strict separation.

In addition to these twenty signatories, Jefferson's report also received support from the legislature. "The legislature published Jefferson's report along with its unanimous approval, a suitable preamble to the legislature's own approval in January 1819 of a real university for the state of Virginia," Gaustad comments. "At the same time, the first board meeting following legislative approval appointed Jefferson as rector of the university."[26] As Rector, or the head of the university, "Jefferson jumped into action—at age seventy-five—with all the vigor of a young man. Adrenalin pumping, he wrote to Madison the next month what was 'immediately necessary,' what had to be done right after that, and what admitted no delay."[27] Though advanced in years by this point, Jefferson clearly cared about the path he was charting. Over the next several years, Jefferson helped raise money, oversee buildings plans and construction, plan university curriculum, locate highly credentialed professors, and more.

Conclusion

Notwithstanding the clarity of Jefferson's views concerning accommodation in the Rockfish Gap Report, no one has ever presented it to the Supreme Court (based on my research). We do see reference in the court records to Jefferson's letter to the Danbury Baptist Association, where he speaks of "a wall of separation between church and state." However, as we have seen, the historical evidence shows that the Court misinterpreted the phrase, which referred only to religious establishment. It could not have indicated the strict separation of church and state because that is not the model that Jefferson himself followed when he founded the University of Virginia. The presentation of Jefferson's report to the Supreme Court could clear up some of the confusion regarding church-state relations in the United States and help to realize the vision that Jefferson, Madison, and others worked for.

CHAPTER ELEVEN

Report to the President and Directors of the Literary Fund

In the previous chapter, I reviewed the Report of the Commissioners for the University of Virginia (the Rockfish Gap Report), concluding that Thomas Jefferson expressly supported a nonsectarian model of public education that would reasonably accommodate students from different religious backgrounds. This finding means that Jefferson could not have meant strict separation when he referred to a "wall of separation between church and state" in his letter to the Danbury Baptist Association, as the majorities in *Everson v. Board of Education* and *McCollum v. Board of Education* claim. Instead, Jefferson was referring to religious establishment. In this chapter, I will continue reviewing relevant writings from Jefferson that speak to his view of the relationship between church and state, or religion and government, giving specific attention to his Report to the President and Directors of the Literary Fund.

Between the period of the Rockfish Gap Report (1818) and the University of Virginia's opening its doors to students (1825), many expressed concern about how the university would deal with the matter of religion. In a report from October 7, 1822, entitled the Report to the President and Directors of the Literary Fund (President-Directors Report), Jefferson elaborated on a plan that he hoped would find acceptance. During this period, Jefferson served as Rector of the university. After giving an account of the buildings' construction, the report explains how the university would work to develop a cordial working relationship between itself and the different religious sects. As we will see, Jefferson's approach clearly demonstrates reasonable accommodation over strict separation.

Rooms for Religious Worship

Concerning the issues of construction, Jefferson writes, "The remaining building necessary to complete the whole establishment and called for by the Report of 1818, which was to contain rooms for religious worship, for public examinations, for a library, and for other associated purposes, is not yet begun for the want of funds."[1] Basically, the university had not yet begun work on one building for lack of funds. Jefferson had also referred to this building in the Rockfish Gap Report, describing it as "a building of somewhat more size in the middle of the grounds."[2]

Significantly, though, he explains that it would contain "rooms for religious worship," in addition to other purposes. If Jefferson had adopted the model of strict church-state separation, he hardly would have given such emphasis to a building that the university could use for, among other things, religious worship. No, he is describing reasonable accommodation. He then describes its completion as being indispensible for opening the university's doors: "The Visitors, from the beginning, have considered it as indispensable to complete all the buildings before opening the institution."[3]

REPORT TO THE PRESIDENT AND DIRECTORS

Jefferson explains that the Board of Visitors believe that postponing the "commencement of the institution" until it is "full and complete" is preferable to beginning "prematurely in an unfinished state," which would be "utterly inadequate to the great purposes which the report of 1818 and the Legislature have hitherto had in contemplation."[4] As the report continues, he makes a plea for more financial assistance to speed up the process of completing the additional building in order to open the university for students.

SUMMARIZING THE ROCKFISH GAP REPORT

Jefferson then shifts to give attention to the best way for the university to manage the subject of religion. He does this by analyzing and further developing the comments he made in the Rockfish Gap Report. Even though we reviewed it at some length in the previous chapter, I will summarize it over the course of this paragraph and the next because Jefferson adds a few interpretive remarks and because it will bear on what he will say next. He repeats his point about the university teaching subjects on which different sects (or denominations) can agree, thereby treating them equally while leaving distinctive theological commitments for individual groups to teach as they believe best.

For that reason, Jefferson proposes that the professor of ethics, instead of a professor of divinity, teach proofs for God's existence, as well as the laws of morality. In the President-Directors Report, he highlights the importance of these "courses of ethical lectures" for "developing those moral obligations in which all sects agree." In addition, the university would provide instruction for the Hebrew, Greek, and Latin languages, which he describes as "the depositories of the originals, and of the earliest and most respected authorities of the faith of every sect."[5] On two separate occasions, he describes his nonsectarian model as conforming to constitutional principles:

"in conformity with the principles of our constitution" and "proceeding thus far without offence to the Constitution."[6]

Instruction in Religious Opinion and Duty

Having summarized material from the Rockfish Gap Report in the President-Directors Report, Jefferson sheds further light on his view of the proper relationship between church and state. As before, I will provide a quotation after which I will analyze it. We will find still further evidence that reasonable accommodation describes Jefferson's basic approach, not strict separation. Immediately after his summary of the Rockfish Gap Report, Jefferson says, "It was not, however, to be understood that instruction in religious opinion and duties was meant to be precluded by the public authorities, as indifferent to the interests of society."[7]

We established in part one that Jefferson predated the phenomenon of secularism, meaning that he was not a secularist in name. Language such as that from the President-Directors Report indicates that he was not a secularist in spirit either. "On the contrary," Jefferson continues, "the relations which exist between man and his Maker, and the duties resulting from those relations, are the most interesting and important to every human being, and the most incumbent on his study and investigation."[8] Far from believing in a strict church-state separation, he states explicitly that public authorities should support instruction in religious opinion and duty because it bears on the interests of man and of society.

Sectarian Instruction within a Nonsectarian Model of Public Education

Jefferson then shifts from talking about nonsectarian to considering sectarian instruction, from basic religious and moral teaching to creedal distinctions. Perhaps surprisingly he says that it warrants a place in a public university: "The want of instruction in the various creeds of religious faith existing among our citizens presents, therefore, a chasm in the general institution of useful sciences."[9] He holds that a university's failure to offer theology would evidence a hole in its educational curriculum. George Marsden summarizes Jefferson's point, saying he "recognize[d] that theology was among the sciences that belonged at a university and provided a means for its practitioners to enjoy benefits of the state-supported academic center without being directly supported by the state."[10]

However, does Jefferson's suggestion not conflict with the nonsectarian model that he has been building? Before explaining precisely how these two ideas fits together, he reviews a point of concern: "But it was thought that this want, and the entrustment to each society of instruction in its own doctrines, were evils of less danger than a permission to the public authorities to dictate modes or principles of religious instruction, or than opportunities furnished them by giving countenance or ascendancy to any one sect over another."[11]

Jefferson acknowledges that a nonsectarian approach to education carries with it some challenges. But those challenges are preferable to the ones created by religious establishment or anything akin to it. As we have considered, Jefferson had explained to the Danbury Baptists that the First Amendment has built a wall of separation between church and state. Again, though, he was referring to religious establishment, not to religious instruction. Additionally, the President-Directors Report indicates that Jefferson does not conflate either nonsectarian or sectarian instruction within an institution of the state, such as a public university, as being tantamount to religious establishment.

Independent Schools of Divinity

Yet the question remains as to how he envisions a nonsectarian institution that nonetheless makes room for "instruction in the various creeds of religious faith." Jefferson begins answering this concern by proposing independent divinity schools: "A remedy, however, has been suggested of promising aspect, which, while it excludes the public authorities from the domain of religious freedom," thereby avoiding the semblance of religious establishment, "will give to the sectarian schools of divinity the full benefit of the public provisions made for instruction in the other branches of science," thereby not effectively penalizing confessional religious instruction. Additionally, he clarifies, "But always understanding that these schools shall be independent of the University and of each other."[12]

Jefferson's suggestion walks well the tightrope of competing aims and tensions. The prospect of omitting sectarian theological instruction would unjustly discriminate against the discipline of theology relative to the other disciplines. In addition, it would unfairly disadvantage those entering into religious professions: "These branches are equally necessary to the divine as to the other professional or civil characters, to enable them to fulfill the duties of their calling with understanding and usefulness."[13] In this way, Jefferson maintains a nonsectarian model of public education while also guarding the religious freedom of the practitioners of confessional theology.

Jefferson continues, explaining that leaders of these schools would "establish their religious schools on the confines of the University." In other words, specific denominations or groups could locate their institutions on the same campus. The effect of that strategy would accomplish two goals: (1) "to give to their students ready and convenient access and attendance on the scientific lectures of the University"; and (2) "to maintain, by that means, those destined for the religious professions on as high a standing of science, and of personal weight and respectability, as may be obtained by others from the benefits of the University."[14] Therefore, students entering religious professions have the advantage of both sacred (eternal) and secular (temporal) instruction.

Jefferson's approach would benefit not only the students of these divinity schools but also the students of the university, meaning that it is mutually beneficial to all parties involved. "Such establishments would offer the further and greater advantage of enabling the students of the University to attend religious exercises with the professor of their particular sect," Jefferson explains, "either in the rooms of the building still to be erected, and destined to that purpose under impartial regulations, as proposed in the same report of the commissioners, or in the lecturing room of such professor."[15] His mention of "rooms of the building still to erected" refers back to the "rooms for religious worship" that we considered at the beginning of the chapter. Thus university students could attend services of religious worship or lectures of religious instruction.

The Board of Visitors

Jefferson then summarizes the position of the Board of Visitors: "To such propositions," referring back to the prospect of religious worship and religious instruction, "the Visitors are disposed to lend a willing ear, and would think it their duty to give every encouragement." The university's overseers agree with his plan. Jefferson continues, saying that they would also assure prospective students "that the regulations of the University should be so modified and *accommodated* as to give every facility of access and attendance to their Students, with such regulated use also as may be permitted to the other students," including "the library which may hereafter be acquired, either by public or private munificence."[16]

Throughout his writings, we have characterized Jefferson's approach as reasonable accommodation. In this passage, he actually uses the word *accommodated*. The sentiment that Jefferson and the Visitors express is that they would bend over backward to see this plan take fruition. Just as Jefferson does not want to err on the side of sanctioning religious establishment, he also does not want to err on the side of denying religious liberty. In Jefferson's words, "Such an arrangement would complete the circle of useful sciences embraced by this institution, and would fill up the chasm now existing, on principles which would leave inviolate the constitutional freedom of religion."[17]

By use of the word *chasm*, Jefferson returns to a theme he introduced earlier in the report. In the language of the First Amendment—"Congress shall make no law respecting the establishment of religion, or prohibiting the free exercise thereof"—non-establishment and free exercise work together.[18] Jefferson goes on to describe religious freedom as "the most inalienable and sacred of all human rights, over which the people and authorities of this state, individually and publicly, have ever manifested the most watchful jealousy."[19] Jefferson had worked on articulating a proper doctrine of religious freedom literally for half a century, from understanding its application in society generally in the Virginia Statute for Religious Freedom, which he drafted in 1777, to its application in public education specifically.

Conformity to Constitutional Principles

Jefferson had begun the President-Directors Report by explaining that his proposals conform to constitutional principles, and now he concludes the report with the same point, saying, "Could this

REPORT TO THE PRESIDENT AND DIRECTORS

jealousy be now alarmed, in the opinion of the legislature, by what is here suggested, the idea will be relinquished on any surmise of disapprobation which they might think proper to express."[20] In other words, any legislature tempted to believe that Jefferson's proposal violates constitutional principles will, upon reflection, give up their supposition of disapproval. In Jefferson's words, they will "relinquish" it precisely because it fits within the parameters of the constitutional order that had been established.

Jefferson demonstrates, in the Report to the President and Directors of the Literary Fund, that he clearly believed that the University of Virginia should make reasonable accommodations to sectarian schools. Yet he thought that they should remain independent from the university and from one another. However, they could all enter into cooperative relationships with each other and, being on the same campus, their students could mutually learn and benefit. Under this arrangement, the university could fill the void in learning so that it would leave out no useful science—confessional theology included.

Ultimately, this arrangement did not come to fruition. James Madison succeeded Jefferson as Rector and suggested a plan "of having chaplains appointed yearly rotating from the four major Protestant denominations."[21] However, the main point is not whether Jefferson's proposal finally succeeded. Our point is to investigate and understand Jefferson's beliefs concerning the church-state relationship in relation to the constitutional principles that the nation and its states established at the founding, since it is to Jefferson that the *Everson* and *McCollum* majorities appealed in their articulation of these subjects.

As we have seen, Jefferson supported the notion of reasonable accommodation rather than that of strict separation. In fact, the principles he established suggest that he would have seen strict separation as an affront to the exercise of religious freedom. Again, the constitution with which Jefferson is interacting is the Virginia Constitution. At this point in history, the First Amendment applied only to the federal Congress. However, had it applied to states at this time, I believe that Jefferson would also have appealed to it, since Virginia law was based on the Virginia Statute, which also served as a significant precursor to the religion clauses in the First Amendment.

JUSTICE REED'S INTERPRETATION

Although the Rockfish Gap Report has not appeared in any Supreme Court case that I have seen, the President-Directors Report has. In the sole dissent of *McCollum* (which we reviewed in chapter seven), Justice Stanley Reed interacts with it, as well as the Regulations of the University from October 4, 1824. In so doing, he introduces some very important information into the record regarding Jefferson's thinking in relation to the founding of the University of Virginia. After describing the university as being "wholly governed, managed and controlled by the State of Virginia," Reed writes, "Mr. Jefferson . . . was faced with the same problem that is before this Court today: The question of the constitutional limitation upon religious education in public schools."[22]

Next, Reed introduces the President-Directors Report, which we have reviewed at some length, and then comments that the Board of Visitors, including Madison, approved Jefferson's views and adopted them into the Regulations of the University, "provided that 'Should the religious sects of this State, or any of them, according to the invitation held out to them, establish within, or adjacent to, the precincts of the University, schools for instruction in the religion of their sect, the students of the University will be free, and expected to attend religious worship at the establishment of their respective sects, in the morning, and in time to meet their school in the University at its stated hour.'"[23] This quotation demonstrates that the ideas Jefferson propounded were not his solely but also received the support of the Board of Visitors. In addition, far from staying out of issues relating to the attendance of worship services, this quotation also shows that the board actually encouraged it, even using the language of *expecting* it.

Although Reed does not interact with this portion, the minutes would go on to say: "The Students of such religious school, if they attend any school of the University, shall be considered as Students of the University, subject to the same regulations, and entitled to the same rights and privileges."[24] These quotations from the minutes of the Board of Visitors, including those with which Reed interacted and those he did not, indicate that these luminaries did not find the reasonable accommodation of church and state within the context of a public university to be contrary to constitutional principles.

Having interacted with the President-Directors Report and the Regulations of the University, Reed offers an interpretation of Jefferson's phrase from his letter to the Danbury Baptists that the First Amendment has built a wall of separation between church and state. "Thus, the 'wall of separation between church and State' that Mr. Jefferson built at the University which he founded did not exclude religious education from that school."[25] As we have seen in previous chapters, the majority decisions in both *Everson* (1947) and *McCollum* (1948) interacted with Jefferson's statement, interpreting it through the lens of strict church-state separation. *Reynolds v. United States* (1878) had also quoted the phrase but did not interact with it. However, Reed's statement in his dissent to *McCollum* demonstrates that he disagreed with the majorities of these cases and, in that way, his interpretation overlaps with my own.

"The difference between the generality of his [Jefferson's] statements on the separation of church and state and the specificity of his conclusions on education are considerable," Reed continues, "A rule of law should not be drawn from a figure of speech."[26] Indeed, justices should not establish rules of law from a figure of speech, particularly when that rule lacks consistency with the point for which it was offered, that is, Jefferson did not offer the figure of speech for the proposition that the majority justices claimed, namely the strict separation of church and state.

Conclusion

Instead, as we have considered in this chapter, Jefferson advocated for reasonable church-state accommodation, even within the context of public education. Jefferson made recommendations for rooms dedicated to religious worship and for independent divinity schools. He aimed to provide the opportunity for sectarian instruction within a nonsectarian institution. He believed in the importance of public educational institutions giving instruction in religious opinion and duty because it bears on man and society. Finally, he believed that these ideas conform to constitutional principles.

CHAPTER TWELVE

Four Letters

Throughout this section of the book, I have argued that Thomas Jefferson advocated for the reasonable accommodation of church and state. We have seen this point illustrated from the Report of the Commissioners for the University of Virginia, which I analyzed in chapter ten. We have also considered this position from the Report to the President and Directors of the Literary Fund in chapter eleven. In this chapter I want to turn to two letters that also bear out this interpretation of Jefferson's position, the first to Thomas Cooper and the second to Arthur Spicer Brockenbrough. In these letters Jefferson maintains his position of reasonable church-state accommodation. He also highlights the importance of people showing kindness and fairness to one another as each seeks to accommodate the other.

Thomas Jefferson's Letter to Dr. Thomas Cooper: Church-state Accommodation and Kindness

In less than a month after Jefferson presented the Report to the President and Directors of the Literary Fund on October 7, 1822, Jefferson wrote a letter to Dr. Thomas Cooper on November 2, 1822, in which he further explains the ideas that he suggested in his reports. Through the course of this section, I will quote from and comment on a portion of the letter. About halfway through the letter, Jefferson summarizes a persistent rumor that had circulated: "In our university you know there is no Professorship of Divinity. A handle has been made of this, to disseminate an idea that this is an institution, not merely of no religion, but against all religion."[1]

This interpretation is more in line with what secularists often say regarding Jefferson's views of church-state relations and public education. However, Jefferson explicitly remarks that that position—namely that the University of Virginia is against all religion—is *not* his position, instead referring to it as "calumny," which carries with it the idea of falsehood, defamation, and/or slander. "Occasion was taken at the last meeting of the Visitors, to bring forward an idea that might silence this calumny, which weighed on the minds of some honest friends to the institution."[2]

Jefferson then offers his summary of the President-Directors Report, which we have just analyzed, saying, "In our annual report to the legislature, after stating the constitutional reasons against a public establishment of any religious instruction, we suggest the expediency of encouraging the different religious sects to establish, each for itself, a professorship of their own tenets." He also explains that these religious sects would establish themselves "on the confines of the university, so near as that their students may attend the lectures there, and have the free use of our library, and every other accommodation we can give them; preserving, however, their independence of us and of each other."[3]

Next, Jefferson iterates his point that theology exists among the useful sciences, "This fills the chasm objected to ours, as a defect in an institution professing to give instruction in *all* useful sciences," after which he offers his prediction concerning how the various sects would receive the idea: "I think the invitation will be accepted, by some sects from candid intentions, and by others from jealousy and rivalship. And by bringing the sects together, and mixing them with the mass of other students, we shall soften their asperities, liberalize and neutralize their prejudices, and make the general religion a religion of peace, reason and morality."[4] As we have seen from previous selections, this example offers further evidence that Jefferson advocated a reasonable church-state accommodation, believing that it consists fully with constitutional principles. Undoubtedly, some of these measures mark a move toward improving public relations among the various sects.

Jefferson saw a pragmatic benefit from having the sects establishing their schools contiguous to the university campus. Students from different churches and sects would exist and learn and engage in theological discussions in close proximity to one another. Such an approach would soften their dispositions, engendering greater kindness. As we have seen, within the context of the university, the ethics professor would not have given attention to confessional theology, although he would have taught proofs for God's existence and the laws of morality, as well as beliefs common to all sects. Still, beyond the context of the university proper, the divinity schools could establish divinity professors, and students from different backgrounds could engage in theological disputes. Before drawing further conclusions and wrapping up this chapter, I want to consider one more letter that Jefferson penned.

Thomas Jefferson's Letter to Arthur Spicer Brockenbrough: Fairness and Modifications

On April 21, 1825, Jefferson wrote a letter to Arthur Brockenbrough, the University of Virginia's proctor. He sent this letter approximately two-and-a-half years subsequent to the one he sent to Cooper. In the letter, Jefferson discusses the prospect of using

Pavilion No. 1 at the University of Virginia for Sunday worship services. As we will see, he will refer to many of the points that we have considered over the course of the last two chapters. Jefferson begins by acknowledging Brockenbrough's request: "In answer to your letter proposing to permit the lecturing room of the Pavilion N° 1 to be used regularly for prayers and preaching on Sundays."[5] From there he makes several observations.

Observations

The first concerns a similar request some three or four years prior at which point "an application was made to permit a sermon to be preached in one of the pavilions on a particular occasion, not now recollected." That episode "brought the subject into consideration with the Visitors." He explains that, "altho' they entered into no formal and written resolution on the occasion," the board's basic sentiment was to reject the request for two reasons: (1) "the concurrent sentiment was that the buildings of the University belong to the state that they were erected for the purposes of an University;" and (2) "that the Visitors, to whose care they are committed for those purposes, have no right to permit their application to any other."[6]

Summarizing the specific resolution of that request, Jefferson writes, "And accordingly, when applied to, on the visit of General La Fayette, I declined at first the request of the use of the Rotunda for his entertainment." But then Jefferson recollects another option, saying, "until it occurred on reflection that the room, in the unfinished state in which it then was, was as open and unenclosed, and as insusceptible of injury, as the field in which it stood."[7] The room to which he refers is one and the same that we considered in the previous chapter. Jefferson had mentioned the prospect of using these rooms for religious worship in the Rockfish Gap Report and the President-Directors Report.

"In the Rockfish report it was stated as probable that a building larger than the Pavilions might be called for in time," he writes, "in which might be rooms for a library, for public examinations, and for religious worship under such impartial regulations as the Visitors should prescribe, the legislature neither sanctioned nor rejected this proposition; and afterwards, in the Report of Oct 1822."[8] That the legislature neither sanctioned nor rejected this proposal does not mean the idea lacked constitutional backing. It means simply what it says. The legislature did not need to sanction or reject it because it represented ideas that Jefferson had brainstormed for the prospective use of certain facilities. The fact remains that Jefferson believed his ideas were consistent with constitutional principles, and nothing exists in the minutes to indicate that the legislature disagreed with his analysis.

Having mentioned the pavilion and the rooms for religious worship, Jefferson shifts to talk about the idea of the divinity schools that he discussed in the President-Directors Report: "The board suggested, as a substitute, that the different religious sects should be invited to establish their separate theological schools in the vicinity of the University, in which the Students might attend religious worship, each in the form of his respective sect, and thus avoid all jealousy of attempts on his religious tenets." An advantage of this approach, he explains, is that it avoids the potential of showing favoritism to one sect over others. In Jefferson's words, it avoids all jealousy, and it encourages equality and impartiality: "Among the enactments of the board is one looking to this object, and superseding the first idea of permitting a room in the Rotunda to be used for religious worship, and of undertaking to frame a set of regulations of equality and impartiality among the multiplied sects."[9]

Undoubtedly, the church-state relationship generally and the sphere of public education specifically require caution because it is such an important subject. Jefferson writes, "I state these things as manifesting the caution which the board of Visitors thinks it a duty to observe on this delicate and jealous subject."[10] On the one hand, Jefferson wants to avoid the problems resulting from religious establishment, some of which Justice Hugo Black outlined in his majority opinion in *Everson*. On the other hand, as I have demonstrated, Jefferson's solution was not strict church-state separation.

Request Denied

With these various observations in mind, Jefferson turns to his answer to Brockenbrough: "Your proposition therefore leading to an application of the University buildings to other than University purposes, and to a partial regulation in favor of two particular sects, would be a deviation from the course which they think it their duty to observe."[11] In other words, he turns down Brockenbrough's request. At first glance, Jefferson's answer may puzzle the reader. If Jefferson advocated for reasonable church-state accommodation, then why does he decline this request?

To begin, appropriate church-state relations are a balancing act. The denial of one proposal does not indicate the rejection of the principle of reasonable accommodation. As I have demonstrated, Jefferson advocated for reasonable accommodation. It just so happens that Brockenbrough's request did not qualify as such. Jefferson points to several issues with it. For one, as the quotation above demonstrates, it would, on its face, favor some sects over others. Jefferson's vision seeks to avoid that when possible. Consequently, Brockenbrough's proposal would result in disorder, Jefferson's second reason for rejecting it: "Nor indeed is it immediately perceived what effect the repeated and habitual assemblages of a great number of strangers at the University might have on its order and tranquility."[12]

A third reason that Jefferson gives for declining the idea concerns the availability of other locations in Charlottesville. "That place has been in long possession of the seat of public worship, a right always deemed strongest until a better can be produced. There too they are building, or about to build, proper churches and meetinghouses, much better adapted to the accommodation of a congregation than a scanty lecturing room. Are these to be abandoned, and the private room to be preferred?" Jefferson asks.[13]

He then argues that the preference of private rooms over proper churches would actually harm the visible unity of the religious congregation. "If not, then the congregations, already too small, would by your proposition be split into halves incompetent to the employment and support of a double set of officiating ministers. Each of course would break up the other, and both fall to the ground." Jefferson concludes the matter with these words: "I think therefore that, independent of our declining to sanction this application, it will not, on further reflection, be thought as advantageous to religious interests as their joint assembly at a single place," after which he assures Brockenbrough of his "great esteem and respect."[14] Thus we see that Jefferson does not reject reasonable church-state accommodation per se.

James Madison's Letter to Edward Everett

Two other letters, written by Madison rather than Jefferson, shed further light on understanding the latter's reasoning to Brockenbrough. Recall that Madison had served on the board of trustees when the university changed from Albemarle Academy to Central College before eventually becoming the University of Virginia. He had also signed the Rockfish Gap Report. Additionally, after Jefferson died, Madison would serve as the university's second Rector. On March 19, 1823, he penned a letter to Edward

Everett, who was also an educator, writing, "I am not surprised at the dilemma produced at your University by making theological professorships an integral part of the System."[15] Everett served at Harvard University, which had not pursued the same nonsectarian model for which the University of Virginia was aiming.

"The anticipation of such an one led to the omission in ours," Madison continues, "the Visitors being merely authorized to open a public Hall for religious occasions, under impartial regulations; with the opportunity to the different sects to establish Theological schools so near that the Students of the University may respectively attend the religious exercises in them." Here Madison summarizes what I have reviewed previously. The founders of the University of Virginia highly valued impartiality and suggested independent divinity schools. He also refers to the same point that Jefferson would make in his letter to Brockenbrough about Charlottesville: "The village of Charlottesville also, where different religious worships will be held, is also so near, that resort may conveniently be had to them."[16]

James Madison's Letter to Frederick Beasley

Madison wrote the second letter I want to consider on December 22, 1824. Writing to Frederick Beasley, Madison first points out that the University of Virginia had not yet put its policies into practice: "The system of polity for the University of Virginia being not yet finally digested and adopted, I cannot venture to say what it will be in its precise form and details." Although various university leaders had spent approximately six years in preparation, the university would not open its doors until 1825. Madison then mentions the point that the university had not proposed a divinity professor: "The peculiarity in the Institution which excites at first most attention, and some animadversion, is the omission of theological professorship."[17]

Undoubtedly, the university's nonsectarian model demonstrated a deviation from the norm for that time, which Madison's letter to Everett illustrates. At the same time, the nonsectarian model signified the university's attempt at impartiality and reasonable church-state accommodation. Additionally, says Madison, public opinion had begun to bend toward their proposal: "The public opinion seems now to have sufficiently yielded to its incompatibility with a State Institution, which necessarily excludes sectarian preferences."[18]

Madison then points to two provisions, both of which we have considered, that the university would make to practice reasonable accommodation: (1) "The best provision which occurred was that of authorizing the Visitors to open the public rooms for Religious uses, under impartial regulations, (a task that may occasionally involve some difficulties)," as well as (2) "admitting the establishment of Theological Seminaries by the respective sects contiguous to the precincts of the University, and within the reach of a familiar intercourse distinct from the obligatory pursuits of the students."[19] Finally, Madison refers, again, to Charlottesville: "The growing village of Charlottesville, also, is not distant more than a mile, and contains already congregations and clergymen of the sects to which the students will mostly belong."[20]

Madison clearly acknowledges that the university would make these public rooms available for religious worship. Yet he also acknowledges that the university's polity is "not yet finally digested and adopted." Madison's clarification has nothing to do with whether the university would adopt the hard line of strict church-state separation. His tone in these letters, like that of Jefferson in his letters and reports, signifies the desire for a nonsectarian model of public education and the reasonable accommodation of church and state. Madison's clarification marks his recognition of the possible need for modification once the university officially opened its doors to students. Educational policy in theory sometimes looks different in practice.

Constructing good educational policy is like building an automobile. Engineers design a given automobile. They follow the scientific principles of engineering to the best of their ability, but then comes the test drive. In the course of this experimentation, they will begin to see that they have to make certain corrective changes. Similarly, Jefferson, Madison, and others served as the engineers of the university who built the institution to the best of their abilities. However, once the university opened up, once administration, faculty, staff, and students began to give it a test drive, its leaders would have to make some corrective changes. By writing, "I cannot venture to say what it will be in its precise form and details," Madison is not discounting the basic model on which the university's leaders had worked for six years; he is simply acknowledging that they may have to make some modification here and there.

Interpreting Jefferson in Light of Madison

With these two letters from Madison in place, I will revisit Jefferson's letter to Brockenbrough from 1825 in which he declines the request of using a pavilion at the university for Sunday worship. In that letter Jefferson gave three specific reasons for his denying the request: the appearance of favoritism, the prospect of disorder, and the reality of alternative locations in Charlottesville—in short, fairness. Madison's letters shed light on an additional reason: the recognition of modification. Unlike Jefferson's two reports and his letter to Cooper, as well as Madison's two letters to Everett

FOUR LETTERS

and Beasley, Jefferson wrote his letter to Brockenbrough *after* the university had opened its doors. The university was putting its theory into practice.

Conclusion

We can appreciate Jefferson's hesitation, while also recognizing that he was not forsaking an approach of reasonable accommodation. We can understand why he would question whether it would be wise to grant this request. The university is in its early stages of operation. Its leaders are setting precedent for the future. They have just begun their test drive, and they are proceeding with care. Remember that the University of Virginia was setting the precedent for a nonsectarian model of public education that sought to avoid the problems that can result from religious establishment. Madison's suspicions that modification might follow the university's opening proved true.

However, that did not mean Jefferson, Madison, and the rest had closed the book on the hope of reasonable accommodation. As we have seen, the reasons he gave for denying the application concerned legitimate questions of the appearance of partiality, the concern for disorder, and the fact of alternate locations. But even if, for the sake of argument, Jefferson, Madison, and the rest were closing the book on the practice of reasonable accommodation at the university—though I do not believe that this is the case—that is ultimately beside the point. The point is that Jefferson affirmed time and again that reasonable church-state accommodation did not violate constitutional principles. All of his writings, from his reports to his letters, demonstrate this point. In the following chapter, I will offer some review and analysis of the argument that we have been building through the course of this book before turning to part four.

CHAPTER THIRTEEN

REVIEWING THE CASE FOR THE REASONABLE ACCOMMODATION OF CHURCH AND STATE

Through the course of parts two and three of this book, we have considered three cases from the Supreme Court: *Reynolds v. United States* (1879), *Everson v. Board of Education* (1947), and *McCollum v. Board of Education* (1948). These cases made reference to four different documents, which we have also reviewed: Patrick Henry's Bill Establishing a Provision for Teachers of the Christian Religion (1784), James Madison's Memorial and Remonstrance against Religious Assessments (1785), and Thomas Jefferson's Virginia Statute for Religious Freedom (1786) and letter to the Danbury Baptist Association (1802).

THE STRICT SEPARATION OF CHURCH AND STATE

Chief Justice Morrison Waite wrote the Court's unanimous opinion in *Reynolds*. One of the questions with which Waite interacted concerned the constitutionality of outlawing bigamy: To what degree does the guarantee of religious freedom require the freedom to pursue bigamy? Two years after the Virginia legislature passed Jefferson's Virginia Statute guaranteeing religious freedom in 1786, it passed a law against bigamy.[1] On the federal level, even though the First Amendment guarantees that Congress shall not prohibit the free exercise of religion, it passed the Morrill Anti-Bigamy Act in 1862.[2] Waite concluded, like the people of Virginia in the 1780s, that anti-bigamy laws were not inconsistent with the doctrine of religious liberty.

One of the evidences to which he pointed for his conclusion is Jefferson's letter to the Danbury Baptists. Waite analyzed in particular the phrase that "the legislative powers of government reach actions only, and not opinions."[3] He interpreted the phrase to mean that the government cannot enforce a law merely against religious ideas but that it can do so if an idea manifests itself in an action that is destructive to the well-being of a civilized society, namely one that does not correspond to social duty or good order.

In the case of *Reynolds*, the Court found that anti-bigamy laws are not inconsistent with religious liberty because bigamy violated social duty and subverted good order. To analyze that phrase about "legislative power" from Jefferson's letter to the Danbury Baptists, Waite quoted the entire letter, including Jefferson's metaphor of a "wall of separation between Church and State."[4] Waite quoted the entire letter to give a fuller context, but he did not otherwise comment about Jefferson's "wall of separation."

Some seventy years later, Justice Hugo Black authored the majority opinions in *Everson* and *McCollum*. Citing *Reynolds*, Black wrote, "The First Amendment has erected a wall between church and state. That wall must be kept high and impregnable. We could not approve the slightest breach," and, "In the words of Jefferson, the clause against establishment of religion by law was intended to erect 'a wall of separation between church and State.'"[5] In their interpretation of the phrase, the majority justices in *Everson* could not rely on any prior Supreme Court case because no earlier case had interpreted the phrase. In Justice Wiley Rutledge's words, "This case forces us to determine squarely for the first time what was 'an establishment of religion' in the First Amendment's conception."[6]

Regrettably, the majority, in its interpretation of Jefferson's statement about a "wall of separation," did not bring into view the full scope of his context or meaning. Black acknowledged the importance of the 1780s, writing, "This Court has previously recognized that the provisions of the First Amendment, in the drafting and adoption of which Madison and Jefferson played such leading roles, had the same objective, and were intended to provide the same protection against governmental intrusion on religious liberty as the Virginia statute."[7] Undoubtedly, Henry's bill, Madison's Remonstrance, and Jefferson's Statute provide a background from which to interpret properly Jefferson's usage of the "wall of separation." However, Black does not seem to have distinguished sufficiently the facts that gave rise to those developments relative to the facts with which he was interacting.

Additionally, his opinion does not deal with Jefferson's work in helping to found the University of Virginia in the 1820s, which provides a vital context for understanding Jefferson's views of church-state relations and his "wall of separation." By the time *McCollum* came around a year later, its majority relied on the authority that they had established in *Everson*. Together these two cases enshrined the legal doctrine of strict church-state separation, presumably but falsely on the authority of Jefferson.

The Reasonable Accommodation of Church and State

Since the rulings of *Everson* and *McCollum*, the Supreme Court has interpreted Jefferson's "wall of separation" to refer to the strict separation of church and state, which has guided its rulings concerning church-state relations in the United States. "I contemplate with sovereign reverence," wrote Jefferson to the Danbury Baptists in 1802, "that act of the whole American people which declared that their legislature should 'make no law respecting an establishment of religion, or prohibiting the free exercise thereof,' thus building a wall of separation between Church and State."[8] However, as I have shown, these cases do not present an open-and-shut case because the opinions that Jefferson put forward in reports and letters during the founding of the University of Virginia conflict with that interpretation. It is more likely that he was referring more narrowly to religious establishment.

An additional question about my viewpoint emerges from a letter that James Madison wrote in 1819 to Robert Walsh in which he actually used the phrase "total separation of church and state."[9] Because I have previously focused my attention on Jefferson, I have not yet interacted with Madison's letter, but I will do so now. In order to give context to what Madison meant by that phrase, I will offer a summary of the entire letter and then begin my analysis several sentences prior to the phrase in question. Through the course of this letter to Walsh, Madison discusses the subjects of slavery, morality, religion, and education.

The phrase in question occurs in the section on religion in which Madison is discussing its growth in Virginia. "The qualifications of the Preachers too among the new sects where there was the greatest deficiency, are understood to be improving," Madison writes. "On a general comparison of the present & former times, the balance is certainly & vastly on the side of the present, as to the number of religious teachers, the zeal which actuates them, the purity of their lives, and the attendance of the people on their instructions."[10] This portion appears within a larger context of his discussing Episcopalians, Presbyterians, Baptists, and Methodists. Relative to the former two, the latter two represented newer sects of Christianity. Thus he argues that preachers were improving in terms of their qualifications, quantity, and quality.

His purpose for making this remark, as well as introducing a comparison between the present and former times, regards the topic of religious establishment. The developing doctrines of non-establishment and religious liberty emerged out of the writings of Madison and Jefferson and culminated in the First Amendment's religion clauses. However, the prospect of non-establishment was a highly contentious issue among some who claimed that it would precipitate the ruin of government and religion. Madison explains, "It was the universal opinion of the Century preceding the last, that Civil Govt. could not stand without the prop of a Religious establishment, & that the Xn religion itself, would perish if not supported by a legal provision for its Clergy."[11]

However, experiment had demonstrated the contrary: "The experience of Virginia conspicuously corroborates the disproof of both opinions." He first addresses the point about government, writing, "The Civil Govt. tho' bereft of everything like an associated hierarchy possesses the requisite Stability and performs its functions with complete success." Then he considers the point about religion, and it is within this context that he mentions the phrase in question: "Whilst the number, the industry, and the morality of the priesthood & the devotion of the people have been manifestly increased by *the total separation of the Church from the State*."[12]

What did Madison mean by this phrase? Did he mean the same thing that the majority justices in *Everson* and *McCollum* would mean by the strict separation of church and state? Interestingly, neither of these cases interacted with this letter. Written about seventeen years after Jefferson's letter to the Danbury Baptists, it is not unlike his expression that the First Amendment has built a "wall of separation between Church and State."[13] But as I have demonstrated, Jefferson did not mean what later justices presumed him to mean. Is the same true with Madison?

These men clearly used these phrases, but we cannot interpret them in a vacuum. We will not find the smoking gun hidden away in a compressed sentence or paragraph somewhere in their writings. Rather, we find the meaning of these expressions by working our way through the numerous materials, reports, and letters, as I have done throughout part three. Unquestionably, the picture that emerges is that of church-state accommodation. Jefferson, Madison, and company plowed new ground when they made the University of Virginia into a reality. No other institution of learning in the history of the world had ever tried to fashion an educational institution for a state that would simultaneously avoid religious establishment while also upholding religious freedom.

In the specific case of Madison, he wrote the letter to Walsh after Jefferson's Report of the Commissioners for the University of Virginia (1818) but before his Report to the President and Directors of the Literary Fund (1822). Among other things, these reports recommended:

(1) that the university not employ a divinity professor, not because it was establishing a secular model of education, but because it was establishing a nonsectarian model and wanted to maintain impartiality;
(2) that it employ an ethics professor to teach proofs for God's existence and the laws of morality upon which different Christian sects would agree;
(3) that it teach the languages of Hebrew, Greek, and Latin, each of which are important for biblical studies;

(4) that it build rooms for various activities, including religious worship;
(5) that it instruct in religious opinion and duty;
(6) that it teach theology alongside the other useful sciences; and
(7) that it provide for establishment of independent divinity schools on the confines of the university's campus and encourage cross-pollination between the institutions.

In short, these two documents recommend an approach of reasonable accommodation, not strict separation. Significantly, Jefferson believed that these ideas did not offend constitutional principles, and neither did the Board of Visitors nor Madison. Concerning Jefferson, many scholars will analyze his letter to the Danbury Baptist Association, for example, as well as his Virginia Statute for Religious Liberty to understand his view of church-state relations. However, they are far less likely to interact with the Rockfish Gap Report and especially the President-Directors Report, and when they do—rare as that is—they do not interact with Jefferson's model of reasonable accommodation. They do not analyze the recommendations that follow from it. In fact, as I will demonstrate in the next chapter, sometimes they appear to ignore them explicitly in order to present Jefferson as saying the opposite of what he actually said.

Returning to Madison, concerning his phrase, "the total separation of church and state," he could not have meant what *Everson* and *McCollum* would mean by the phrase because Madison's work with the founding of the university makes that interpretation impossible. So what did Madison mean by the phrase? His meaning is fairly plain from the broader context of his letter: When Madison refers to the "total separation of church and state," he is not referring to the prospect of secularism; he is referring, explicitly, to the phenomenon of religious establishment. Rather than non-establishment harming the areas of government and religion, Madison argues that it had helped them.

In sum, when Jefferson refers to a "wall of separation" and when Madison refers to "total separation," they are not arguing for secular church-state relations as the secularists would interpret these statements, or as those who follow the majority opinion of *McCollum* would interpret them. They are arguing against the type of religious establishment that was common in Europe. Contrary to secular ideology, Jefferson and Madison, while standing resolutely against establishment, nonetheless contended for reasonable church-state accommodation.

Summarizing My Case

Throughout these chapters, I have interacted with numerous documents. Although the United States ratified the First Amendment in 1791, the Supreme Court would not interpret the Establishment Clause until 1947 in *Everson*. In the words of Justice Rutledge, "This case forces us to determine squarely for the first time what was 'an establishment of religion' in the First Amendment's conception."[14] So far as I know, no one has challenged Rutledge's observation. In answering this question, Justice Black and the majority interpreted Jefferson's "wall of separation" to refer to the strict separation of church and state, which has set legal precedent since that time.

This interpretation, however, is inaccurate. It fails to take into account a holistic view of Jefferson's beliefs and actions on the subject. To understand Jefferson's meaning fully, I have consulted his other reports and letters on the subject. Most significant among these are those written in conjunction with the founding of the University of Virginia. All of these documents shed light on his view of church-state relations: the Virginia Statute, the Rockfish Gap Report, and the President-Directors Report, as well as the numerous letters that he wrote on the subject through the decades, not to mention Madison's Memorial and Remonstrance, as well as his letters.

The full facts demonstrate that Jefferson's "wall of separation," as well as Madison's "total separation," did not refer to the strict church-state separation that *Everson* and *McCollum* enshrined into American jurisprudence. These men consciously laid out an approach to public education that would accommodate church and state, or religion and government, in a manner that they believed conformed to constitutional principles. This point is beyond doubt. How then can we reconcile this vision of reasonable accommodation with *Everson-McCollum's* vision of strict separation? The answer is that we cannot. Despite the interpretation of these cases, Jefferson did not set forth that view.

Jefferson promoted a view that would avoid religious establishment. He aimed to promote a scenario in which people of differing religious beliefs could freely exercise their religion within the setting of public education. He did not support a situation in which a public university would preempt people from practicing their religion; that would be the opposite of religious freedom. As the Virginia Statute demonstrates, he strongly supported the doctrine of religious freedom. As his work in establishing a nonsectarian model of education indicates, he believed that societies could realize this ideal while also promoting reasonable church-state accommodation. In fact, it is accommodation that best protects this freedom.

I have also argued that Jefferson's Virginia Statute influenced the meaning and adoption of the religion clauses in the First

Amendment. Each of these documents had the same objectives. Justice Black said as much in *Everson*: "This Court has previously recognized," referring to *Reynolds*, "that the provisions of the First Amendment, in the drafting and adoption of which Madison and Jefferson played such leading roles, had the same objective, and were intended to provide the same protection against governmental intrusion on religious liberty as the Virginia statute."[15]

Jefferson believed that reasonable accommodation was consistent with the aims of the Virginia Statute and best protected a society's interests in religious liberty. It is then reasonable to conclude that he would have believed the same concerning the First Amendment's religion clauses since they have the same objectives. The reason the First Amendment did not apply at the time of Jefferson's writing is that the Court had not yet incorporated it against the states. As a result, when we interpret Jefferson's statement in his letter to the Danbury Baptists or Madison's phrase in his letter to Walsh, we must take these various points into account.

We do not interpret Jefferson and Madison in a vacuum or out of context concerning their views of church-state relations. Instead, we do so in light of all of their writings. What we find is that the view of strict church-state separation is inconsistent with their views because they opted for reasonable church-state accommodation. Undoubtedly, the broader context changes our views of Jefferson. He is not the separationist that we have been led to believe he was. Instead, he supported accommodation. In light of the evidence, the Supreme Court should reevaluate the way it interprets the First Amendment with regard to the relationship of church and state from strict separation to reasonable accommodation.

PART IV

Closing Argument: Summing It Up

CHAPTER FOURTEEN

Reasonable Accommodation v. Strict Separation of Church and State

In these next two chapters, I will reflect on the argument that I have developed more fully throughout the book. I will begin with some remarks about the term *secular* before reviewing the arguments for strict separation versus reasonable accommodation of church and state. The motivation for launching this research project, which has evolved into a book, occurred when I read Warren C. Young's article on secularism in the *Baker's Dictionary of Theology*.[1] He pointed out that George Jacob Holyoake had coined the term *secularism* in 1846. Holyoake then founded the British Secular Movement in 1851–52, marking the beginning of "Secular Societies" in Britain. The Leicester Secular Society, formed in 1851, is the world's oldest secular society. In the United States, secularist leaders used the term *secular union* rather than secular societies. The first secular union was organized in 1885 with Robert Ingersoll as its first president.

Many claim that the United States was founded on secularism. However, the fact that the movement of secularism did not begin to emerge until the mid-1850s creates problems of chronology for those arguing that claim since the United States ratified its Constitution in 1788. This discovery about the origins of secularism ignited in me a determination to understand the history of the word *secular* and its derivatives. I have concluded and believe that this book demonstrates that secularism, as we understand it today, did not exist prior to the mid-1800s.

SECULAR AND ITS DERIVATIVES

I have not found the first time that the term *secular government* appears in public speech.[2] I have found no occurrence in which the founding fathers referred to American civil government as a secular government. The first time that the terms *secularism* or *secular government* appear in any Supreme Court cases was in 1963: *Abington School District. v. Schempp* and *Sherbert v. Verner*.[3]

Regarding the term *secular*, only about 150 Supreme Court cases in United States history have even used the word. The first did not occur until 1845.[4] From 1845 until 1948, the word appeared only twenty-nine times; the remaining 120-plus instances have occurred since 1948. Nothing up to that time in the use of the word *secular* indicated that the Supreme Court justices were assuming that the Constitution was founded on secularism.

In addition, the only use of the term that I have found predating the founding fathers was by Martin Luther. In *On Secular Authority*, Luther used the word *weltlich*, which translates as secular.[5] He distinguished between secular authorities and governments, and between ecclesiastical or spiritual authorities and governments.[6] By secular, Luther meant civil or temporal, which may be less confusing; he was not referring to the absence of religion or spiritual matters.

ACCOMMODATION V. STRICT SEPARATION

THE CASE FOR THE STRICT SEPARATION OF CHURCH AND STATE

While many figures made significant contributions to formulating the legal relationship between the state and church in the United States, the most important were Thomas Jefferson and James Madison. They guided the "ship of state" to safe anchorage, and their contributions complement one another.[7] While justices of the Supreme Court have relied on both Jefferson and Madison in their decisions, they have relied more on Jefferson. What the justices say matters, especially when it occurs in their majority opinions because what they say carries significant weight for the country. As this book demonstrates, the Court set forth a vision for the strict separation of church-state relations in the 1940s, a position that I challenge.

In 1948 the Court decided its landmark *McCollum v. Board of Education*. Previous cases using the term *secular* or any of its derivatives offer little help for our analysis. They do not adequately explain how a majority of the Supreme Court justices arrived at the position of strict church-state separation. As we have seen, Jefferson, when founding the University of Virginia, suggested an approach for reasonable church-state accommodation.

Although the Court handed down its interpretation of strict separation in *McCollum*, it laid much of the groundwork in *Everson v. Board of Education* (1947). In *Everson*, Justice Wiley Rutledge observed, "This case forces us to determine squarely for the first time what was 'an establishment of religion' in the First Amendment's conception."[8] In other words, this question was a brand new one for the Court. Rutledge's phrase signals to us to pay careful attention to how the Court carried it out.

At the founding, the Bill of Rights, including the First Amendment, did not apply to the states; it applied only to Congress. As

Justice Hugo Black, author of the majority opinion in *Everson*, explains, "Prior to the adoption of the Fourteenth Amendment, the First Amendment did not apply as a restraint against the states."[9] However, the adoption of the Fourteenth Amendment opened the door for the Court to incorporate the Bill of Rights, phrase-by-phrase, against the states.

When reading Black's opinion for the first time, it sounds as if he is going to rule against the Board of Education's action of reimbursing to Catholic parents the money that they spent on bus fare in sending their children to Catholic parochial schools. However, he famously declared, "The First Amendment has erected a wall between church and state. That wall must be kept high and impregnable. We could not approve the slightest breach. New Jersey has not breached it here."[10] So, although the majority justices put forward the principle of strict separation in *Everson*, they did not find that it had been breached in this case.

Four Major Documents

Historically, four major documents have shaped the Supreme Court's understanding of the relationship between church and state, or religion and government. All four are mentioned in *Everson*. First, Patrick Henry's Bill Establishing a Provision for Teachers of the Christian Religion (1784) proposed that the state tax its citizens to pay teachers and preachers of Christianity. The Court considered Henry's proposal as giving the government too much authority into matters of religion. The second major document was Madison's Memorial and Remonstrance against Religious Assessments (1785), which defeated Henry's bill. Madison's work contains a powerful argument for keeping the government out of church affairs, either in helping or opposing.

ACCOMMODATION V. STRICT SEPARATION

Third, Jefferson's Virginia Statute for Religious Freedom (1786, first written in 1777) has also played an important role in the Court's articulation of the church-state relationship. Whereas Madison's Memorial and Remonstrance explained what this relationship should not be, Jefferson's Virginia Statute explained what it should be. Jefferson elaborated on what religious freedom means, thus helping to establish what should guide the Court in deciding what is and what is not consistent with the promotion of religious freedom. Justice Black refers to this document in *Everson*: "This Court has previously recognized," referencing *Reynolds v. United States* (1878), "that the provisions of the First Amendment, in the drafting and adoption of which Madison and Jefferson played leading roles, had the same objective and were intended to provide the same protection against governmental intrusion on religious liberty as the Virginia statute."[11]

Finally, the fourth important document is Jefferson's letter to the Baptist Association of Danbury, Connecticut (January 1, 1802), in which he wrote, "I contemplate with sovereign reverence that act of the whole American people which declared that their legislature should 'make no law respecting an establishment of religion, or prohibiting the free exercise thereof,' *thus building a wall of separation between Church and State.*"[12] The *Everson* decision used this phrase to construct the legal doctrine of strict church-state separation: "In the words of Jefferson, the clause against establishment of religion by law was intended to erect 'a wall of separation between Church and State.'"[13] *Everson* does not mention the letter by name, but *Reynolds* quoted it in its entirety, although it analyzed the phrase, "the legislative powers of government reach actions only, and not opinions," rather than the phrase, "a wall of separation." Thus the Court uses Jefferson's words to form the basis of its interpretation of the Establishment Clause in the First Amendment.

SECULARISM AND THE AMERICAN REPUBLIC

The Case for the Reasonable Accommodation of Church and State

The time has come for the Supreme Court to reconsider its interpretation of the strict separation of church and state. Because *Everson* and *McCollum* relied particularly on Jefferson and Madison with respect to the First Amendment and church-state relations, we have also considered them and their intentions.

Jefferson and Madison on Religion and Secularism

Lenni Brenner edited a volume provocatively entitled *Jefferson and Madison on the Separation of Church and State: Writings on Religion and Secularism*. This collection of letters and documents comprises several of the documents that have been key in my research. The back cover asserts, "This book is the most complete collection of these forefathers's writings on religion and secularism."[14] It states further that Jefferson and Madison are the founders of modern secularism. Yet ironically, the term *secularism*, in this most complete collection of Jefferson's and Madison's writings on religion and secularism, does not appear. It would not appear until Holyoake coined it in 1846, more than fifty years after the ratification of the First Amendment.

Additionally, neither does the word *secular* nor any of its derivatives appear in any of Jefferson's writings. In Madison's writings, the word occurs once: "Torrents of blood have been spilt in the old world, by vain attempts of the *secular arm* to extinguish Religious discord, by proscribing all difference in Religious opinions."[15] By no stretch of the imagination can Madison's reference to the "secular arm" be said to refer to secularism. It would seem that many secularists have interpreted the writings of Jefferson and Madison against religious establishment as being tantamount to secularism. However, non-establishment is not secularism. Instead, they carved out a position between those two extremes, which I have referred to as reasonable accommodation.

Jefferson's Report of the Commissioners for the University of Virginia

Invaluably beneficial to my proposal of an approach of accommodation is Jefferson's Report of the Commissioners for the University of Virginia of August 4, 1818. This report totals about six thousand words and represents the most significant discovery I made as I researched for writing this book. Jefferson's report appears to me to offer the greatest hope of the Supreme Court rethinking its approach to church-state relations. After Jefferson presented the report, Jefferson, Madison, and nineteen other luminaries of Virginia signed it.

In the Rockfish Gap Report, Jefferson stated:

> *In conformity with the principles of our Constitution*, which places all sects of religion on an equal footing, with the jealousies of the different sects in guarding that equality from encroachment and surprise, and with the sentiments of the Legislature in favor of freedom of religion, manifested on former occasions, *we have proposed no professor of divinity*; and the rather as *the proofs of the being of a God*, the creator, preserver and supreme ruler of the universe, the author of all the *relations of morality*, and of the laws and obligations these infer, *will be within the province of the professor of ethics* to which adding the developments of these moral obligations, of those in which all sects agree, with a knowledge of the languages, Hebrew, Greek, and Latin, a basis will be formed common to all sects. *Proceeding thus far without offence to the Constitution*, we have thought it proper at this point to leave every side sect to provide, as

they think fittest, the means of further instruction in their own peculiar tenets.[16]

My internal Richter scale registered a reading of "9" when first reading this. The cogs in my mind began turning. This document calls for a direction very different from what *McCollum* offered. In fact, Jefferson's Rockfish Gap Report stands in direct conflict with Justice Black's decision, permitting then what state-supported educational institutions would not permit today. Significantly, it was presented and signed by some of America's founders. The report amplifies our understanding regarding Jefferson's view of the church-state relationship because it shows that he followed principles of reasonable accommodation in founding the University of Virginia.

Why has no one brought the Rockfish Gap Report before the Supreme Court? Why was it not one of the major documents shaping the Court's understanding of church-state relations? Few scholars interacting with the topic of secularism appear to have spent much time with it or to have realized the importance of this document. Some have plainly misinterpreted it, which I illustrate below. Perhaps others do not even know of its existence. Although none of the opinions from *McCollum* considered the Rockfish Gap Report, its dissent referenced some of the other documents from the founding of the University of Virginia.

Establishing the relevance between the university and the facts of *McCollum*, Justice Stanley Reed writes, "Mr. Jefferson, as one of the founders of the University of Virginia, a school which from its establishment in 1819 has been wholly governed, managed and controlled by the State of Virginia, was faced with the same problem that is before this Court today: The question of the constitutional limitation upon religious education in public

ACCOMMODATION V. STRICT SEPARATION

schools." Reed then explained that Jefferson himself set forth his views "at some length" in his "annual report as Rector, to the President and Directors of the Literary Fund, dated October 7, 1822, approved by the Visitors of the University of whom Mr. Madison was one," and that Jefferson's suggestions "were adopted."[17]

In addition to referring to the President-Directors Report, *McCollum's* dissent quoted from a second document: "Should the religious sects of this State, or any of them, according to the invitation held out to them, establish within, or adjacent to, the precincts of the University, schools for instruction in the religion of their sect," the Regulations of the University, dated October 4, 1824, provide, *"the students of the University will be free, and expected to attend religious worship at the establishment of their respective sects, in the morning, and in time to meet their school in the University at its stated hour."*[18]

Commenting on these regulations, Reed concluded, "Thus, the 'wall of separation between church and State' that Mr. Jefferson built at the University which he founded did not exclude religious education from that school. The difference between the generality of his statements on the separation of church and state and the specificity of his conclusions on education are considerable. *A rule of law should not be drawn from a figure of speech."*[19]

Reed's statement in italics refers to the Court's reliance on Jefferson's words in his letter to the Danbury Baptists, which includes the phrase, "building a wall of separation between church and State." In some ways, the majorities in *Everson* and *McCollum* based their holdings on Jefferson's wall of separation. However, the evidence of these reports concerning the founding of the University of Virginia demonstrates that they misinterpreted his meaning and exculpates Jefferson from the charge of strict separation. Beyond Reed's references in *McCollum*, the Court has not given further attention to Jefferson's reports from 1822 and 1824.

Still, why did Jefferson use the expression of a "wall of separation"? The documents from the university's founding indicate that Jefferson was not setting forth a position consonant with the strict separation of church and state. Instead, he clearly proposed and followed a position of reasonable accommodation. The answer then is that Jefferson was denying a church-state union in the United States as was common in Europe. The United States disestablished church and state, thereby introducing legal separation between them. However, disestablishment is much different from the strict separation of secularism.

Introducing Jefferson's Rockfish Gap Report to the Supreme Court

As noted above, the Supreme Court based its interpretation of strict separation on four major documents: Patrick Henry's bill, Madison's Memorial and Remonstrance, Jefferson's Virginia Statute, and his letter to the Danbury Baptists. If these were the only documents available, or if Jefferson had never addressed the church-state relationship after his letter, then the majority Court's interpretation in *McCollum* could make sense. However, that is not the end of the story.

Jefferson addressed the subject again, and he did so specifically in the context of state-sponsored higher education. In a fifth document, the Rockfish Gap Report, he gave further meaning to how he believed that religious freedom could constitutionally function in state-sponsored educational institutions. Can there be any doubt that Jefferson and Madison promoted a model of church-state accommodation in the founding and the development of the University of Virginia?

A misinterpretation of Jefferson's letter to the Danbury Baptists has ruled supreme since 1948. However, his Rockfish Gap Report, written after the letter, offers a worthy change of scenery.

ACCOMMODATION V. STRICT SEPARATION

I believe the time has come for someone to introduce Jefferson's report for consideration before the public forum, before the Supreme Court. Perhaps the justices will not brush it aside, unlike the 1822 and 1824 documents that Justice Reed introduced. The *McCollum* majority did not have an ill intent in arriving at a position of strict church-state separation. Much of the data that I have introduced in this book was presumably not available to them. One would think that the founding documents of the University of Virginia were lost from circulation. However, as I illustrate, it is not that they were lost; it is that they were ignored.

Leonard Levy and Jefferson's Rockfish Gap Report

From my research on the relationship between church and state in the United States, I found only one person from the twentieth century to give significant attention to Jefferson's Report of the Commissioners for the University of Virginia: Leonard Levy. Others have given some attention to it but not *significant* attention. Yet I am puzzled as to why this scholar who received the Pulitzer Prize for History in 1969 dealt with the report in the manner he did. In his book, *The Establishment Clause: Religion and the First Amendment*, he characterized Jefferson's curricular vision for the university: "In 1818, for instance, his academic plan for the newly authorized state university included ten professorships and thirty-four subjects, none of them relating to religion. This curriculum, which was adopted, was laid out in a report, written by Jefferson as chairman of the commissioners for the University of Virginia." The report to which Levy referred was Jefferson's Rockfish Gap Report.[20]

Levy proceeded to quote from the report. "In conformity with the principles of our Constitution, which places all sects of religion on an equal footing... we have proposed no professor of divinity.... Proceeding thus far without offence to the Constitution, we have thought it proper at this point to leave every sect to provide, as they think fittest, the means of further instruction in their own peculiar tenets." Levy then wrote, "The report also stated: 'It is supposed probable, that a building... may be called for in time, in which may be rooms for religious worship... for public examinations, for a library.'"²¹ The ellipses in these quotations, which I will comment on below, are original with Levy.

Levy analyzed Jefferson's report, explaining, "The conditional phrasing of this sentence suggests that Jefferson was seeking to fend off an anticipated barrage of criticism against the university as a 'godless' institution. In fact he was under constant pressure from church groups to make suitable provision for theological training and religious worship at the university." Levy continues, "The 'supposed probable' room that might in time be a place of worship was a concession to those who, as Jefferson reported in a letter to Dr. Thomas Cooper, used the absence of a professorship of divinity to spread the idea that the university was 'not merely of no religion, but against all religion.'"²²

Regrettably, Levy omitted critical key information by his use of ellipses. Before commenting on Levy's omission and interpretation, I will review the entire section with which he was interacting, italicizing the portions he omitted:

> In conformity with the principles of our Constitution, which places all sects of religion on an equal footing, *with the jealousies of the different sects in guarding that equality from encroachment and surprise, and with the sentiments of the Legislature in favor of freedom of religion, manifested on former occasions,* we have proposed no professor of divinity; *and the rather as the proofs of the being of a God, the creator, preserver, and supreme ruler of the universe, the author of all*

ACCOMMODATION V. STRICT SEPARATION

the relations of morality, and of the laws and obligations these infer, will be within the province of the professor of ethics to which adding the developments of these moral obligations, of those in which all sects agree, with a knowledge of the languages, Hebrew, Greek, and Latin, a basis will be formed common to all sects. Proceeding thus far without offence to the Constitution, we have thought it proper at this point to leave every side sect to provide, as they think fittest, the means of further instruction in their own peculiar tenets.[23]

The italicized portion clearly suggests a different conclusion than that which Levy draws. Am I missing something? Can someone explain how a scholar such as Leonard Levy with his credentials could have justified these glaring omissions? To use ellipses and omissions in a manner that will distort the meaning of what is being quoted is inappropriate. Do Levy's omissions not distort what Jefferson was saying in his report? Furthermore, of the multitude of historians who have gone over Jefferson's writings with a fine-toothed comb, why have the vast majority of them given little to no consideration to these penetratingly relevant passages?

The source that Levy used for his research was Roy Honeywell's *The Educational Work of Jefferson*, first published in 1931. Levy's source proves that he was not interacting with a faulty source of the Rockfish Gap Report, since Honeywell provided in his book a full copy of the report, entitled "Report of the Commissioners Appointed to Fix the Site of the University of Virginia." Honeywell wrote, "This report was written by Jefferson before the meeting and was adopted by the commissioners with only minor changes."[24] We can wonder why Levy made these deletions from the report. Nevertheless, he did, and I hope that this book can set the record straight.

Jefferson undoubtedly acknowledged a "wall of separation between church and state" in his letter to the Danbury Baptists. Because most of the justices were convinced that Jefferson's wall was inconsistent with reasonable accommodation, they settled for the position of strict separation. Even so, the justices in *Everson* and *McCollum* expressed concern about the people who would be adversely affected by those who would misunderstand and misapply their ruling. One of the benefits of reading Supreme Court cases is that you can feel the struggles and concerns that the justices experience. The time has come for us, as Americans, to think and to feel our way through these issues with this new information in mind.

The Supreme Court should abandon its approach of strict separation concerning church-state relations in favor of their reasonable accommodation for three reasons. First, Jefferson and Madison themselves advocate for that strategy. Second, the claim that Jefferson founded the University of Virginia on secularism is impossible owing to the fact that the concept would not emerge until several decades after that period. Third, agnosticism and atheism did not command a significant following in the United States until well after the mid-nineteenth century. As late as 1869, Charles Eliot Norton, nursing doubts about God's existence and immortality, penned a letter to John Ruskin, asking, "What education in these matters ought I to give my children? . . . It is in some *respects a new experiment.*"[25] For these reasons, I believe that the time has come for someone to introduce Jefferson's report to the Supreme Court.

A Final Observation from the United States Constitution

Some point out that the American founders mentioned neither God nor Jesus Christ in the Constitution. However, it nonetheless

ACCOMMODATION V. STRICT SEPARATION

accommodates religion in general and Christianity in particular. Article I, which concerns the legislative branch, provides for how a bill can become law even if the president vetoes it: "If any Bill shall not be returned by the President within ten Days (Sundays excepted) after it shall have been presented to him, the same shall be a Law, in like Manner as if he had signed it, unless the Congress by their Adjournment prevent its Return, in which Case it shall not be a Law."[26]

The parenthetical statement, "Sundays excepted," is not without consequence. It refers to the day of the week on which most Christians worship. Either the framers themselves recognized it as a day of worship, or they respected the rights of others who observe it enough to set it aside. In short, the framers not only respected religion but also, significantly, accommodated it.

Conclusion

In this chapter, I have reviewed some of the key material that I have developed through the course of this book, including my motivation for launching this project, origins into the word *secular* and its derivatives, and the competing cases of strict separation versus reasonable accommodation in relation to church-state relations. I also reviewed the four main documents with which the Supreme Court has interacted in its articulation of strict separation, including Henry's bill, Madison's Memorial and Remonstrance, Jefferson's Virginia Statute, and his letter to the Danbury Baptists.

Additionally, I have argued that the Court should give greater attention to the documents that resulted from the founding of the University of Virginia, including, specifically, the Rockfish Gap Report and the President-Directors Report. These documents are significant for appreciating these founders' beliefs concerning the interplay of church and state, religion and government, in light of constitutional principles. Honest consideration of the implications from these documents would change the trajectory of church-state relations in the United States generally and in the space of public education specifically, a topic to which I turn in the final chapter of this book. In particular, I will conclude by considering implications for higher education, secular humanism, and liberty.

CHAPTER FIFTEEN

IMPLICATIONS FOR PUBLIC EDUCATION, SECULAR HUMANISM, AND LIBERTY

EDUCATION: WHERE DO WE GO FROM HERE?

The Report of the Commissioners for the University of Virginia

In the late 1970s and the early 1980s, a series of television advertisements promoted the stock brokerage firm, E. F. Hutton and Company. The firm was best known for the phrase, "When E. F. Hutton talks, people listen."[1] When Thomas Jefferson and James Madison speak, people listen—or at least they should. I hope the Supreme Court will reverse *McCollum v. Board of Education* (1948), which interpreted the First Amendment to require the strict separation of church and state.

A major factor that could contribute to this reversal is Jefferson's Report of the Commissioners for the University of Virginia, dated August 4, 1818, signed by both Jefferson and Madison, the two founders most consequential for the United States' vision of religious freedom. Their signatures to the report should settle the case for their vision of church-state relations. In addition, nineteen other luminaries, the likes of which includes lawyers, judges, and politicians, signed their names to the document.

If any other president after Jefferson or Madison had written the Rockfish Gap Report, its significance would pale in comparison in its potential to influence the Court to reverse *McCollum*. The reason for this assertion is that the Court based its conclusions regarding the First Amendment and church-state relations on Jefferson and Madison. They had paved the way for religious liberty in the United States in the 1780s. They did the work, they prepared the documents, and they left a paper trail. Madison's Memorial and Remonstrance against Religious Assessments (1785) responded to Patrick Henry's Bill Establishing a Provision for Teachers of the Christian Religion (1784). Jefferson then reintroduced the Virginia Statute for Religious Freedom (1777), which the Virginia General Assembly adopted in 1786.

Then in *Everson v. Board of Education* (1947), Justice Hugo Black, author of the majority opinion, cited *Reynolds v. United States* (1878) for the proposition that Jefferson's Virginia Statute carries the same meaning and purpose as the First Amendment: "This Court has previously recognized that the provisions of the First Amendment, in the drafting and adoption of which Madison and Jefferson played such leading roles, had the same objective and were intended to provide the same protection against governmental intrusion on religious liberty as the Virginia statute."[2] However, Jefferson never intended that the view of religious liberty he put forward in the Virginia statute be used to support the strict separation of church and state.

Instead, Jefferson interpreted the First Amendment to permit the reasonable accommodation of church and state. The Court should acknowledge that the Rockfish Gap Report is a

IMPLICATIONS

valid source of data that goes against its faulty interpretation of Jefferson's letter to the Danbury Baptists. The justices should hear a case on this issue and rule on it with integrity. Of all the founders, Jefferson and Madison exercised the greatest influence on the question of church-state relations. I believe the time has come to call them back to the witness stand. Considering the magnitude of the potential influence of the report, the justices may want to validate its credibility and investigate why it has not appeared in the public arena.[3]

Since first reading the Rockfish Gap Report, I have worked through its implications. The evidence supports the conclusion that the framers who founded the nation were open to and comfortable with theism and with Christian thought in public institutions. I have considered this conclusion only recently. The belief system of theism served as the backdrop for the American founders. In Jefferson's university, the professor of ethics could offer proofs for the existence of God: "The proofs of the being of a God, the creator, preserver and supreme ruler of the universe, the author of all the relations of morality, and of the laws and obligations these infer, will be within the province of the professor of ethics to which adding the developments of these moral obligations, of those in which all sects agree, with a knowledge of the languages, Hebrew, Greek, and Latin, a basis will be formed common to all sects."[4]

While questions may exist as to what degree the government may or may not enforce morality, Jefferson affirmed that public educational institutions could constitutionally teach courses on theistic morality. In addition, they could require marks of high character to bring faculty, administration, and staff into their employ. Finally, Jefferson's mention of Hebrew, Greek, and Latin demonstrates still further evidence of his accommodating

Christian studies, since, as he acknowledged, the Old Testament is written in Hebrew, the New Testament is written in Greek, and theology and the scholarly works are written in Latin.

Jefferson stated that he believed that his vision was consistent with constitutional principles. Specifically, he mentioned the Constitution of Virginia. However, since the Supreme Court has acknowledged that the freedom of religion in the First Amendment is the same as that in the Virginia Statute for Religious Freedom, Jefferson's statement is tantamount to his saying that it is consistent with the First Amendment. Jefferson's vision for the university offers an instructive model for us today.

Implications for Public Education

I now offer some suggestions for the Court to consider in light of Jefferson's plan for the University of Virginia in the Rockfish Report: Institutions of public education should not support specific religious sects. Yet they should legally offer more freedom and opportunity—reasonable accommodation—in matters of religion. These principles mean that both theists and non-theists should properly hold equal rights. The law should recognize, for example, the right of public institutions of education to adopt policy, hire faculty, and build courses that accommodate different worldviews equally, including theistic ones, including Christian ones. Morals based on traditional theistic belief should have the same rights to be heard as those rooted in other systems of thought, whether agnosticism, atheism, feminism, Marxism, or others.

Jefferson proposed that the University of Virginia not employ a professor of divinity. Wisdom suggests that we follow that model. However, that principle does not mean that professors should not be permitted to refer to the Bible and theology in their courses. Freedom of speech and academic liberty means that we can permit

IMPLICATIONS

other areas of thought, whether in favor of or in opposition to Christian thought, with decency and order. Public schools should not require that Christian professors awkwardly avoid their honest thoughts and beliefs, just as they should not require the same of non-Christian professors. The government should not require that public schools follow modernist or postmodernist philosophical assumptions as the only valid models for academic research capable of producing facts and truth.

The leadership of public schools and universities should permit professors to teach on the subjects of absolute empiricism and rationalism, agnosticism and atheism, and materialism and naturalism, as well as those of theism and Christianity and other religions, in a manner consistent with their beliefs in the classroom, assuming that they do not violate concerns for public policy. Non-theists should not be forbidden from teaching in a manner that is informed by their atheistic beliefs, and theists should not be forbidden from teaching according to their beliefs. Public schools should permit professors to share their views of life and the world. Additionally, they should permit students to ask questions freely concerning these matters.

Thus the government should constitutionally recognize the right of public schools to permit open discussion to occur concerning belief in the existence of God and the implications of that belief for morals, just as rights are granted to secularists and their beliefs. Such discussions should not result in any restriction of the freedom of speech as it now exists on campuses of public education. The government should remove the muzzle from those who would like to give voice to Christian belief and morality. A professor who is a Christian should be able to acknowledge that he or she is a Christian. In fact, all professors should be able to acknowledge their views of life and the world.

SECULARISM AND THE AMERICAN REPUBLIC

I am not asking that the government deny a voice to non-Christian worldviews, nor am I asking for it to place any limitations on philosophies of life such as secularism and secular humanism. Rather I am asking that the government exercise consistency in its application of freedom in public educational institutions. The government should grant the same freedom that secularism currently experiences, the same freedom that Christianity could experience, to other religions and worldviews as well. To be sure, the government should grant to Christianity the same freedoms that it grants to non-Christian and non-theistic worldviews, especially since secularism as such was non-existent when America's founders ratified the Constitution.

The Growth of Secularism in Public Education

Popular and Epistemological Secularism

The question remains how secularism came to dominate modern institutions of public education, including colleges and universities. I refer to the Englishman George Jacob Holyoake's form of secularism, which he introduced in 1846 and Robert Ingersoll promoted in the United States in the late nineteenth century as "popular secularism." This use of the term *secularism* has caused much confusion in the United States because it now refers to the absence of religion, whereas historically it referred simply to that which occurs beyond the religious cloister. In any case, popular secularism was short-lived. It fizzled out around 1890, though its essence still occupies a continued presence in our culture.

More influential regarding the question of how secularism came to dominate is "epistemological secularism." Colleges and universities began strictly adhering to an absolute epistemological empiricism. This type of secularism has had a greater influence on American culture than popular secularism. However, it did not become a significant force until after World War II.[5]

The University of Virginia and Secularism

Part of the chronological challenge is that secularists did not have a seat at the table at the United States founding because, as we have just reviewed, secularism as such had not yet emerged. The same holds true with respect to the founding of the University of Virginia. Jefferson could not have staffed the faculty of the university with agnostics or atheists, even if he wanted to, when it opened in 1825. That would have been true even if he had drawn from the whole world of scholarship.

If anyone in the Western world could have come close to qualifying as an agnostic, it would have been Auguste Comte (1798–1857). He was about twenty-seven-years-old when the University of Virginia opened, and likely a non-theist by that point. Michel Bourdeau comments that Comte "thought of emigrating to the United States to teach at a school that Jefferson was planning to open and which was to be modeled on the École Polytechnique."[6] He even attempted to establish contact with Jefferson. However, nothing came of it.

According to American diplomat Nicholas Philip Trist (1800–1874), who also worked in Jefferson's law office, Comte mailed a small manuscript to Jefferson explaining his views. However, by the time the manuscript arrived, Jefferson had died. For Trist's part, he opened the package and was impressed by what he saw.[7] Comte was the only scholar, or likely professor, then living who might have qualified as a non-theist. Even so, Jefferson likely would not have given a non-theist a position on the faculty of the university. He was also aware of David Hume (1711–1776) and Immanuel Kant (1724–1804) and their rejection of proofs for the existence of God.[8] But he likewise did not follow them.

Constitutional Freedoms for Secularism as a Religion

Even though secularism did not have a seat at the table when the country or Jefferson's university was founded, it nonetheless finds freedom to exist in the constitutional freedoms of speech guaranteed in the First Amendment: "Congress shall make no law respecting an establishment of religion, or prohibiting the free exercise thereof; or abridging the freedom of speech, or of the press. . . ."[9]

While secularism did not exist at the founding, the First Amendment nonetheless applies to it. Once secularism made its appearance, the First Amendment preempted Congress from denying to secularism a voice in the public square and, as a result, in public institutions of education. Historically the freedom of speech has granted secularism its First Amendment freedoms. However, a recent court case from 2014 has extended this protection even to the religion clauses, granting to secular humanism the status of religion.

Secularism as a Religion

Some interesting developments have occurred in recent court battles regarding the legal definition of secular humanism. In *American Humanist Association v. United States*, Senior District Judge Ancer Haggerty found that the First Amendment protects adherents to humanism.[10] Judge Haggerty was trying to improve matters for an inmate, Jason Michael Holden, a secular humanist who had been denied the right to meet with other secular humanist inmates to celebrate special days and events, a right that had otherwise been granted to approved religions. Jack Jenkins says that the *American Humanist Association* is "paving the way for the non-theistic community to obtain the same legal rights as groups such as Christianity."[11] Steven Dubois explains, "Federal prisoners who identify as humanist can now celebrate Darwin Day and get accommodations typically afforded to those inmates who believe in a deity."[12]

Few people seem to know that Judge Haggerty has declared that humanism is a religion under the Establishment Clause. Haggerty understandably desired to offer relief to Holden and his fellow inmates. I would have wanted the same. However, the way in which he granted the relief has confused the issue at hand, as well as the driving question of this book: Is the United States founded on secularism to the point that it does not recognize a place for theism?

Nicholas Little, Ronald Lindsay, and Tom Flynn challenge Judge Haggerty's "bizarre" holding, opining that secular humanism is not a religion. Yet some secularists view secularism as religious. Little, Lindsay, and Flynn divide the "humanist community" into three camps: First, religious humanism "views Humanism as a religious commitment and may include assent to objectively unprovable propositions, such as the perfectibility of human beings." Second, congregational humanism "describes a growing group of humanists who eschew any form of religious faith but desire to take part in ceremonies and rituals drawn from the life of church or synagogue congregations." Finally, secular humanism refers to "an explicitly nonreligious life stance that rejects all form of supernaturalism or spirituality and is often uninterested in practices borrowed from congregational life."[13]

Secularists often designate themselves as non-theists or as following a natural religion. However, congregational humanists have recognized the social value of religious observances, as evidenced by secular baby dedications, secular weddings, and secular funeral services. In some ways, they are attempting to provide for their adherents something similar to what Christianity and other organized religions provide for their adherents.

Implications for Public Education

Where are these developments taking us? If secular humanism receives the same rights as other religions, then does it also receive the same restrictions? What about the limitations of freedom that the government has placed upon Christianity as a religion? Do secular humanists meet with the same limitations that the government has imposed on Christians? Do Christians have the same freedom to advance a Christian view of life and the world in university classrooms as that given to secular humanists? To these questions: If not, why not?

For example, many in society move to restrict Christians in the area of sexual ethics, such as forcing them to keep silent on matters related to same-sex weddings and transgender issues. But if these Christians were to follow the lead of society, they would violate their longstanding convictions. To be sure, concerned parties will have to reach an understanding on some issues now and then. Thus responsible people on both sides should offer input so as to reach workable solutions to these difficult challenges. However, one side should not be silenced in favor of the other. True reasonable accommodation would permit the voice of all sides.

In recent history humanists are riding a wave of victory. They have won some legal victories against those who would not agree to offer them services, and they are rejoicing in their triumphs. Nevertheless, their cries of victory may have come too soon. Over the years, secular humanists have succeeded in restricting Christians to keep them from Bible readings, prayer, and other such

IMPLICATIONS

practices in institutions of public education. However, if indeed secularism is a religion, then secularists should also experience the strong arm of the law. If secularism and theism are competing visions for life and the world, then one of two results should follow: Either the government should permit each equal freedoms in public institutions, or else it should require equal restrictions.

FACING THE FUTURE OF PUBLIC EDUCATION IN THE UNITED STATES

The prevailing view among many is that the United States of America was not founded as a Christian, or even a religious, nation. As examined in part one, a sizable number of people believe that it was founded as a secularist nation. However, honest interaction with the chronological incompatibility of the founding of secularism relative to that of the United States should nullify that claim. My guiding concern for this book has been to lay a legal foundation that will prepare the way to overthrow the doctrine of strict church-state separation that *McCollum* announced. As Americans we are strong advocates of religious liberty. However, true liberty will have bounds because it is not mere license. An important case from the Supreme Court to clarify its limits was *Reynolds v. United States* (1878), which I analyzed in chapter nine.

In that case opinion, which concerned the constitutionality of bigamy, Chief Justice Morrison Waite developed a distinction that Jefferson had made between actions and opinions. He explained that religious liberty does not extend to actions that conflict with social duty and result in social unrest. In cases where actions accord with proper duty but still cause unrest, legislatures do not have the true authority to forbid them since they reflect what is right. However, legislatures have the proper authority to interfere in actions, even if they are based on genuine religious belief that subvert social duty and order, which was (and is) the case with bigamy. Waite also gave other examples that illustrate these principles, such as the practice of human sacrifice or of sati.[14]

In the past several decades, some secularists have restricted Christians from giving voice to their convictions and morals within institutions of public education. However, as Jefferson and Waite would remind us, "the legislative powers of government reach actions only, and not opinions."[15] The government may place civil limits upon what people may practice (action) in the name of their religion or philosophy when that practice does not accord with social duty or subverts good order. However, it should permit them to express their beliefs (opinions).

If the government permits secular humanists to express their beliefs within public education, it should grant the same freedom to Christianity, as well as to other religions and belief systems. Likewise, if the government restricts the voice of Christianity, it should also restrict that of secularism. Belief in the freedoms of religion and speech does not require that we affirm all expressions of those freedoms according to the parameters I have considered above. However, we should value the freedom of people to express what they believe is right and good.

If these principles hold true for public schools and universities, then they should also hold true for private institutions, which are not controlled by the state to the same degree. As we considered in part three, Jefferson envisioned the University of Virginia as a nonsectarian institution but believed that the state should recognize the freedom of private institutions to teach the creeds of their particular sects. In fact, as the Rockfish Gap and the President-Directors Report make plain, he even affirmed cross-pollination between public and private institutions. However, the point is that the state should not presume to restrict the rights of public or private

IMPLICATIONS

institutions from teaching that which accords with their theological, philosophical, and ethical beliefs, whether with regard to life, marriage, sexuality, or something else. Such implications follow from the principles established by the tradition following Jefferson and Waite.

Conclusion

This book has explored elements related to secularism and the American republic. Although the creed of secularism has grown in institutions of public education, the vision of American founders such as Thomas Jefferson demonstrate a better way. Contrary to the assertion of some scholars, secularism per se did not exert a strong influence on the founders, largely owing to chronological incompatibility that such a position presents, to say nothing of their personal epistemologies. Notwithstanding this point, Justice Hugo Black and colleagues enshrined the creed into American jurisprudence with two key Supreme Court decisions by interpreting Jefferson's letter to the Association of Danbury Baptists to mean the strict separation of church and state.

However, Jefferson's writings, including his Report of the Commissioners for the University of Virginia and Report to the President and Directors of the Literary Fund, signal a considerably different vision for church-state relations. It is not one of strict separation but rather one of reasonable accommodation; it is not one of coercion but rather one of liberty. Although the implications for these principles are far-reaching, I have focused on church-state relations within the sphere of education. By attending to the principles that Jefferson laid out, I believe that we as a nation can succeed in accommodating a large and diverse populace that holds assorted philosophical and religious viewpoints in a fair, honest, and respectful manner that accords with constitutional principles.

Appendices

In Search of the Secular John Locke

Gregory Sergent

John Locke (1632–1704) is important to this study because he was an especially important influence on the thinking of the American founders. In this appendix I want to consider the questions: Would this father of classical liberalism qualify as a card-carrying secularist today? Would the display of religious symbols in the public square appall him? Would an invocation offered at a public school graduation or references to God on currency offend him? Or would he call for the privatization of religion? How would he weigh-in on the current debate over church-state relations?

I will argue that Locke was not a secularist. He did not support a forceful, corrupt state church that imposed dogma upon its citizens, but neither did he promote a secular state that was absolute and would silence the voice of religious consciousness, reason, and moral principle. Instead, Locke, to some extent, aligned himself, both ideologically and theologically, with much of the dissenting free-church tradition. In addition, he affirmed some basic Christian doctrine, which contributed to his political philosophy. In order to demonstrate these points, I will begin by considering the education and teachings of Locke.

The Education and Teachings of John Locke

Upbringing and Education

Locke was born in Somerset, England, in an era of political and theological upheaval. The Lockes were zealously Puritan and Calvinistic in belief. Their minister, the Puritan intellectual Dr. Samuel Crook, baptized young John. The senior Locke served as a captain in Oliver Cromwell's Parliamentary Army, affording the young Locke a place at the prestigious Westminster School, where he studied under Richard Busly. Under his tutelage, Locke learned to think critically and to "beware of persuasion, and never accept without reflection the pretensions of men of power."[1]

Noted Lockean scholar Maurice Cranston says that, by the age of twenty-four, Locke began budding as an empiricist. As such, he viewed the thoughtless adherence to tradition and emotional conviction as a basis of truth as sources of error throughout history. However, Locke's empiricism did not exclude supernaturalism. Locke believed that both divine revelation and rational reflection reveal truth.

Cranston attributes Jeremy Taylor's discourse on the liberty of prophesying as having converted Locke to affirm religious toleration. However, the influence may also have resulted from the Puritan divine John Owen who led the Oxford chapels, where Locke frequently heard sermons and addressed theo-political themes. Owen reportedly said that all "men should be free to think and worship as they please so long as their faith did not lead them to disturb peace and order. The duty of the Government... was to maintain order and not to impose religion."[2] Locke received a typical Puritan upbringing and a classical education that involved the study of Scripture, philosophy, and the sciences. In other words, he was certainly not raised in the throes of secularism.

The Reasonableness of Christianity

Although Locke would come to hold some unorthodox views, he identified himself as a Christian. He possessed an internal tenacity that questioned conventional wisdom and authorities. Yet he was an apt student of the Bible and follower of a rational Christianity. Locke thus defended Christianity in *The Reasonableness of Christianity, as Delivered in the Scriptures* (1695).

Because he disagreed with many of the edicts of the formal organized religion of his day and instead approached apologetics from an empiricist perspective, many of his contemporaries interpreted him as controversial and even mysterious. Nevertheless, Cardinal Avery Dulles listed Locke as an apologist in *The History of Apologetics*, asserting that Locke was a "convinced Christian" who accepted a doctrine of Christian revelation.[3] We might then refer to Locke as an evidentialist apologist who appealed to human reason to establish the rationality of Christian faith and to divine revelation, which he believed to be rational.

Like most early scientists in the Christian tradition, Locke believed that the conclusions he drew from the empirical sciences better enabled him to understand the divine truth that God had specially revealed as well as the natural law that He had ordered. Locke argued that the gospel is believable because it is reasonable. In an era marked by suspicion, intolerance, persecution, and theological upheaval, he drew attention to the simplicity of the Christian gospel. He described the nature of faith as follows: "[B]elieving on the Son, is the believing that Jesus was the Messiah; giving Credit to the Miracles he did, and the profession he made of himself."[4] The prophecies of the Old Testament and the witness of the apostles and the early church concerning the gospel include belief in Jesus' death, burial, and resurrection from the dead.[5] Locke's point in defending the simplicity of Christianity was to show its empirical reasonableness as "a religion suited to vulgar Capacities."[6]

God entrusts the message of the gospel to common people, unlearned and unschooled yet with ordinary rational ability.[7] Locke's vision stood in contrast to that of his contemporaries who argued from ontological presuppositions and tight creedal formulations and imposed belief systems. He did not appeal to the established authority of ecclesial institutions, theologians, and philosophers but rather to the capability of ordinary people to understand the Bible. Locke emphasized the rational appeal of empirical evidence.

He thus challenged the strongly held Calvinistic doctrine of election by divine decree on one hand, as well as the extremes of "pure natural religion" espoused by the Deists that "do violence" to the New Testament message on the other.[8] Locke was not attempting per se to undermine Christianity. Instead, he sought to promote forbearance, peace, and unity.

Personal and Political Liberty

Locke's view of the Christian gospel and his study of Christianity, especially of the Pauline corpus, led him to affirm both personal and political liberty. His affirmation of personal liberty resulted from his study of human reason and the Bible. He held that physical reality consists in the interplay of a material-immaterial dichotomy. Consequently, human nature consists in the material aspect of the body and the immaterial aspect of the spirit, which gives rise to liberty. Locke explained that the "ideas we have belonging and peculiar to spirit, are thinking, and will, or a power of putting body into motion by thought, and, which is consequent to it, liberty."[9]

He held further that man's basic liberty permits him to know that God exists. In contrast to the materialism of Hobbes, Locke believed that reason leads to the knowledge of God: "Thus from the consideration of ourselves, and what we infallibly find in our own constitutions, our reason leads us to the knowledge of this certain and evident truth, that there is an eternal, most powerful, and most knowing Being."[10] The author of human reason is God the Creator, who endows human beings with liberty, which functions as their personal governor, informing their consciences and concepts of morality. God never coerced people into embracing a new religion.[11] Even Old Testament Israel did not compel strangers to embrace the Mosaic Law by force.

As a result of affirming man's rational capacity of choice and belief, Locke advocated a vision of religious toleration for society. Political liberty follows personal liberty. It grants individuals the power of choosing political leaders. However, Locke was far removed from the late-modern secularist who would privatize religious expression and exclude moral persuasion from the public square. Personal liberty is not license for "carnality," which undermines the very foundation of political liberty. It is "not a liberty for ambition to pull down well-framed constitutions, that out of its ruins they may build themselves fortunes."[12] For the law of the state to result in a "happy state" and a "pure church," it must be consistent with the law of God.[13]

Religious Toleration in the Church and State

Whereas a modern-day secularist aims to suppress the public expression of religious sentiment, Locke appealed specifically to religious sentiment to build his case for legal and social toleration. Locke lived in the midst of much controversy regarding church-state relations. The Protestant Reformation had stripped the Roman Catholic Church of its institutional authority in the eyes of many, instead emphasizing the authority of the Bible. In addition, scholars began translating the Bible into the language of the common person in the seventeenth century.

The Reformation manifested itself in England in the Anglican Church. Yet numerous dissenting sects were still suspicious and even distrustful of the Church of England, which they viewed as oppressive. In fact, England often used the threat of the sword to compel dissenters' religious adherence. If they did not obey, England persecuted them, depriving them of property rights and civil participation.

Within this broader context, Locke penned *A Letter Concerning Toleration*. He lamented that neither governors nor dissenters understood, much less practiced, toleration and liberty. However, "absolute liberty, just and true liberty, equal and impartial liberty, is the thing that we stand in need of."[14] Human reason demonstrates a dichotomy between the material and immaterial, which parallels the body and spirit.[15] The immaterial spirit motivates the mobility of the material body. Thus the church should appeal to the "inward persuasion of the mind" with "light and evidence" rather than with force.[16] The church should care for the needs of the soul through the power of persuasion, substantiating the need for religious toleration.

Locke extended his material-immaterial dichotomy to the church-state relationship. Through the equal protection of the law, the civil magistrate should safeguard toleration for civil interests, which includes religious liberty: "life, liberty, health, and indolency of body; and the possession of outward things, such as money, lands, houses, furniture, and the like."[17] The magistrate has the power of external force but not of internal force. He cannot impose belief, which flows not from outward constraints or penalties but rather from inward conviction.[18]

Locke also advocated for a limited governmental authority that acknowledges the public good as the "rule and measure of all law-making."[19] The authority of God supersedes that of the civil magistrates who would impose laws violating personal conscience, as well as of either establishing or restricting religious rites.[20] In this way, Locke, despite his Puritan upbringing, deviated from the teachings of Calvin and the divines who followed him in this regard, instead emphasizing liberty of conscience. Furthermore, as Victor Nuovo has shown, Locke's views on toleration were influenced by the Remonstrants, the successors to Jacobus Arminius in the Netherlands.[21]

For Locke, religious belief is not the grounds for persecution but rather for the expression of personal liberty. Thus the magistrate should step into religious affairs only when the public good, peace, or safety is at risk, in which case he has the power of executing the full authority of the law. Magistrates should never misuse authority to oppress the church in the pretense of public good. Locke understood that the public good involves the protection of civil rights and the possession of worldly goods. The magistrate does not possess indiscriminate authority to punish sin.[22]

Locke did not write as a churchman of the established hierarchy but rather as a layman, as well as a philosopher who was concerned for the integrity of Christian belief, which he believed invariably includes freedom. He argued that the church is not a political machine to impose its belief on the populace through establishment. Instead, it is a "free and voluntary society" that God gives man the choice of joining only by mutual consent.[23] Locke thus aimed to preserve ecclesiastical liberty, which he described as the church's legal right of existence and the state's legal duty of religious toleration toward both churches and individuals without prejudice or loss of civil enjoyment.[24]

Locke argued that the gospel compels men to charity, bounty, and liberality toward one another.[25] Toleration is the chief characteristic of the true church. He called upon "pulpits everywhere" to sound the doctrine of peace and toleration.[26] He likewise reminded church leaders that they would one day give an account to the Prince of Peace.[27] As individuals should live in tolerance of one another, so churches should live in "peace, equity, and friendship" toward one another without superiority or prejudice.[28] Persuasion should depend upon the strength of argument that confounds the errors of men rather than upon force.[29]

The nature of the church's influence in culture or the individual's religious expression in the public square is perhaps the crucial question of our day in church-state relations. Locke believed that the church's authority is confined to the bounds of the church; it is not extended to the commonwealth.[30] Yet he also affirmed that the church's ideas (e.g., beliefs, dogmas, traditions, and rituals) are open to the public for evaluation and the "persuasion of the mind." Free societies, as such, permit the free expression of ideas. Not all ideas are equally believable. Nevertheless, free societies allow practitioners to present their ideas in an intellectually reasonable fashion to persuade and convince, and they allow free citizens to make informed, rational choices regarding those ideas. Free societies permit the public expression even of unpopular opinions.[31]

The church has the power not only of public expression but also of moral influence. The church is not an "ecclesiastical dominion" that has the power of domination and force to persecute others. However, it may persuade men to live according to morality, piety, and virtue. "It is in vain for any man to usurp the name of Christian, without holiness of life, purity of manners, and benignity and meekness of spirit."[32] Religious liberty is not a license for impure and immoral living under the guise of religious sentiment but rather for mutual toleration.

The Religious Base of a Society that Promotes Religious Toleration

Locke taught that man would preserve civil society only through an underlying morality that is informed by belief in God and Scripture: "No opinions contrary to human society, or to those moral rules which are necessary to the preservation of civil society, are to be tolerated by the magistrate."[33] Moral actions belong both to the public and to the private realms. Man requires the authority of the law to guide the outward governance of the magistrate and the inward governance of an informed conscience.[34]

Thus questions of religion and morality are not solely private matters but rather are public concerns for the civil government. Magistrates rightly concern themselves with morality for societal preservation. In addition, the conscience that is informed by religion helps protect social decency. This background means that Locke never espoused a secular, "godless" government. Instead, he grounded civil rights and decency within a theistic belief system.

The denial of God's existence is tantamount to the denial of belief in the essence of divine law. Locke believed that such denials undermine the very foundations of human law. He held that atheists could not think of social promises, such as contracts, in the same way as theists because they deny natural law. Locke thus supported a state that upholds the existence of God and the necessity of Christian moral principle yet also that tolerates variant worldviews, permits open expression and debate, and privileges reason.[35]

Perhaps the Fundamental Constitutions of Carolina best summarize Locke's views of government. They identify several prerequisites for state office holders, including belief in God, recognition of divine justice and human responsibility, and church membership.[36] The state may recognize the significance of faith expressions, but it should not coerce people into religious belief with public penalties.[37] Neither belief nor unbelief should offend a culture of toleration. Instead, society should permit human reason to judge each worldview as either reasonable or unreasonable.

Finally, government is rightfully concerned with the individual's "good life." Locke summarized this kind of life clearly and concisely: "A good life, in which consist not the least part of religion and true piety, concerns also the civil government; and in it lies the safety both of men's souls, and of the commonwealth. Moral actions belong therefore to the jurisdiction both of the outward and inward court, both of the civil and domestic governor, I mean, both of the magistrate and conscience."[38] The individual has a right to govern his or her life by the dictates of a conscience that is informed by an inward court and an outward court: religious principle and the magistrate who serves as the domestic governor of the public safety and good life.

Conclusion

John Locke was not a *secularist* as we understand the term today but rather was a person who identified himself as a Christian and espoused the virtue of religion for public morality. His background, education, and training were thoroughly Christian. Even though his rationalism was controversial with some established Christian thinkers, including those of his Calvinist background, Locke nonetheless appealed frequently to the Bible in his writings. In addition, he explicitly established a biblical basis for his concept of liberty, linking it directly to the gospel. Incidentally, he was perhaps the most prominent political theorist to influence the American founders.

With the secularist push to privatize religious expression and to minimize its role in public life, much historical evidence exists from Locke's writing that religious sentiment begins as a matter of personal conscience. Locke was perhaps the most influential political theorist on the founding of the United States. For him, a conscience informed by religion has an important place in public expression. Religious expression in the public square requires toleration (a vital Christian ethic), not suppression. The truth (which appeals to human reason) not only arises but flourishes in such an environment.

Locke would have agreed that the secularist worldview fares better in the world of Christian toleration rather than in a hypothetical state devoid of public religious expression and morality. The very essence of true religion and citizenship respects, not suppresses, public expression. In other words, even the secularist worldview requires a certain moral base as influenced by religion that enables the survival of secularism as a worldview.

If secularists succeed in privatizing religion and suppressing public religious expression, then something other than a culture that values legal and social toleration will evolve. Locke was thoroughly convinced that truth, whether acquired through revelation or reason, would stand when persuasion results from hearty dialogue rather than physical coercion. Rational people do not need to be told what to believe but are free to think and choose. The power of words through rational dialogue, and even through preaching, persuades the conscience and enables internal transformation in a way the sword or physical threat cannot.

This spirit molded the newly formed democratic republic of the United States through free elections. The evangelical tradition (that supported the individual moral consciousness helping sustain the public good) flourished in America and particularly in the most rural and isolated parts of the republic. This moral fabric sustained a nation torn apart by civil strife, and it was the ethos for reconciliation and rebuilding. Locke's theo-political contribution not only provided the basis of founding documents but also guided a classic philosophy of education and contributed in guiding the Supreme Court in deciphering church and state issues for almost 160 years. Perhaps the most persuasive summation of John Locke's life and philosophy are the words inscribed on his gravestone:

> Near this place lieth John Locke. If you ask what kind of man he was, he answers that he lived content with his own small fortune. Bred a scholar, he made his learning subservient only to the cause of truth. This thou will learn from his writings, which will show thee everything else concerning him, with greater truth, than the suspect praises of an epitaph. His virtues, indeed, if he had any, were too little for him to propose as matter of praise to himself, or as an example to you. Let his vices be buried together. As to an example of manners, if you seek that, you have it in the Gospels; of vices, to wish you have one nowhere; if mortality, certainly, (and may it profit thee), thou hast one here and everywhere.[39]

SECULARISM AND THE AMERICAN EXPERIENCE

Garrett Sheldon

As this book has demonstrated, secularism as such did not exist in early American society, nor did it exist at the forming and framing of the Constitution of the United States. Instead, the topic of religious liberty filled the founders' deliberations. Advocates of the doctrine viewed it as presenting a middle way between competing extremes, as well as a means by which to teach true morals and virtues in society.

The predominantly Calvinist theology of early American churches emphasized the importance of Christian participation in politics as a "calling" and a duty, and it placed the status of the Christian magistrate on the same level as a church minister.[1] In addition, the Protestant doctrine of "liberty of conscience" meant that a single official ("established") church would not dominate the Christian political involvement. For the founders, then, non-establishment meant that a greater Christian citizenry could ensue in public life since one sect would not dominate. Thus the founders' articulation of religious liberty preempted religious establishment, but it did not require secularism.

SECULARISM AND THE AMERICAN REPUBLIC

We see this theme from Thomas Jefferson (1743–1826), who authored the Declaration of Independence and the Virginia Statute for Religious Freedom. We also see it from James Madison (1751–1836), the father of the Constitution who also authored the Memorial and Remonstrance against Religious Assessments. Other writers and documents also show this conception of religious liberty at the founding. However, this appendix will review Jefferson and Madison specifically and provide additional information to support the argument presented by Leroy Forlines.

The writings of these key figures demonstrate that the doctrine of religious liberty never implied a secular rejection of religion in the public square. Instead, Jefferson and Madison viewed religious liberty as the best way to promote Christian morality and virtue. Even Thomas Paine (1737–1809), whom some have called an atheist but who was actually a Deist, accepted the moral role that religion should play in society, to the point that the radicals of the French Revolution persecuted him for it.

This appendix will focus primarily on Madison, examining his education in Christian thought and his defense of religious liberty as the best means of advancing a Christian faith and commonwealth. It will then look briefly at Jefferson's Virginia Statute through which he sought to unshackle the true Christian religion from corrupt state control. Finally, the appendix will demonstrate how the religion clauses of the First Amendment situate this American conception of religious liberty by placing it between the extremes of religious establishment and secularism. Throughout the appendix, I will offer examples for how the ideal that Madison and Jefferson put forward benefits the Christian faith, which views God as its Sovereign and Providence, but by no means are these benefits limited to the Christian religion.

James Madison: Education and the Case for Religious Liberty

Madison's Christian Education

Madison received a consistently Christian upbringing and education. Beginning with a devout and attentive paternal grandmother, Frances Taylor Madison, Madison's education was directed toward Christian ideals. Drawing on a library at his father's estate, Montpelier, which boasted nearly one hundred volumes, Madison imbued an intellectual and religious temperament from an early age. These volumes included bound copies of a British Christian literary magazine, as well as Joseph Addison's *Spectator*. At age twelve, he was boarded at the school of a Protestant clergyman, the Reverend Donald Robertson, who had received his education in the Scottish universities of Aberdeen and Edinburgh.[2]

Under Robertson, Madison studied the classics and Christian theology.[3] Everything he learned was from a Christian perspective, as a logical syllogism from one of his student notebooks reveals:

I. No sinners are happy;
II. Angels are happy; therefore
III. Angels are not sinners.[4]

Madison later described Robertson as "a man of extensive learning, and a distinguished teacher" and added that "all that I have been in life I owe largely to that man."[5]

At age sixteen, Madison continued his education with another clergyman, the Reverend Thomas Martin, an evangelical Christian minister who had recently graduated from the (then) fervently Calvinist Princeton College, which was imbued with the spirit of the

Great Awakening and where Madison would later attend.[6] In addition to Martin's influencing this decision, Robertson would also influence it because he convinced the Madison family to send James to Princeton rather than to the reputedly morally lax William and Mary College.[7] A family friend would later confirm that he entered into the lively Christian spirit of his college, returning home to lead family worship.[8]

At Princeton, Madison studied with the new President John Witherspoon (1723–1794), a dynamic Reformed minister from Scotland. Known for his fiery orthodoxy and intellectual acumen, Witherspoon integrated all studies with the Christian faith.[9] Continuing the Great Awakening tradition that formed Princeton, Witherspoon emphasized a simple Christian faith: human sin and rebellion against God, repentance and acceptance of God's forgiveness through the atoning sacrifice of Jesus Christ, the "new birth" of the indwelling Holy Spirit within believers, and the sharing of that gospel of love to others through Christian evangelism.[10]

Central to the spread of the Christian faith was liberty of conscience and the freedom of religion so that people could freely hear and voluntarily accept God's grace. As the Scripture says in Romans 10:17, "So then faith comes by hearing, and hearing by the word of God." For Witherspoon, then, as well as for Madison, which I will consider below, religious liberty was part and parcel of civil, political, and economic liberty and justice. Together these basic liberties precipitate the prosperity of a society. Additionally, people best realize the gifts and callings that God has given them by virtue of religious liberty. In the words of Witherspoon, such liberty "promotes industry, and ... happiness." It "produces every latent quality, and improves the human mind,—Liberty is the nurse of riches, literature and heroism."[11]

Madison's Case for Religious Liberty

With the lessons he learned at Princeton, Madison went back to Virginia (1) to liberate it from its bondage to religious establishment and (2) to frame the American conception of religious liberty. First, he applied his Christian education to the "diabolical Hell," as he called it, of religious persecution in Virginia.[12] As a colony of Great Britain, the "Old Dominion" continued the established Anglican Church. Consequently, the state granted privileges to a single official church, while slightly tolerating dissenting Christian denominations. The state forced citizens to support the Church of England financially through taxes.[13] The state also required that the clergy of the official state church perform important ceremonies such as weddings and funerals. Dissenting ministers were legally restricted as to where and when they could preach, build churches, and teach doctrine.

For Madison, an exclusive state church, combined with restrictions on individuals to express their faith freely, contributed to the distortion of Christianity. It also substituted an unchristian means of salvation, namely by state coercion rather than by prayer and persuasion. It encouraged a worldly pride and wealth in the church, contrasting sharply with Jesus' humility and poverty. Finally, it made ordinary believers lazy and apathetic since the state legally recognized only officially ordained clergy as ministers.[14]

Faith came through Christian witness and testimony, not through coercion and violence, and it came through clergy and laymen alike, not just through ministers. The idea that all Christians have equality to share their beliefs reflects the Reformation doctrine of the priesthood of all believers. This doctrine teaches that every Christian is a minister and evangelist in some sense and is commanded by the Lord Jesus Christ to proclaim the gospel. As Jesus said to His disciples in the Great Commission, "Go therefore and make disciples of all the nations, baptizing them in the name of the Father and of the Son and of the Holy Spirit, teaching them to observe all things that I have commanded you" (Matthew 28:19–20a). From Madison's vantage point, the spread of Christianity—indeed, the spread of any religious opinion—results best from liberty rather than from law.[15]

Madison believed that these principles have implications for statecraft. He had witnessed the jailing of a Baptist minister who was preaching to his flock through the bars of his jail window in Culpepper, Virginia.[16] This episode greatly impressed him as a sterling example of how state restrictions on religious expression harm the faith rather than help it. Religious liberty would promote a vital, lively Christianity that could change people's lives. In fact, the revival movements of the Great Awakening in the American colonies involving Jonathan Edwards and George Whitefield, as well as the founding of Princeton, had demonstrated that very point.[17]

A Christian faith that is freely expressed and led by the Holy Spirit causes people to see their sin and prompts them to repent and lead new lives in accord with true morality. Madison's teacher, Witherspoon, held that the doctrine of religious liberty primarily benefits the spreading of the "knowledge of divine truth."[18] In addition, Madison pointed out that its benefits also extend to private and public life. It leads not only to the decrease of crime and abuse but also to the increase of committed and loving marriages and families, honest and productive businesses, and dedicated and dutiful government agencies. Integral to the liberty of person and property is the basic liberty of religious expression, which promotes true morals to establish a virtuous and just society. Religious liberty is thus a solemn, sacred duty for creating the conditions of a happy member of the republic.

Leaders of state and society must not restrict or confine people's ability to speak and write freely about their faith. Leaders should recognize a full and free expression of people's beliefs, both in private and in public. In a free republic, citizens must demonstrate confidence in, rather than offense from, the free exchange of ideas, even if those ideas differ from their own. In fact, intelligent members of a free republic will welcome alternative viewpoints that challenge and/or strengthen their own. This approach keeps interactions fair and honest. British philosopher John Stuart Mill (1806–1873) would later articulate this notion, known as the "free marketplace of ideas," in his essay *On Liberty*.[19] Only a weak, oppressed people require legal sanctions to protect their fondly held ideals. But a healthy, robust citizenry values and encourages a strong people who can accept free expressions of religious opinions without fear or offense as part of a mature and virtuous republic.

Madison contrasted the religious and social "slavery" of religious establishment in Virginia with the healthy and free environment of Pennsylvania. William Penn (1644–1718) had founded the colony with such ideals. Writing to his Princeton classmate, William Bradford (1755–1795), a Pennsylvania native, Madison requested documents on that colony's tradition of religious liberty and praised the "free air" of Penn's experiment. Madison looked to Pennsylvania as a bellwether. He also contrasted the tolerant, clean, hardworking, educated culture of Pennsylvania with the "corruption" and "ignorance" of Virginia. The difference, he believed, was the free, confident, independent nature of the Mid-Atlantic colony.[20]

Virginia's narrow suppression of religious expression promoted "pride, ignorance and knavery" amongst the clergy and "Vice and Wickedness" among the people in Virginia. Such religious and intellectual bondage, Madison wrote, "shackles and debilitates the mind and unfits it for noble enterprise." By contrast, competition among the congregations promotes "industry and virtue" among the churches, keeping them honest and morally responsible. This trajectory, in turn, spills over into other areas of society: economics, education, and politics, where "commerce and the Arts have flourished."[21]

Religious liberty and respect of individual conscience reflects the mature attitude of a society's citizenry: one that dearly holds cherished beliefs but is also confident enough to live peaceably among others who do not share those beliefs. Adherence to the doctrine of religious liberty demonstrates faith in God's ultimate goodness and power to correct and advance His truth. It shows a respect for reasoned persuasion and private prayer, rather than legal restrictions and violent threats, to convert others. "That religion," Madison wrote, "or the duty which we owe our Creator, and the manner of discharging it, can be directed only by reason and conviction, not by force or violence; and therefore, all men are equally entitled to the free exercise of religion, according to the dictates of conscience."[22]

Madison's views commend the "mutual duty of all to practice Christian forbearance, love and charity towards each other."[23] Those virtues allow for the testimony of the simple Christian faith: that humans are sinful and rebellious against God's laws, that this sin hurts others and deserves punishment, but that God loves man and provides an atonement for sin and that the acceptance of this atonement grants forgiveness and eternal life. Religious liberty provides for the promotion of that gospel message, which is not simply a private good but also a public good that leads to a moral and virtuous citizenry.

The Memorial and Remonstrance against Religious Assessments

The Presbyterian petitions in favor of ending the established Anglican Church argued for a Virginia that benefited from "the virtuous of every [Christian] denomination."[24] The victory for religious liberty in Virginia would come with the defeat of a bill to assess citizens for state payment to ministers. Such a "support" of religion would have actually regulated the church by permitting state officials to define Christianity. Madison's famous document, the Memorial and Remonstrance against Religious Assessments (1785), provides the classic arguments for religious liberty, which promote Christian evangelism and prevent government corruption of religion.[25]

Madison reinforces the idea that individuals have a duty before God to understand their nature and relation to the Creator through "reason and conviction," not through "force or violence."[26] Madison observes, "Whilst we assert for ourselves a freedom to embrace, to profess and to observe the Religion which we believe to be of divine origin, we cannot deny an equal freedom to those whose minds have not yet yielded to the evidence which has convinced us."[27] In this view, people must choose religious faith voluntarily for it to be true, genuine, and pleasing to God.

The Universal Sovereign is not fooled by mere outward appearances or observances of religious belief, including coercion by state actors. Every person must give an account to God for his perseverance in knowing and obeying his Creator: "To God, therefore, not to man, must an account of it be rendered."[28] A just society will ensure that that pursuit is unencumbered by laws favoring the narrow religiosity of religious establishment. Religious liberty provides societies with the greatest opportunity to explore religious belief and learn true religion.

Madison believes that forced "conversions" constitute an "unhallowed perversion" of the otherwise gentle "means of salvation."[29] Personal testimonies, prayer, and preaching demonstrate the proper means of sharing the faith—not threats, bribes, and persecution.

Madison describes the disastrous history of government control over religion as corrupting both church and state. Christianity flourishes when it is independent of the world's authorities and under "the ordinary care of Providence."[30] The teaching of Christianity shines "in its greatest lustre" when it is freed from state control.[31] Madison's orientation rests upon that Reformation doctrine of the priesthood of all believers. Any restriction on the freedom of individual religious expression would harm the spreading of religious truth and, as Madison wrote elsewhere, create "a monster feeding and thriving on its own venom, gradually swell[ing] to a size and strength overwhelming all laws human and divine."[32]

On the basis of Madison's arguments that religious liberty would advance Christianity more effectively than an official state church or public subsidies to ministers, the assessment bill was defeated. Jefferson reflected many of these same arguments for liberty of conscience and religious liberty in the Virginia Statute for Religious Freedom, which would become the basis for the Free Exercise Clause in the First Amendment.[33]

Madison's Commitment to Religious Liberty

Forty years later, Madison wrote that the rapid spread of evangelical Christianity in the United States proved the efficacy of religious liberty: "[T]here has been an increase of religious instruction . . . [which] is now diffused throughout the community by preachers of every sect with almost equal zeal . . . at private homes and open stations." The "zeal which actuates them" and "the purity of their lives and the attendance of the people" has resulted from the condition of religious liberty.[34] Notice his emphasis on the zeal of these believers, which refers to their enthusiasm and commitment to a healthy, lively life. These kinds of traits were often missing in the sometimes cold, formal official church.

Sixty years after his original advocacy for religious liberty, Madison wrote that Christianity was "the best and purest religion" and that the Christian faith was advanced by the freedom of belief and the liberty to profess one's faith without governmental restrictions.[35] Government restrictions on religious expression violate the American tradition. Madison continued to praise the doctrine of religious liberty as the fourth President of the United States. An American Jewish rabbi, Mordecai Noah (1785–1851), had written to Madison expressing gratitude that religious liberty allowed the people of the Jewish faith to practice their religion without fear of prosecution. Madison wrote in reply, "Having ever regarded the freedom of religious opinions and worship as . . . the best human provision for bringing all either into the same way of thinking, or into that mutual charity which is the only substitute, I observe with pleasure the view you give of the spirit in which your Sect partake of the blessings offered by our [Government] and Laws."[36]

This statement encapsulates Madison's views concerning religious liberty in the United States. He believed that it offers the best means through which people would hear the gospel and come to faith in Jesus Christ. He knew that people would arrive at true faith only if they do it voluntarily. Religious liberty encourages "mutual charity" and respect. This vision avoids the oppression of religious establishment, but it does not devolve into postmodern relativism. It requires a citizenry who are intellectually and spiritually mature, who are confident in their beliefs, and who rely on the power of persuasion, prayer, and Providence to propagate the faith in a free and charitable manner.

Jefferson's Statute for Religious Freedom

Jefferson's famous Virginia Statute for Religious Freedom reflects these same sensibilities and values, which later became the basis for the Free Exercise Clause in the First Amendment.[37] Jefferson expressed the divine basis of religious liberty in the statute's first words: "Almighty God has created the mind free" by His "supreme will." Therefore, the mind is "insusceptible of restraint." Official attempts to influence it produce "habits of hypocrisy and meanness."[38]

Jefferson demonstrated the religious dimension of this freedom when he ascribed it to "the plan of the holy author of our religion" and said that the "propagation" of the faith cannot be achieved by "coercion." The Virginia Statute reflects the traditional Christian doctrine that man is sinful when it says that "rulers" are "fallible." It goes on to say that it is "sinful" for rulers to "compel" others to subscribe to certain beliefs rather than to leave the question of belief to individuals who are exposed to a variety of faiths in a free, competitive environment.[39]

Similarly, Jefferson believed that the state should recognize the freedom of individuals to support the pastor financially that they think best provides knowledge of God. Consequently, a general tax to fund churches or clergy violates this individual right. For Jefferson, this idea also provides "an incitement to earnest and unremitting labours" of ministers "for the instruction of mankind" in religious truth and duties. Such incentives help the clergy to avoid seduction by "worldly honours and emoluments."[40]

A free marketplace of religious thought and practice is as important to a healthy, vibrant faith and society as a free marketplace with a competitive economy is to material prosperity. Governmental monopoly in either produces inefficiency, sloth, oppression, and, ultimately, poverty (material and spiritual). For the state to support a single church exclusively will "corrupt that *very* religion [Christianity] it is meant to encourage" because it emphasizes and rewards external conformity rather than internal

SECULARISM AND THE AMERICAN EXPERIENCE

faith, and it "bribes" people to subscribe to a worldly religion while branding those who "withstand such temptation" as "criminal."[41]

The truth of the Christian gospel "will prevail if left to herself." Truth "has nothing to fear from the conflict unless by human interposition disarmed of her natural weapons, free argument and debate; errors ceasing to be dangerous when it is permitted freely to contradict them." In other words, the Christian faith will spread most effectively by the free profession of its beliefs by all believers. Therefore, the Virginia Statute for Religious Freedom states "that all men shall be free to profess, and by argument [not violence] to maintain" their religious beliefs without government restrictions.[42]

Jefferson described the positive effects of this vision in his portrayal of religious liberty in the town of Charlottesville, Virginia, where four denominations, without individual church buildings, worshipped together in the county Courthouse: "In our village of Charlottesville there is a good deal of religion.... The courthouse is the common temple.... Episcopalian and Presbyterian, Methodist and Baptist, meet together, join in hymning their Maker ... and all mix in society with perfect harmony."[43] Jefferson's remark offers another example of reasonable church-state accommodation. He did not consider the use of public property to be a violation of religious liberty so long as it was open to all.

THE FIRST AMENDMENT

The religion clauses of the First Amendment perfectly express the ideals of non-establishment and religious liberty as Madison and Jefferson conceived them: "Congress shall make no law respecting the establishment of religion, or prohibiting the free exercise thereof."[44] This amendment addresses the problem of the imposition of a single official state religion by its Establishment Clause.

It also addresses the problem of the forced absence of religious expression by its Free Exercise Clause. Thus the amendment guards against the religious establishment of its day, or the dominance of a single, official state religion or church. It also provides protection against the secularism of our day, or the total absence of religion in public life.

In many ways, religious establishment and modern secularism are two sides of the same coin. The non-establishment and religious liberty of the First Amendment paves a moderate, middle position between the extremes of exclusive establishment and exclusive secularism. According to this vision, citizens may express their deeply held beliefs by persuasion and prayer but not by the coercion of others through legal proclivities or violence. Again, this view implies a mature, tolerant citizenry. For the founders, this vision followed from a belief that such freedom would promote the Christian religion and Christian morals and virtues, thus contributing to a just society.

Conclusion

Before concluding this appendix, I want to offer just one modern-day example of the implications of these ideas. According to the ideal of religious liberty put forward by Madison and Jefferson, an individual high school student praying at a football game or a graduation is permissible in a free republic. It is not tantamount to religious establishment. However, the denial of such an expression is tantamount to the imposition of secularism, and it violates the vision of the founders. The exercise of religious liberty is not only restricted to the private sphere but also finds expression in the public sphere, as Jefferson's letter about the courthouse illustrates. In conclusion, a mature citizenry will permit the expression of differing perspectives about life and religion.

Studies in Secularism: An Overview

Matthew Steven Bracey

Through the years myriad scholars have given themselves to some aspect of the topic of secularism. By no means will I consider all of these scholars, but I will offer an overview of some in order to situate the work of Leroy Forlines. Studies in secularism run the gamut. These scholars examine the subject from multiple perspectives: philosophical, anthropological, ethical, historical, cultural, sociological, scientific, legal, political, moral, and more. Usually, they approach their theses through a primary lens but also bring others to bear on their inquiry. For example, one study may investigate the issue through the overarching perspective of philosophy while also reviewing points of history. Another may approach the theme of secularism primarily through the lens of sociology but also fill out his or her examination with moral deliberations.

In short, books about this subject usually include an amalgamation of disciplines—in that sense, this branch of study is truly interdisciplinary—but a given author will treat one field of study (or two) as the primary frame(s). For that reason, philosophers, theologians, ethicists, historians, and scientists, as well as others, all contribute to secularism studies. As we have seen,

Forlines investigates the subject primarily through historical and legal lenses. Generally speaking, he examines the period from the 1780s to the 1820s and analyzes several key Supreme Court cases from the mid-twentieth century. However, before considering his contribution specifically, I will review the work of some of these other scholars, comparing and/or contrasting Forlines's work to theirs to situate his unique contribution.

Secularism and the United States

University of Notre Dame historian James Turner's *Without God, Without Creed* assesses the origins of unbelief in America. He identifies 1500–1865 as a period of modern belief, 1840–1870 as a period of great confusion for Christianity, and 1865–1890 as a period of modern unbelief. "America in 1840 was a Christian nation."[1] He argues that atheism and agnosticism slowly emerged through the course of the nineteenth century because people were grappling with how to fit the theory of God within the increasingly popular ideas of modernity. Even if the topic of secularism is not one of Turner's primary burdens in *Without God, Without Creed*, it is still present. Additionally, the work serves as an important backdrop to contemporary discussions of secularism. For his part, Turner demonstrates that secularism, to some extent, describes the beliefs of those who lack belief in God: without God, without creed.

Forlines interacts with Turner when he gives attention to the etymology of the term *secular*, as well as its derivatives. Forlines distinguishes the "secular" from "secularism." Additionally, he distinguishes the popular secularism of George Jacob Holyoake and Robert Ingersoll from the epistemological secularism that has come to dominate university campuses and American culture more generally. That distinction allows Forlines to acknowledge the developments in the late 1800s that Turner discusses.

STUDIES IN SECULARISM: AN OVERVIEW

However, rather than characterizing them as marking a period of modern unbelief, as Turner does, he sees them simply as precursors to later developments in the twentieth century. Forlines does not deny that religious unbelief characterized the lives of individuals in the late 1800s; his point is that it does not characterize the period as a whole.

Although Forlines touches on this distinction in the present volume, when he considers the categories of religious belief and unbelief, those concerns factor much more extensively in his broader body of work in secularism studies. Instead, the central focus of this book is the advent of secularism in relation to the founding of the United States and its implications for the proper relationship of church and state. Invariably, the question of religion and government arises when examining the American founding and church-state relations.

As an example of this theme, Isaac Kramnick and R. Laurence Moore, historians from Cornell University, published *The Godless Constitution* in 1997. Through the years, this controversial book would have multiple subtitles, including *The Case Against Religious Correctness* and *A Moral Defense of the Secular State*. Part history, part legal analysis, and part moral case, *The Godless Constitution* argues for the "secularism of the Constitution" and explains that the "underdocumented and underremembered controversy of 1787–88 over the godless Constitution was one of the most important public debates ever held in America over the place of religion in politics. The advocates of a secular state won, and it is their Constitution we revere today."[2] Kramnick and Moore appeal to such figures as Roger Williams, John Locke, and Thomas Jefferson, and they point to the English roots of the secular state.

Forlines contends with Kramnick and Moore in his argument, interacting with Locke and especially Jefferson, as well as with the text of the Constitution. However, Forlines says that Kramnick and Moore have conflated the secular state with secularism. Forlines maintains that the secular state refers simply to a state that is not controlled by an ecclesiastical body, to a state that is disestablished from an ecclesiastical body but may still reasonably accommodate religion.

By contrast, secularism as such describes a specific movement that would not emerge within the United States until the mid-nineteenth century with figures such as Holyoake and Ingersoll. Philip Hamburger, law professor at Columbia Law School, explains that "secularism was a term popularized for polemical purposes in the mid-nineteenth century precisely in order to minimize the differences among quite divergent tendencies, many of which were candidly religious."[3] According to Forlines, then, when scholars, such as Kramnick and Moore, point to examples of secularism prior to that point, they are guilty of anachronism, even if they are interacting with important antecedents to the movement that became secularism.

Authors such as Susan Jacoby in *Freethinkers: A History of American Secularism* and Andrew L. Seidel in *The Founding Myth: Why Christian Nationalism Is Un-American* take a more polemical approach to the question of the American founding and church-state relations. Jacoby points to the absence of God in the Constitution and argues that the United States was founded on secularism. In one chapter, "Revolutionary Secularism," she explains that John Adams and Thomas Jefferson, whom she refers to as secularists, were instrumental in establishing a secular government in the United States. Throughout the book, she also interacts with Thomas Paine, Abraham Lincoln, and Robert Ingersoll.[4]

Likewise, Forlines interacts with Adams, Paine, and Ingersoll, although Jefferson is his primary focus. Again, according to

STUDIES IN SECULARISM: AN OVERVIEW

Forlines, to say that the American founders established a *secular* government is not tantamount to saying that they established a *secularist* government or that they themselves were secularists; disestablished government is not necessarily secularist government. Forlines distinguishes these characteristics where some conflate them. Additionally, freethinkers are not historically equivalent to secularists. Since secularism would not emerge on the American scene until well after the founding, Forlines posits that a chronological incompatibility exists for the claim that the United States was founded on it. In his telling, the history of American secularism is not as old as people like Jacoby would have it to be.

Additionally, the fact that the word *God* does not appear in the text of the Constitution does not mean that the document was established on the bedrock of secularism, although it does signify that the founders intended to disestablish the church and state. In addition to the anachronism it presents, Forlines argues that that position signifies a superficial reading of the Constitution, which otherwise refers to and seeks to accommodate the practice of religion. Even if it is a secular document, in the sense that it avoids religious establishment, it is not a secularist document. Again, one of the things that Forlines does well is to avoid conflating terms like *secular* and *secularism*. To be clear, by holding that the founders did not legally establish a secularist nation, he is not asserting that they legally established a Christian one. In fact, he explicitly but briefly disclaims that point.

Were he to wade into that debate, based on the larger manuscript of which this book is only a part, he would generally agree with the position put forward by Mark David Hall of George Fox University. In *Did America Have a Christian Founding?* Hall aims to separate modern myth from historical fact. Thus he explicitly debunks the claims of people like Kramnick and Moore, as well as that of Jacoby, in a chapter entitled "the United States does not have a godless Constitution."[5] Hall sensibly argues that Christian themes influenced the American founders but not that the founders legally established a Christian nation, or even that they were all consistently orthodox Christians. Readers interested in this subject will find Hall's contribution to the topic helpful. Forlines spends considerable time with the founding. However, his specific interest concerns a proper interpretation of the First Amendment in reference to the relationship between church and state.

A final publication dealing specifically with the phenomenon of American secularism is a book aptly titled *American Secularism* by Joseph O. Baker and Buster G. Smith. A work in the sociology of religion, *American Secularism* examines secularism from the vantage points of classification: culture; history; religion; ethnicity, social class, and immigration; gender and sexuality; marriage, family, and social networks; and politics. Whereas James Turner uses the categories of belief and unbelief, arguing that the latter has displaced the former, Baker and Smith focus on the notion of belief, a position that philosopher Charles Taylor, whom I will survey below, had posited approximately ten years prior. Baker and Smith highlight that even secularism is a form of belief, albeit nonreligious belief, especially among the religious nones.[6] Also, they describe the secular as a "general description" for that which is "*not* religious," whereas they define secularism as a "cosmic belief system that is explicitly nonreligious in orientation."[7]

Like Baker and Smith, Forlines distinguishes the secular from secularism, though he articulates them differently. Forlines does not necessarily associate the secular with the nonreligious. Instead, he associates the secular, based on an etymological study of the term, with that which is opposite of the religious cloister. In addition, he differentiates the secular from subsequent movements of secularism, which, as mentioned, he distinguishes further between popular secularism and epistemological secularism. Finally, the topic of nonreligious belief—or, as Turner described it, religious unbelief—warrants significant attention within Forlines's broader work on secularism, although not as much in this publication.

A Secular Age

I will now shift from authors who explore the subject of secularism specifically within the American context to the contributions of the Catholic philosopher Charles Taylor of McGill University, who has authored what is perhaps the most significant book to emerge in secularism studies this side of the millennium: *A Secular Age*, published in 2007. Taylor's project is similar to that of Turner's in that he explores the origins of religious unbelief/nonreligious belief. However, at approximately nine hundred pages in length, Taylor's work is much more expansive. As he says elsewhere about *A Secular Age*, "My book lays out, unashamedly, a master narrative."[8]

Taylor proposes that secularity has arisen within a secular age, and he proposes three meanings of the term *secularity*: One meaning concerns the separation of religion from other spheres, where "public spaces" have "been allegedly emptied of God, or of any reference to ultimate reality." A second meaning defines secularity as the "falling off of religious belief and practice."[9] These two interpretations reflect subtraction theories or "stories" of secularization, which refer to the belief that the people of a given society will subtract religion from their individual and collectives lives in favor of an idolized version of science. In Taylor's words, it is the "story that a convert to unbelief may tell, about being convinced to abandon religion by science"[10] Many secularist scholars follow this thesis, including, for example, the new atheists, such as Richard Dawkins and Christopher Hitchens.[11] On the other hand, sociologists such as Rodney Stark argue against this interpretation of secularization.[12]

In any case, Taylor proposes that such understandings of secularism are incomplete, pointing, instead, to a third meaning of secularity that concerns "conditions of belief. The shift to secularity in this sense consists, among other things, of a move from a society where belief in God is unchallenged and indeed, unproblematic, to one in which it is understood to be one option among others, and frequently not the easiest to embrace," or, as he alternatively describes it, "from a society in which it was virtually impossible not to believe in God, to one in which faith, even for the staunchest believer, is one human possibility among others."[13] For example, throughout the book, he traces the shift in Western civilization from belief in theism to belief in deism to belief in atheism. Thus, in Taylor's telling, a secular age is not one in which its occupants have simply subtracted religious belief but rather one in which they have exchanged one belief system for another.

So significant is Taylor's work that numerous volumes of summary and analysis have followed it. For example, Michael Warner, Jonathan VanAntwerpen, and Craig Calhoun edited a work in 2010 entitled *Varieties of Secularism in a Secular Age*. They hope that their book "will suggest something of the complexity of the question of secularity, the analytic density of Taylor's take on it, and the variety of discussions that *A Secular Age* opens up."[14] Coming from a multiplicity of academic disciplines, the contributors to *Varieties* explore the topics and themes of modernity, the sacred-secular divide, competing notions of secularism, and enchantment and disenchantment, among others. Another publication to interact with Taylor's work is Calvin University philosopher James K. A. Smith's *How (Not) to Be Secular* from 2014. As with the authors of

Varieties, Smith examines *A Secular Age* and provides an apologetic for it. He describes Taylor as a "reliable cartographer who provides genuine orientation in our secular age."[15]

More recently in 2017, Collin Hansen has edited a volume entitled *Our Secular Age: Ten Years of Reading and Applying Charles Taylor*, whose contributors analyze specific issues of concern to the church in light of the broader frame of secularism.[16] These include Reformation theology, preaching, belief, piety, church attendance, politics and public life, human flourishing, and art, among others. Even though a secular age may discourage Christians, Hansen holds that Christians may nonetheless profess hope. Another contributor, theologian and historian Carl Trueman, echoes the point of complexity that others have emphasized: "Christians need to understand that the dramatic changes we are witnessing in the West are the fruit of a long and complicated history," which leads him to say, "Any responses we offer must take full account of this complexity."[17] Trueman's remark, as well as this survey of the literature more generally, should remind the reader that the topic of secularism is truly intricate and resists simplistic formulations.

In fact, Trueman has recently expanded upon some of these ideas in *The Rise and Triumph of the Modern Self*, a work for which Taylor looms large in the background. Trueman considers how figures such as Jean-Jacques Rousseau, William Blake, Percy Bysshe Shelley, Charles Darwin, Karl Marx, Friedrich Nietzsche, and Sigmund Freud have contributed to the secular state and to secularism. He also focuses on the crisis of identity, particularly sexual identity, of the contemporary world. Thus, for Trueman, the historical emergence of a secular age and secularism has not been without consequence. As he writes, "The sexual revolution is as much a symptom as it is a cause of the culture that now surrounds us everywhere we look, from sitcoms to Congress."[18]

By no means is Forlines's interest as broad as or as sweeping as that of Taylor's and those who have followed in his steps. Forlines's central question concerns the influence of secularism during the period of the American founding and its implications for church-state relations. Still, Forlines would appreciate the care with which Taylor and his interpreters have engaged the subject of secularism. Forlines, like Taylor, carefully parses the concept of the secular from that of secularism.

However, whereas Taylor's view is more conceptual, Forlines's is more technical. For example, Taylor interprets the notion of secularity with that of "conditions of belief," which permits him to explore periods of time that predate the emergence of secularism per se. By contrast, Forlines, as mentioned previously, distinguishes the secular from the religious cloister, as well as from subsequent movements of secularism. The secular, which is consistent with a broadly Reformed doctrine of vocation that resists a hierarchical sacred-secular divide, may still be religious even if it is not ecclesiastical per se. Conventional understanding may view the secular and the religious as antonyms, but Forlines takes a more nuanced approach based on the etymology of the word *secular* and its historical usage. From his perspective, a secular state may have wide-ranging tolerance and accommodation for religion, provided it does not formally favor a specific church, such as is the case with religious establishment.

In many ways, Forlines has pursued a separate project from Taylor, at least in the present volume. However, as his broader research that is not yet published from which this book is extracted makes plain, Forlines would not deny Taylor's broader thesis. Forlines would agree with Turner and Taylor and Trueman that secularism has not emerged in a vacuum but rather has resulted from that which preceded it. However, he would distinguish secularism proper from its antecedents. Also, he would especially appreciate volumes such as those edited by Hansen and authored by Trueman because they examine the ministry of the church within the context of the contemporary culture.

In addition, while Forlines would recognize the utter complexity of the topic of secularism, he engages primarily with those who would interpret secularism to mean the absence of religion in the public square, and especially with those who make constitutional arguments of strict church-state separation to that effect. Against such positions, Forlines argues for the reasonable accommodation of church and state, which he views as the middle way between religious establishment and strict separation. Thus Forlines envisions a public square that respects multiple views of life and the world and, in a manner of speaking, calls for the end of secularism.

Secularism and Pluralism

In fact, political scientist Hunter Baker of Union University released a book by that very title in 2009: *The End of Secularism*. Secularists propose a so-called "neutral public square," or what Protestant-turned-Catholic writer Richard John Neuhaus referred to as a "naked public square."[19] Emblematic of that position is professor of law and philosophy Paul Cliteur, who argues for moral and political secularism in his book *The Secular Outlook*, which was published the year after Baker's. Defining secularism as a "normative or ethical creed," Cliteur states, "The secularist contends that the best way to deal with religious differences is a morally *neutral* vocabulary that we all share and a morality that is not based on religion."[20] Sociologist Steve Bruce of the University of Aberdeen argues similarly in *Secularization: In Defence of an Unfashionable Theory*.[21]

Contrary to such positions, Baker argues that secularism is a "failed strategy for social peace."[22] Undoubtedly, the question of religious pluralism stemming from the Protestant Reformation has created challenges within societies. Nevertheless, the answer of secularism is "a dead end," and "there are better ways to deal with religious pluralism than removing religion from public life." In addition, "the case for secularism is partisan, shallow, and under-examined," a point that Neuhaus and others have also made.[23] Against the thesis of a so-called neutral public square, Baker argues for a "contested public square" in which Christianity, environmentalism, feminism, Marxism, secularism, and other philosophical and religious viewpoints vie for acceptance.[24]

Forlines's project fits comfortably with Baker's, but its scope is much narrower, both in terms of setting (United States) and focus (education). Nevertheless, like Baker, as well as Neuhaus before him and those who have followed in that interpretive tradition, Forlines would argue against the notion of a neutral public square. Neither language (contra Cliteur) nor the public square can ever truly be neutral, philosophically speaking, because participants necessarily fill them with the beliefs of their worldviews. As a result, a so-called "neutral" public square is, in fact, a closed one because it engenders a space where people are coerced rather than convinced of a given viewpoint.

A neutral public square is not only philosophically impossible but also constitutionally unjustified in the United States. Secularists have interpreted Jefferson's statement that the First Amendment has built a wall of separation between church and state to mean that they should be strictly, or literally, separated, as opposed merely to their legal separation. On the contrary, Forlines contends that these figures have fundamentally misinterpreted Jefferson's meaning. Consequently, Forlines argues for an open public square rather than a closed one, a free society rather than a captive one. In short, he advocates for a society whose participants adhere to belief in true freedom of conscience, which has fundamental implications for true freedom of religion.

In the year following the publication of Cliteur's *The Secular Outlook*, Oxford University Press released *Rethinking Secularism* in 2011, edited by Craig Calhoun, Mark Juergensmeyer, and Jonathan VanAntwerpen. This multi-author, interdisciplinary work analyzes the multiple and often conflicting views of secularism within the scholarship. Not unlike Taylor, these authors question the utter ascendency of science and seek to situate the fact of religious expression within contemporary societies. They challenge the secularization thesis, which holds that traditional religious belief declines in modern societies.

They also call into question the traditional understanding of secularism. A "host of political activists," the editors explain, are "calling into question a supposedly clear division between the religious and the secular."[25] As a result, instead of discussing secularism (singular), they propose multiple secularisms (plural). For example, the editors write that secularism can "designate a framework for religious pluralism, but this is by no means always the case."[26] Thus their view of secularism is, in a manner of speaking, pluralistic and reflective of a postmodern milieu in its admitting varied and even contradictory understandings.

Three years later, sociologist Peter Berger of Rutgers University and Boston University released *The Many Altars of Modernity* in 2014, also affirming this basic descriptive narrative of pluralism. Approximately fifty years prior, he had advanced a secularization thesis in *The Sacred Canopy* (1967), arguing that modernity leads to secularism and predicting the secularization of the modern world. He based his views partly on what he believed he saw from the historical-sociological data from Europe, which he then transferred to other modernized societies.

However, that same year, Arnold E. Loen's *Secularization* was translated from the German, in which he discussed how secularization, which he defined as the "historical process by which the world is de-divinized," was occurring in the domains of cosmology, physics, biology, psychology, history, philosophy, and even theology.[27] Rather than predicting the inevitability of secularization, Loen suggested that readers "not accept secularization as unavoidable" and "den[ied] that secularization is an indisputable historical process."[28] The scholarship through the intervening decades has confirmed Loen's ideas.

Consequently, Berger, for his part, came to believe that his theories concerning secularization in *The Sacred Canopy* were inaccurate, and he retracted them in *Altars of Modernity*. Rather than leading to secularization, secularism has given rise to pluralism, which he describes as "an empirical fact in society experienced by ordinary people."[29] Rather than displacing the phenomenon of belief, modernity has generated a multiplicity of beliefs, leading Berger to point to the existence of "multiple modernities."[30]

Notwithstanding the proposals of Calhoun, Juergensmeyer, and VanAntwerpen, as well as those of Berger and others, about multiple secularisms-modernities, philosopher J. P. Moreland remains concerned about the veneration of science in his 2018 release of *Scientism and Secularism*. He certainly does not deny the value of the discipline of science, but he dubs its wrongful elevation as scientism, referring to it as a "dangerous ideology." Moreland defines scientism as the view that "the hard sciences alone have the intellectual authority to give us knowledge of reality."[31] Scientism claims to be "vastly superior to what we can know from any other discipline." Also, according to scientism, "the claim that ethical and religious conclusions can be just as factual as science, and therefore ought to be affirmed like scientific truths, may be a sign of bigotry and intolerance."[32]

Moreland also discusses the implications of scientism and secularism for Christianity, and he challenges Christians' engagement with these subjects: "The disastrous implications of the secularization of our culture, with scientism being the primary mover here, are largely due to evangelical ignorance of this issue. Scientism is a silent yet deadly killer of Christianity."[33] Like Moreland, Forlines analyzes the relationship of science and secularism within his broader manuscript, although not as much in the present volume. In particular, he spends considerable time examining the false dichotomy that some scholars construct between religion and science. Also like Moreland, Forlines affirms that Christians must engage these issues, though his answers and his view about the nature of engagement differ from those of Moreland.

Forlines would appreciate the nuanced approach that Berger and the contributors of *Rethinking Secularism* follow. However, his scope is narrower and different from theirs. Therefore, Forlines does not engage the idea of multiple secularisms or multiple modernities. He deals with a specific form of secularism, namely the separation of religion from the state, owing principally to the nature of his project. However, in this particular book, he does engage a broader cultural study. Even so, Forlines would likely find unhelpful the idea of giving distinct and often conflicting definitions to a single word, such as secularism.

Rather, he would give different names to these different expressions to avoid conflating them and to distinguish them carefully. As an example, he would likely demur at Calhoun, Juergensmeyer, and VanAntwerpen's notion that secularism can (or should) "designate a framework for religious pluralism." Forlines would see secularism as a threat to pluralism, as would Baker in *The End of Secularism*. In any case, regardless of the battle of definitions among the scholars of secularism studies, Forlines affirms a prescriptive vision for pluralism, although he prefers the language of *accommodation*.

Another book that discusses the themes of pluralism and secularism is *Secularism and Freedom of Conscience*, authored by Jocelyn Maclure and Charles Taylor and released several years after *A Secular Age* and several months after *Rethinking Secularism*. They argue for a "moral pluralism," which refers to the "phenomenon of individuals adopting different and sometimes incompatible value systems and conceptions of the good."[34] They undergird their vision with two principles and two operative modes. The two principles are equality of respect and freedom of conscience, and the two operative modes are church-state separation and state neutrality toward religions. By "church-state separation," they are not affirming the literal separation but rather the legal separation of church and state. Thus they indicate the importance of a disestablished state rather than one that is devoid of all things religious.

Maclure and Taylor tease out their notion of moral pluralism by considering the state's disposition toward questions of religious heritage, rituals, and symbols. For example, speaking specifically about the prospect of a state official wearing religious symbols, they argue that it "does not pose any particular challenge to republican conceptions of secularism."[35] However, that position is not to say that the "wearing of all religious symbols by all public officials must be accepted. Rather, it implies that wearing a religious symbol should not be prohibited simply because it is religious."[36] Their broader point is that moral pluralism is preferable to its absence: "Peaceful coexistence in a diverse society requires that we learn to find normal a range of identity-related differences."[37]

Maclure and Taylor also argue for the "legal obligation for reasonable accommodation." This position results from the affirmation of true freedom of conscience and freedom of religion, which "includes the freedom to *practice* one's religion."[38] They explain further that the "principle of accommodation" proceeds from "more general rights, namely, the right to equality and non-discrimination or freedom of conscience and religion."[39] Their vision bears some similarities to that of John Rawls, political philosopher of Harvard University, with whom they specifically interact.

In his book, *Political Liberalism*, which was originally published in 1993, Rawls pointed to the "fact of reasonable pluralism," in which a diverse people peaceably occupy the same public space.[40] Undoubtedly, such realities may result in "intractable struggles" about the "highest things: for religion, for philosophical views of the world, and for different moral conceptions of the good." While some will grumble about such conflicts, Rawls tied the preservation of reasonable pluralism to justice: "We should find it remarkable that, so deeply opposed in these ways, just cooperation among free and equal citizens is possible at all."[41] As was the case with Taylor's *A Secular Age*, a host of volumes followed the publication of Rawls's *Political Liberalism*, in which scholars responded to Rawls's ideas.[42]

Like Maclure and Taylor and Rawls, Forlines emphasizes the importance of freedom of conscience and religious disestablishment. However, his emphasis lies particularly with the freedom of religion, especially with respect to Thomas Jefferson's and James Madison's conceptions of it. Also, Forlines would affirm what Maclure and Taylor say about a state's making reasonable accommodations for both private and public expressions of religious heritage, rituals, and symbols. In fact, *accommodation* is a significant buzzword for Forlines, who adopts the phrase from Jefferson himself.

Forlines would also agree with thinkers like Rawls and Berger, among others, who observe that pluralism is a fact of communal life. However, as already mentioned, Forlines prefers the language of *accommodation*, which, for him, is a prescriptive vision. Consequently, government should not separate religious expression from the public square or even from the state itself, thereby coercing the presumed (but false) neutrality of secularism. Rather, it should accommodate varying viewpoints and encourage a genuine meeting of the minds. Undoubtedly, that proposal will result in disagreement among those of a given society, but such dispute can be respectful and kind. Forlines would reject the liberal basis that Rawls gives to pluralism and instead would affirm something more akin to the "principled pluralism" of Bruce Ashford and Chris Pappalardo.

Ashford and Pappalardo argue for "principled pluralism" in *One Nation Under God: A Christian Hope for American Politics*, published in 2015. According to this proposal, governments should neither "actively promote secular zealotry" nor "deny religious liberty and promote the interests of the few over the interests of the many."[43] Ashford and Pappalardo thus criticize a "normative directional pluralism." However, like these aforementioned scholars, they note that a "descriptive directional pluralism" is a fact of life and that "Christianity enables its adherents to tolerate plurality in a way that other worldviews find more difficult."[44] Their remark offers insight into why secularists often find true, equitable pluralism impalpable; they refer specifically to "Rawls's secular liberalism" as a "jealous god." Contrariwise, they suggest a principled pluralism in which the "public square should be both *convictional* (contra Rawls) and *plural* (contra theocrats)."[45]

Generally speaking, Forlines would agree with these sentiments, although they do not really characterize his research interests.

SECULARISM, POLITICS, AND RELIGION

As we have considered, some studies of secularism center on the founding and history of the United States. Others are broader in scope, focusing on the West more generally, such as *A Secular Age* and those following in its wake. Still other studies have sought to understand the relationship between secularism and pluralism. Another field, which I have not reviewed, emerging within studies of secularism concerns secularism and education. While many other foci emerge within this subject, I will consider only one more, namely the interplay of politics and religion within the broader field of studies in secularism.

In 2017 Oxford University Press released *The Oxford Handbook of Secularism*, edited by Phil Zuckerman and John R. Shook. At nearly eight hundred pages and with nearly fifty separate contributors, it is an ambitious project. After identifying what terms like *secular, secularity, secularization,* and *secularism* mean, they examine numerous secular governments throughout the world, as well as analyze the multi-faceted topics of political secularism, the politics of church and state, secularity and society, and morality and secular ethics.

Ethicist John Perry of the University of St. Andrews writes specifically about the Anglo-American expression of secular government, particularly evaluating John Locke, with whom Forlines also interacts, and John Rawls. In so doing, Perry recognizes the persisting ambiguity that exists around words like *secular* and *secularism*: "The English word 'secularism' as it appears in the title of this volume was not widely used until after the Second World War," which corresponds to Forlines's articulation of epistemological secularism, "so using it to describe early debates could create confusion."[46]

Perry makes an important observation here, one with which Forlines would agree wholeheartedly. In fact, it is one of the reasons why Forlines's exploration of secularism looks so much different from some of these other authors. For his part, Forlines carefully associates secularism only with movements that have actually borne that name, which first emerged in the mid-nineteenth century (popular secularism) but would not gain momentum, as Perry has pointed out, until the mid-twentieth century (epistemological secularism). By contrast, other authors have applied the term *secularism* retroactively to describe beliefs that did not, at the time, go by that name, such as rationalism, empiricism, or freethinking. What is more, these identifications do not even describe the same phenomenon as secularism, even if they may overlap with it at times.

For example, in his book *Secularism and Its Opponents from Augustine to Solzhenitsyn*, historian Emmet Kennedy writes about "Thomas Aquinas's Christian secularism," "Dante and lay secularism of the High Middle Ages," and "Immanuel Kant's ambiguous secularism."[47] Similarly, he asserts that "secularism" was a "strong component of French revolutionary ideology."[48] To be fair, Kennedy does acknowledge, "In the nineteenth century, secularism denoted the exclusion, or at least the reduction, of the role of religion in public life, in politics, in education, and in all branches learning. It is the cultural component of the separation of church and state."[49]

However, the point remains that Kennedy appears to take the term *secularism* somewhat for granted, associating it too strongly with the related but distinct concept of the *saeculum* and, consequently, applying it anachronistically. As Perry said, such approaches have generated much confusion. Also, they lack the carefulness of Forlines, who conducts an etymological and historical study in his analysis of the phenomenon and usage of *secularism*. On the other hand, Steve Bruce (mentioned above), who contends explicitly for secularization, argues, "Social scientists spend far too much time quibbling over words."[50] However, it is precisely this level of meticulousness that avoids sloppy scholarship.

Within a year of the release of *The Oxford Handbook of Secularism*, Andrew Copson published *Secularism: Politics, Religion, and Freedom*. Through the course of this work, he defines secularism, surveys its manifestation in Western societies, reviews the diversification of its meaning, examines the cases for and against it, considers various conceptions of it, and engages hard questions and new conflicts about it. Incidentally, Copson begins his book with a reference to George Jacob Holyoake, a figure with whom Forlines spends considerable time: "Inspired by a previous generation of Enlightenment thinkers, he [Holyoake] popularized a this-worldly attitude to personal morals, to philosophy, and to the organization of society and politics." Significantly, Copson writes, "He coined the word 'secularism' to describe his approach."[51] Forlines makes much of this same point in his work. In addition, it provides further evidence for Perry's remark that the ex post facto use of the term results in imprecision.

While Copson recognizes the challenges of defining the term *secularism*, he nonetheless adopts a "good provisional modern definition" from French sociologist Jean Baubérot, which he gives in three parts: (1) "separation of religious institutions from the institutions of the state and no domination of the political sphere by religious institutions": (2) "freedom of thought, conscience, and religion for all, with everyone free to change their beliefs and manifest their beliefs within the limits of public order and the rights of others"; and (3) "no state discrimination against anyone on grounds of their religion or non-religious world view, with everyone receiving equal treatment on these grounds."[52] Generally speaking, Forlines would agree that society should promote the second component of Copson's definition.

However, he may demur at the first and third parts, depending partly on what Copson means by his terms. For example, Forlines contends at length with the doctrine of the strict separation of church and state as developed by Justice Hugo Black in the mid-twentieth century, instead favoring the reasonable accommodation between them that figures like Thomas Jefferson and James Madison promoted. Thus, if Copson follows in that tradition by his use of the term *separation*, then Forlines would disagree with it. On the other hand, if Copson is referring merely to the legal separation of church and state, then he is not talking about anything more than religious disestablishment, which Forlines would affirm. In fact, Forlines spends considerable time interacting with and praising Madison's Memorial and Remonstrance against Religious Assessments and Jefferson's Virginia Statute for Religious Liberty, both of which promote religious liberty over religious establishment.

Additionally, Forlines would articulate Copson's third component differently. Forlines would not deny a general presumption for freedom of conscience and religion. However, insofar as those liberties manifest themselves into actions, he would not say that they are absolute because true liberty has limitations. Specifically, he interacts with Chief Justice Morrison Waite in *Reynolds v. United States* (1878), who, developing the argument from the writings of Jefferson, posits that the state may rightfully interfere in its citizens' freedoms when they use them in a manner that is contrary to social duty and that subverts good order. Also, Forlines would add that that which is right could not, by definition, go against social duty. Thus the state may have a presumption of equal treatment, but it has its definite limitations.

Finally, a persisting challenge of this discussion is that some secularists uphold the proposal of treating religious belief and unbelief (or, alternatively, religious and nonreligious belief) equally in theory but not necessarily in practice. In the event that a state attempts to pursue a broad vision of reasonable accommodation and a certain religious expression gains too deep a foothold within that society, some secularists will cry foul, acting as though the state's support of religious liberty is tantamount to religious establishment. The myriad lawsuits filed by organizations such as the American Civil Liberties Union and the Freedom from Religion Foundation demonstrate this point. In contrast, Forlines would distinguish strongly between reasonable accommodation, which necessarily includes religious liberty, and religious establishment, seeing accommodation as the via media between secularism on the one hand and establishment on the other.

A final publication demonstrates the overtly politically partisan flavor that these kinds of works can assume. In the fall of 2020, the Secular Democrats of America published a document entitled *Restoring Constitutional Secularism and Patriotic Pluralism in the White House*, in which they refer, over and again, to the apparent "constitutional secularism" of the United States. It lambasts "dogmatic religious chauvinism" while promoting a "unifying patriotic pluralism." Additionally, it reads, "We urge you [the Biden-Harris administration] to champion America's original constitutional secularism and the separation of church and state as core governing principles that protect religious freedom for people of all faiths—and none at all."[53]

At times the document reads incoherently. For example, Forlines would point out that the United States Constitution is not a secularist document because secularism proper did not yet exist. To be sure, it, with its amendments, is a document that is premised on religious disestablishment and religious liberty. However, that proposition is quite different from saying it is a secularist document. Forlines would say that the authors of "Restoring Constitutional Secularism" have committed an anachronism—and a false one at that. Again, to Perry's point, the imprecise usage of the term serves to confuse rather than to clarify the issues at stake.

Conclusion

As this overview of the literature has demonstrated, the field of secularism is exciting and vast. This survey is admittedly selective but representative, serving to orient the reader and to situate the work of Forlines. Clearly, people approach this subject from numerous disciplines and vantage points and pursue distinct theses and methodologies. Also, so much of this discussion is wrapped into how a given person defines terms like *secular, secularism, secularization, secularity*, and so forth. Nevertheless, Forlines contributes meaningfully to the subject of secularism through the course of *Secularism and the American Republic*.

Notes

Preface

1 See Matthew Steven Bracey and W. Jackson Watts, eds., *The Promise of Arminian Theology: Essays in Honor of F. Leroy Forlines* (Nashville: Randall House Academic, 2016).

Editor's Introduction

1 See, for example, George M. Marsden and Bradley J. Longfield, eds., *The Secularization of the Academy* (Oxford: Oxford University Press, 1992); Jon H. Roberts and James Turner, *The Sacred and the Secular University* (Princeton: Princeton University Press, 2000); C. John Sommerville, *The Decline of the Secular University* (Oxford: Oxford University Press, 2006); and Michael D. Waggoner, *Sacred and Secular Tensions in Higher Education* (New York: Routledge, 2011).
2 John Perry, "Anglo-American Secular Government," in *The Oxford Handbook of Secularism*, ed. Phil Zuckerman and John R. Shook (Oxford: Oxford University Press, 2017), 126.
3 Noah Feldman, *Divided By God: America's Church-State Problem—And What We Should Do About It* (New York: Farrar, Straus and Giroux, 2006), 113.
4 U.S. Constitution, amend. I.
5 *Everson v. Board of Education*, 330 U.S. 1, 58 (1947) (Rutledge, W., dissenting).
6 *McCollum v. Board of Education*, 333 U.S. 203, 237 (1948) (Jackson, R., concurring).
7 Id. at 235–36.
8 Id. at 247 (Reed, S., dissenting).
9 Philip Hamburger, *Separation of Church and State* (Cambridge: Harvard University Press, 2004), 3.
10 Ibid., 481.
11 Ibid., 492.
12 Henry Stephens Randall, *The Life of Thomas Jefferson*, vol. 3 (Philadelphia: J. B. Lippincott, 1871), 469.

13 See Edwin S. Gaustad, *Sworn on the Altar of God* (Grand Rapids, Mich.: Eerdmans, 1996); George M. Marsden, *The Soul of the American University: From Protestant Establishment to Established Nonbelief* (New York: Oxford University Press, 1994); and Leonard W. Levy, *The Establishment Clause: Religion and the First Amendment*, 2nd ed. rev. (Chapel Hill, N.C.: The University of North Carolina Press, 1994).

14 See John A. Ragosta, Peter S. Onuf, and Andrew J. O'Shaughnessy, *The Founding of Thomas Jefferson's University* (Charlottesville: University of Virginia Press, 2019); and Harry Y. Gamble, *God on the Grounds: A History of Religion at Thomas Jefferson's University* (Charlottesville: University of Virginia Press, 2020); as well as Peter S. Onuf, "Thomas Jefferson's Prayer for the Future: A Look Back at His Forward-Looking Mission for the University," *University of Virginia Magazine*, https://uvamagazine.org/articles/thomas_jeffersons_prayer_for_the_future, accessed February 4, 2021; and Matt Kelly, "200 Years Ago, Jefferson Left Nothing to Chance at Rockfish Gap Conference," *The University of Virginia Today*, July 27, 2018, https://news.virginia.edu/content/200-years-ago-jefferson-left-nothing-chance-rockfish-gap-conference, accessed February 4, 2021.

15 Gamble, 24–54. I want to acknowledge and thank J. Matthew Pinson for referring this volume to me, as well as *The Life of Thomas Jefferson* by Henry Stephens Randall, mentioned above, and for his overall encouragement and support in this project.

16 Ibid., ix.

17 For Gamble's discussion of the Rockfish Gap Report, see pp. 32–35 (cf. 41, 48, 73, 78, 160); and, for the President-Directors Report, see 41–44.

18 Ibid., 41.

19 Ibid., 42.

20 Ibid., 43.

21 Ibid., 44.

CHAPTER ONE

1 Isaac Kramnick and Laurence Moore, *The Godless Constitution: The Case against Religious Correctness* (New York: W.W. Norton, 1997), 14.

2 Lenni Brenner, ed., "Scholar's Afterword," in *Jefferson & Madison on Separation of Church and State: Writings on Religion and Secularism* (Fort Lee, N.J.: Barricade, 2004), 400.

3 Frank Lambert, *The Founding Fathers and the Place of Religion in America* (Princeton: Princeton University Press, 2003), 1.

4 Ibid., 2.

5 Ibid., 11.

NOTES

6 Quoted in Seymour D. Thompson and Leonard A. Jones, eds., *American Law Review* 32 (St. Louis: Review, 1898), 540.
7 The First Barbary War would furnish the occasion for inspiring the "Marine's Hymn" and "When the Warrior Returns."
8 U. S. Constitution, art. VI, § 3; U. S. Constitution, amend. I.
9 *Abington School District v. Schempp*, 374 U.S. 203, 260 (1963).
10 "The Campaign for Secularism," *Free Inquiry* 28, no. 3 (April/May 2008), 5.
11 Warren C. Young, "Secularism," in *Baker's Dictionary of Theology*, ed. Everett F. Harrison (Grand Rapids, Mich.: Baker, 1960), 477–78.
12 *The Oxford English Dictionary: Being a Corrected Re-issue with an Introduction, Supplement, and Bibliography of a New English Dictionary on Historical Principles Founded Mainly on the Materials Collected by the Philological Society*, vol. 9, S–Soldo, s.v. "Secular" (Oxford: Oxford University Press, 1961), 365.
13 Auguste Boudinhon, "Secular Clergy," *The Catholic Encyclopedia*, vol. 12 (New York: Robert Appleton, 1912), http://www.newadvent.org/cathen/13675a.htm, accessed July 17, 2018.
14 James Turner, *Without God, Without Creed: The Origins of Unbelief in America*, New Studies in American Intellectual and Cultural History, ed. Thomas Bender (Baltimore: Johns Hopkins University Press, 1985), 9.
15 Harro Höpfl, Introduction to John Calvin and Martin Luther, in *Luther and Calvin on Secular Authority*, Cambridge Texts in the History of Political Thought, ed. and trans. Harro Höpfl (Cambridge: Cambridge University Press, 1991), xxxviii (in-text references removed).
16 The fact that I have not seen it does not mean that it could not have happened. However, if it had been in popular usage, I think I would have found it. If someone does find it, I can say with certainty that it would not refer to a secularism as presently conceived.
17 *Abington School District*, 374 U.S. at 295.
18 *The Oxford English Dictionary*, vol. 9, S–Soldo, s.v. "Secular," 365.
19 Ibid., 366.
20 Ibid.
21 Ibid.
22 Ibid.
23 David Lyon, "Secularization," in *New Dictionary of Theology*, ed. Sinclair B. Ferguson and David F. Wright (Leicester: InterVarsity, 1988), 634–35. See also *The New Schaff-Herzog Encyclopedia of Religious Knowledge*, vol. 10, Reusch-Son of God, s.v. "Secularization" (Grand Rapids, Mich.: Baker Book House, 1977), 27; and *The Oxford English Dictionary*, vol. 9, S–Soldo, s.v. "Secularization," 366.

SECULARISM AND THE AMERICAN REPUBLIC

24 George Jacob Holyoake, ed., *The Reasoner: Gazette of Secularism*, vol. 16 (London: Holyoake and Co., 1854), 17.
25 *The New Schaff-Herzog Encyclopedia of Religious Knowledge*, vol. 10, Reusch-Son of God, s.v. "Secularism," 326–27 (in-text references removed).
26 *The Oxford English Dictionary*, vol. 9, S–Soldo, s.v. "Secularism," 366.
27 Ibid.
28 George Jacob Holyoake, *The Origin and Nature of Secularism: Showing That Where Freethought Commonly Ends Secularism Begins* (London: Watts & Co., 1896), 51.
29 W. E. Gladstone, "The Course of Religious Thoughts" (June 1876), in *The Contemporary Review* 28, June-November 1876 (London: Henry S. King and Co., 1876), 22.
30 *The Oxford English Dictionary*, vol. 9, S–Soldo, s.v. "Secularism," 366.

CHAPTER TWO

1 John Adams, "Thoughts on Government" (1776), in Charles Francis Adams, *The Works of John Adams, Second President of the United States: With a Life of the Author, Notes and Illustratations*, 10 vols. (Boston: Charles C. Little and James Brown, 1850–56), 4:193.
2 Frank Lambert, *The Founding Fathers and the Place of Religion in America* (Princeton: Princeton University Press, 2003), 247 (italics added).
3 Ibid., 247–48 (italics added).
4 Adams, "Thoughts on Government," 4:194.
5 U. S. Constitution, art. I, § 7, cl. 2.
6 Edwin S. Gaustad, *Sworn on the Altar of God* (Grand Rapids, Mich.: Eerdmans, 1996), 20.
7 Stephen Gaukroger, *Francis Bacon and the Transformation of Early-Modern Philosophy* (Cambridge: Cambridge University Press, 2001), 16–18, 121–22.
8 Francis Bacon, *The Advancement of Learning*, in *The Squashed Philosophers: The 45 Great Classics of Philosophy Abridged into Readable Little Epitomes*, ed. Glyn Hughes (Morrisville, N.C.: Lulu, 2016), 102.
9 Alfred Weber, *History of Philosophy*, trans. Frank Thilly (New York: Charles Scribner's Sons, 1896), 296.
10 Ibid., 298.
11 Actually, Roger Bacon had expressed the concept in the thirteenth century.
12 Weber, 299.
13 Francis Bacon, *The Advancement of Learning*, Book I, in The Works of Francis Bacon, ed. James Spedding et al. (London: Longmans and Company, 1870), 3:267.
14 Ibid., 268.

NOTES

15 Ibid., 479, 483.
16 Isaac Newton, *Newton's Principia: The Mathematical Principles of Natural Philosophy*, trans. Andrew Motte (New York: Putnam, 1850), 506–07.
17 Ibid., 504.
18 Ibid., 505–06.
19 Alex Tuckness, "Locke's Political Philosophy," *Stanford Encyclopedia of Philosophy*, January 11, 2016, https://plato.stanford.edu/entries/locke-political/, accessed August 17, 2018.
20 Isaac Kramnick and Laurence Moore, *The Godless Constitution: The Case Against Religious Correctness* (New York: W.W. Norton, 1997), 73.
21 Garrett Ward Sheldon, "Liberalism, Classicism, and Christianity in Jefferson's Political Thought," in *Religion and Political Culture in Jefferson's Virginia*, ed. Garrett Ward Sheldon and Daniel L. Dreisbach (Lanham, Md.: Rowman & Littlefield, 2000), 97.
22 Kramnick and Moore, 73.
23 Ibid.
24 Peter Laslett, ed., Introduction to John Locke, *Two Treatises of Government*, Cambridge Texts in the History of Political Thought (Cambridge: Cambridge University Press, 2003), 112–13 (italics added and in-text references removed).
25 Ibid., 113.
26 Garrett Ward Sheldon, *The Political Philosophy of Thomas Jefferson* (Baltimore: Johns Hopkins University Press, 1993), 14.
27 Eugenie C. Scott, "Creationism, Ideology, and Science," in *The Flight from Science and Reason*, ed. Paul R. Gross, Norman Levitt, and Martin W. Lewis (Baltimore: Johns Hopkins University Press, 1996), 518–19.
28 John Locke, *An Essay Concerning Human Understanding* (Philadelphia: Kay and Troutman, 1846), 207.
29 Alex Rosenberg, *Philosophy of Science: A Contemporary Introduction* (London: Routledge, 2000), 108.
30 Locke, *Essay Concerning Human Understanding*, 11.
31 Ibid., 99. For observations on Locke's epistemology set within the context of my apologetics, see F. Leroy Forlines and J. Matthew Pinson, *The Apologetics of Leroy Forlines* (Gallatin, Tenn.: Welch College Press, 2019), 7–9, 175–76.
32 Tuckness.
33 Locke, *Essay Concerning Human Understanding*, 161 (italics added).
34 John Locke, *A Letter Concerning Toleration*, ed. Mario Montuori (The Hague, Netherlands: Martinus Nijhoff, 1963), 21.

SECULARISM AND THE AMERICAN REPUBLIC

CHAPTER THREE

1 Susan Jacoby, *Freethinkers: A History of American Secularism* (New York: Henry Holt, 2004), 2n.
2 Ibid.
3 Noah Feldman, *Divided By God: America's Church-State Problem—And What We Should Do About It* (New York: Farrar, Straus and Giroux, 2005), 113.
4 Ibid., 272n11.
5 Declaration of Independence (U.S, 1776).
6 Lenni Brenner, ed., *Jefferson & Madison on Separation of Church and State: Writings on Religion and Secularism* (Fort Lee, N.J.: Barricade, 2004), back cover.
7 James Madison, Memorial and Remonstrance Against Religious Assessments, June 20, 1785, in *Jefferson & Madison on Separation of Church and State: Writings on Religion and Secularism*, ed. Lenni Brenner (Fort Lee, N.J.: Barricade, 2004), 71 (italics added).
8 Readers may view these panels at "Quotations on the Jefferson Memorial," Monticello, https://www.monticello.org/site/jefferson/quotations-jefferson-memorial, accessed September 7, 2018.
9 Edwin S. Gaustad, *Sworn on the Altar of God* (Grand Rapids, Mich.: Eerdmans, 1996), 36. See also Gary Scott, *Faith and the Presidency from George Washington to George W. Bush* (Oxford: Oxford University Press, 2006).
10 Gaustad, xiii.
11 Ibid., 36–37.
12 Ibid., 47–48.
13 Ibid., 32 (brackets in original; italics added).
14 Thomas Jefferson, Draft of the Virginia Statute for Religious Freedom, in *Jefferson & Madison on Separation of Church and State: Writings on Religion and Secularism*, ed. Lenni Brenner (Fort Lee, N.J.: Barricade, 2004), 48.
15 Quoted in Gaustad, 94.
16 Gaustad, 94 (italics added).
17 Ibid., 134–35.
18 Ibid., 135.
19 Ibid., 138.
20 Ibid., 143.
21 Ibid., 100.

CHAPTER FOUR

1 *Everson v. Board of Education*, 330 U.S. 1, 29 (1947) (Rutledge, W., dissenting).
2 Id. at 3.
3 Id. at 18 (italics added).

NOTES

4   Id.
5   Id. at 8–9.
6   Id. at 9.
7   Id.
8   Id.
9   Id. at 9–10.
10 Id. at 10–11.
11 U.S. Constitution, amend. I.
12 *Everson*, 330 U.S. at 11.
13 Id. at 11–12.
14 Id. at 12.
15 Cited in Id. at 12–13 (italics added; in-text citations removed throughout chapter; ellipses in original).
16 Id. at 13.
17 *Permoli v. Municipality No. 1 of City of New Orleans*, 44 U.S. 589, 609 (1845). In this case, the city of New Orleans charged three Catholic priests with violating a law against open casket funerals in instances where it might contribute to the spread of diseases. However, the priests claimed that this law violated the requirement placed on the territory northwest of the Ohio River, according to the Northwest Ordinance, which Congress had passed on July 13, 1787. The priests argued that the city had to grant them religious liberty and that New Orleans had violated their religious liberties. However, the Supreme Court held that, upon Congress's approving the constitution of the state of Louisiana in 1812, the Court had no authority to apply the First Amendment against the states. Instead, such issues were left to the states. *Permoli* represented an application of *Barron v. Baltimore* (1833), which held that the Bill of Rights did not apply to the states.
18 U.S. Constitution, amend. XIV, § 1.
19 *Everson*, 330 U.S. at 13–14.
20 U.S. Constitution, amend. I.
21 *Everson*, 330 U.S. at 14.
22 Id. at 15–16.
23 Id. at 18.
24 Id.

CHAPTER FIVE

1   *Everson v. Board of Education*, 330 U.S. 1, 22 (1947) (Jackson, R., dissenting).
2   Id. at 23.
3   Id.

4   Id. at 23–24.
5   Id. at 24.
6   Id. at 27.
7   Id.
8   Id. at 27–28.
9   Id. at 58 (Rutledge, W, dissenting).
10 Id.
11 Id. at 58–59.
12 Id. at 59.
13 *Pierce v. Society of Sisters*, 268 U.S. 510, 535 (1925).
14 Id. at 532.
15 *Everson*, 330 U.S. at 59 (Rutledge, W., dissenting).
16 Id.
17 Id.
18 Id.
19 Id. at 29.

CHAPTER SIX

1   *McCollum v. Board of Education*, 333 U.S. 203, 204–05 (1948).
2   U.S. Constitution, amend. I.
3   *McCollum*, 333 U.S. at 205.
4   Id.
5   Id. at 207.
6   Id. at 207–08 (in-text citations removed throughout chapter).
7   Id. at 209.
8   Id. at 209–10.
9   Id. at 210.
10 Id. at 210–11; *Everson v. Board of Education*, 330 U.S. 1, 15–16 (1947).
11 *McCollum*, 333 U.S. at 211; *Everson*, 330 U.S. at 16.
12 *McCollum*, 333 U.S. at 211.
13 Id. at 211–12.
14 John Adams to the Officers of the First Brigade of the Third Division of the Militia of Massachusetts, October 11, 1798, in *The Works of John Adams, Second President of the United States*, vol. 9, ed. Charles Francis Adams (Boston: Little, Brown, and Company, 1854), 229.
15 *McCollum*, 333 U.S. at 212.
16 Id. at 213 (Frankfurter, F., concurring; italics added).
17 Id.
18 Id. at 214.

NOTES

19 Id. at 213.
20 U.S. Constitution, amend. I.
21 *McCollum*, 333 U.S. at 213 (Frankfurter, F., concurring).
22 Id.
23 U.S. Constitution, amend. XIV, § 1.
24 *McCollum*, 333 U.S. at 215 (Frankfurter, F., concurring).
25 Id. at 216.
26 Id.
27 Id.
28 Id. at 216–17.
29 Id. at 217 (italics added).
30 Id.
31 Id.
32 Id.
33 Id.
34 Id. at 218 (italics added).
35 Id. at 218–19.

CHAPTER SEVEN

1 *McCollum v. Board of Education*, 333 U.S. 203, 322–21 (1948) (Frankfurter, F., concurring).
2 Id. at 220–21.
3 Id. at 221–22.
4 Id. at 222.
5 Id.
6 Id. at 222–23.
7 Id. at 223.
8 Id. at 224.
9 Id. at 224–25.
10 Id. at 230.
11 Id.
12 Id. at 230–31.
13 Id. at 231 (italics added).
14 Id.
15 Id.
16 Id.
17 Id. at 232.
18 Id. (Jackson, R., concurring).
19 Id.

20 Id. at 232–33.
21 Id. at 234.
22 Id. at 234–35.
23 Id. at 235 (italics removed from quotation).
24 Id.
25 Id.
26 Id.
27 Id. at 235–36.
28 Id. at 236 (italics added).
29 Id. at 236–37.
30 Id. at 237.
31 Id.
32 Id.
33 Id.
34 Id. at 237–38.
35 Id. at 238.
36 Id. at 238–39 (Reed, S., dissenting).
37 Id. at 240.
38 Id. at 241.
39 Id. at 244.
40 Id. at 245.
41 Id. at 246.
42 Id. at 247.
43 Id.
44 Id. at 248–49.

CHAPTER EIGHT

1 James Madison to Marquis De La Fayette, November 24, 1826, in *Jefferson & Madison on Separation of Church and State: Writings on Religion and Secularism*, ed. Lenni Brenner (Fort Lee, N.J.: Barricade, 2004), 392.
2 Ibid.
3 James Madison, Memorial and Remonstrance Against Religious Assessments, June 20, 1785, in *Jefferson & Madison on Separation of Church and State: Writings on Religion and Secularism*, ed. Lenni Brenner (Fort Lee, N.J.: Barricade, 2004), 68.
4 *McCollum v. Board of Education*, 333 U.S. 203, 216 (1948) (Frankfurter, F., concurring).
5 Madison, Memorial and Remonstrance, 68.
6 Ibid.

NOTES

7   Ibid., 69.
8   Ibid.
9   Ibid.
10 Noah Feldman, *Divided by God: America's Church-State Problem—And What We Should Do About It* (New York: Farrar, Straus and Giroux, 2005), 51. Although dictionary definitions of Deism suggest the idea of an impersonal God, the religion of Deism was more multifaceted than that. Jefferson's thinking about God certainly does not support the view of an impersonal God.
11 Madison, Memorial and Remonstrance, 69.
12 Ibid., 70.
13 Ibid.
14 Ibid., 71.
15 Ibid.
16 Ibid., 71–72.
17 Ibid., 72.
18 *Everson v. Board of Education*, 330 U.S. 1, 13 (1947).
19 Thomas Jefferson, Draft of the Virginia Statute for Religious Freedom [1777–1779], in *Jefferson & Madison on Separation of Church and State: Writings on Religion and Secularism*, ed. Lenni Brenner (Fort Lee, N.J.: Barricade, 2004), 48–50. Brenner includes portions that appeared in previous drafts but that did not make the final draft. I have omitted those here because they do not concern our present purposes.
20 Jefferson evidently misunderstood the doctrine of the Trinity because he refers to it as tritheism, a belief in three gods. Very few people in the history of the church have ever held this view. See Thomas Jefferson to John Adams, April 11, 1823, in *Jefferson & Madison on Separation of Church and State: Writings on Religion and Secularism*, ed. Lenni Brenner (Fort Lee, N.J.: Barricade, 2004), 370. According to Christian orthodoxy, the doctrine of the Trinity is properly understood as follows: "By the Trinity is meant that the Father, Son, and Holy Spirit are three co-eternal and co-equal persons, who experience interpersonal relationships, existing in one divine essence with each sharing the entire essence" (F. Leroy Forlines, *The Quest For Truth: Answering Life's Inescapable Questions* [Nashville: Randall House, 2001], 90).

CHAPTER NINE

1   Ralph Ketcham, *James Madison: A Biography* (Charlottesville: The University Press of Virginia, 1990), 229.
2   James H. Read, *Power versus Liberty: Madison, Hamilton, Wilson, and Jefferson* (Charlottesville: The University Press of Virginia, 2000), 30.

SECULARISM AND THE AMERICAN REPUBLIC

3   U.S. Constitution, amend. I.
4   *Everson v. Board of Education*, 330 U.S. 1, 18 (1947).
5   Daniel L. Dreisbach, "'Sowing Useful Truths and Principles': The Danbury Baptists, Thomas Jefferson, and the 'Wall of Separation,'" *Journal of Church and State*, 39 (1997): 460–61. This quotation has been updated to reflect modern conventions of grammar and spelling.
6   Ibid., 461.
7   Thomas Jefferson to the Danbury Baptist Association, January 1, 1802, in *Jefferson: Political Writings*, ed. Joyce Appleby and Terence Ball, Cambridge Texts in the History of Political Thought, ed. Raymond Geuss and Quentin Skinner (New York: Cambridge University Press, 1999), 396–97 (italics added). Interestingly, Brenner's inclusion of the report uses the word *legitimate* rather than *legislative* in the phrase: "that the legitimate powers of government reach actions only." See Thomas Jefferson to the Danbury Baptist Association, January 1, 1802, in *Jefferson & Madison on Separation of Church and State: Writings on Religion and Secularism*, ed. Lenni Brenner (Fort Lee, N.J.: Barricade, 2004), 163.
8   *Everson*, 330 U.S. at 29 (Rutledge, W., dissenting).
9   *Reynolds v. United States*, 98 U.S. 145, 163 (1878).
10 Id. at 163.
11 *Everson*, 330 U.S. at 13.
12 *Reynolds*, 98 U.S. at 163.
13 Id.
14 Id. at 164.
15 Id. (italics added).
16 Jefferson to the Danbury Baptist Association, in *Jefferson: Political Writings*, 397; *Reynolds*, 98 U.S. at 164.
17 *Reynolds*, 98 U.S. at 165.
18 Id.
19 Id.
20 Id. at 166.
21 Id. at 165.
22 Id. at 165–66.
23 Id. at 166 (italics added).
24 *Everson*, 330 U.S. at 16.

CHAPTER TEN

1   Readers should not construe this comment to mean that it has received no attention. I have demonstrated that it does. Examples of scholars who

NOTES

do give it attention include Edwin S. Gaustad (*Sworn on the Altar of God: A Religious Biography of Thomas Jefferson*), George Marsden (*The Soul of the American University: From Protestant Establishment to Established Nonbelief*), Leonard Levy (*The Establishment Clause: Religion and the First Amendment*), and Perry L. Glanzer, Nathan F. Alleman, and Todd C. Ream (*Restoring the Soul of the University: Unifying Christian Higher Education in a Fragmented Age*). However, the point remains that it does not receive the attention it should.

2   Herbert Baxter Adams, *Thomas Jefferson and the University of Virginia* (Washington: Government Printing Office, 1888), 68.

3   Edwin S. Gaustad, *Sworn on the Altar of God: A Religious Biography of Thomas Jefferson* (Grand Rapids, Mich.: Eerdmans, 1996), 171–72.

4   Adams, 68.

5   *Early History of the University of Virginia as Contained in the Letters of Thomas Jefferson and Joseph C. Cabell, Hitherto Unpublished; with an Appendix, consisting of Mr. Jefferson's Bill for a Complete System of Education, and Other Illustrative Documents; and an Introduction, Comprising a Brief Historical Sketch of the University, and a Biographical Notice of Joseph C. Cabell* (Richmond: J. W. Randolph, 1856), xxxiii.

6   Adams, 68.

7   Gaustad, 172.

8   Thomas Jefferson, Report of the Commissioners for the University of Virginia, August 4, 1818, in *Jefferson: Political Writings*, ed. Joyce Appleby and Terence Ball, Cambridge Texts in the History of Political Thought, ed. Raymond Geuss and Quentin Skinner (Cambridge: Cambridge University Press, 1999), 301. Some of Jefferson's thematic content concerning natives, as well as his analysis of culture and tradition, leaves much to be desired. However, I have omitted it because it does not concern our present discussion.

9   Gaustad, 173.

10 Jefferson, Report of the Commissioners for the University of Virginia, 306.

11 George M. Marsden, *The Soul of the American University: From Protestant Establishment to Established Nonbelief* (New York: Oxford University Press, 1994), 73.

12 Jefferson, Report of the Commissioners for the University of Virginia, 306. Interestingly, Perry L. Glanzer, Nathan F. Alleman, and Todd C. Ream argue the following, "Jefferson's curriculum abolished Latin and theology courses" (*Restoring the Soul of the University: Unifying Christian Higher Education in a Fragmented Age* [Downers Grove: IVP, 2017], 83). What is odd is that they make this statement within the context of discussing the Rockfish Gap Report. They even quote from the report less than a page prior, although not from the same portion that I have quoted here. Nevertheless, Jefferson's own

statements in the report seem to indicate the contrary of Glanzer et al.'s position. In addition, both Gaustad and Marsden affirm the interpretation that I have taken. For example, Gaustad writes, "Jefferson gladly included Latin, Greek, and Hebrew in his curriculum" (150; see also Marsden, 73).

13 Gaustad, 173; see also Marsden, 73.
14 Thomas Jefferson, Report to the President and Directors of the Literary Fund, October 7, 1822, in *Jefferson & Madison on Separation of Church and State: Writings on Religion and Secularism*, ed. Lenni Brenner (Fort Lee, N.J.: Barricade, 2004), 364.
15 Thomas Jefferson to the Danbury Baptist Association, January 1, 1802, in *Jefferson: Political Writings*, ed. Joyce Appleby and Terence Ball, Cambridge Texts in the History of Political Thought, ed. Raymond Geuss and Quentin Skinner (Cambridge: Cambridge University Press, 1999), 397.
16 Adams, 157.
17 Ibid.
18 See Thomas Paine, *The Age of Reason* (New York: Kensington, 1988), 50.
19 Adams, 157.
20 Ibid., 171.
21 Ibid.
22 Ibid., 157.
23 Jefferson, Report of the Commissioners for the University of Virginia, 306.
24 Thomas Jefferson to Martha Jefferson Randolph, August 4, 1818, in *The Papers of Thomas Jefferson*, Retirement Series, vol. 13, ed. J. Jefferson Looney (Princeton: Princeton University Press, 2016), 226.
25 "Report of the Commissioners Appointed to Fix the Site of the University of Virginia," in Roy J. Honeywell, *Educational Work of Thomas Jefferson*, vol. 16, Harvard Studies in Education (New York: Russel & Russel, 1964), 260. Readers may also access this document online at the following: Report of the Board of Commissioners for the University of Virginia to the Virginia General Assembly, [4 August] 1818, *Founders Online*, https://founders.archives.gov/documents/Madison/04-01-02-0289, accessed January 17, 2019. I would mention that several differences exist between the Honeywell citation and the *Founders Online* citation. One is the order of the names. Second, Honeywell lists "Wm. A. C. Dade" whereas *Founders Online* lists "Wm. A. G. Dade." Finally, Honeywell lists "A. T. Mason," whereas *Founders Online* lists "Armistead T. Mason."
26 Gaustad, 173.
27 Ibid., 173–74.

NOTES

CHAPTER ELEVEN

1 Thomas Jefferson, Report to the President and Directors of the Literary Fund, October 7, 1822, in *Jefferson & Madison on Separation of Church and State: Writings on Religion and Secularism*, ed. Lenni Brenner (Fort Lee, N.J.: Barricade, 2004), 364.
2 Thomas Jefferson, Report of the Commissioners for the University of Virginia, August 4, 1818, in *Jefferson: Political Writings*, ed. Joyce Appleby and Terence Ball, Cambridge Texts in the History of Political Thought, ed. Raymond Geuss and Quentin Skinner (Cambridge: Cambridge University Press, 1999), 298.
3 Ibid., Report to the President and Directors of the Literary Fund, 364.
4 Ibid.
5 Ibid.
6 Ibid., Report of the Commissioners for the University of Virginia, 306.
7 Ibid., Report to the President and Directors of the Literary Fund, 364.
8 Ibid.
9 Ibid.
10 George M. Marsden, *The Soul of the American University: From Protestant Establishment to Established Nonbelief* (New York: Oxford University Press, 1994), 73.
11 Jefferson, Report to the President and Directors of the Literary Fund, 364.
12 Ibid., 365.
13 Ibid., 364.
14 Ibid.
15 Ibid., 364–65.
16 Ibid., 365 (italics added).
17 Ibid., 365.
18 U.S. Constitution, amend. I.
19 Jefferson, Report to the President and Directors of the Literary Fund, 365.
20 Ibid.
21 Marsden, 78n20.
22 *McCollum v. Board of Education*, 333 U.S. 203, 245 (Reed, S., dissenting).
23 Id. at 246.
24 "Meeting Minutes of University of Virginia Board of Visitors, 4–5 Oct. 1824," *Founders Online*, https://founders.archives.gov/documents/Jefferson/98-01-02-4598, accessed February 9, 2021.
25 *McCollum*, 333 U.S. at 247.
26 Id.

SECULARISM AND THE AMERICAN REPUBLIC

CHAPTER TWELVE

1 Thomas Jefferson to Dr. Thomas Cooper, Monticello, November 2, 1822, in *Jefferson: Political Writings*, ed. Joyce Appleby and Terence Ball, Cambridge Texts in the History of Political Thought, ed. Raymond Geuss and Quentin Skinner (Cambridge: Cambridge University Press, 1999), 406–07.
2 Ibid., 407.
3 Ibid.
4 Ibid.
5 Thomas Jefferson to Arthur S. Brockenbrough, April 21, 1825, *Founders Online*, https://founders.archives.gov/documents/Jefferson/98-01-02-5152, accessed January 15, 2021. I have updated conventions for grammar and spelling throughout this letter.
6 Ibid.
7 Ibid.
8 Ibid.
9 Ibid.
10 Ibid.
11 Ibid.
12 Ibid.
13 Ibid.
14 Ibid.
15 James Madison to Edward Everett, March 19, 1823, in *Jefferson & Madison on Separation of Church and State: Writings on Religion and Secularism*, ed. Lenni Brenner (Fort Lee, N.J.: Barricade, 2004), 367.
16 Ibid.
17 James Madison to Frederick Beasley, December 22, 1824, in *Jefferson & Madison on Separation of Church and State: Writings on Religion and Secularism*, ed. Lenni Brenner (Fort Lee, N.J.: Barricade, 2004), 383.
18 Ibid.
19 Ibid., 383–84.
20 Ibid., 384.

CHAPTER THIRTEEN

1 *Reynolds v. United States*, 98 U.S. 145, 165 (1878).
2 U.S. Constitution, amend. I.
3 Thomas Jefferson to the Danbury Baptist Association, January 1, 1802, in *Jefferson: Political Writings*, ed. Joyce Appleby and Terence Ball, Cambridge

NOTES

Texts in the History of Political Thought, ed. Raymond Geuss and Quentin Skinner (Cambridge: Cambridge University Press, 1999), 397.
4   Ibid.
5   *Everson v. Board of Education*, 330 U.S. 1, 18 (1947); *McCollum v. Board of Education*, 333 U.S. 203, 211 (1948).
6   *Everson*, 330 U.S. at 29 (Rutledge, W., dissenting).
7   Id. at 13.
8   Jefferson, 397.
9   James Madison to Robert Walsh, March 2, 1819, in *Jefferson & Madison on Separation of Church and State: Writings on Religion and Secularism*, ed. Lenni Brenner (Fort Lee, N.J.: Barricade, 2004), 272.
10 Ibid.
11 Ibid.
12 Ibid. (italics added).
13 Jefferson, 397.
14 *Everson*, 330 U.S. at 29 (Rutledge, W., dissenting).
15 Id. at 13.

CHAPTER FOURTEEN
1   Warren C. Young, "Secularism," in *Baker's Dictionary of Theology*, ed. Everett F. Harrison (Grand Rapids, Mich.: Baker, 1960), 477–78.
2   I hope that someone will give attention to the chronology of the term *secular government* in public discourse.
3   See *Abington School District v. Schempp*, 374 U.S. 203 (1963); and *Sherbert v. Verner*, 374 U.S. 398 (1963).
4   *Permoli v. Municipality No. 1 of City of New Orleans*, 44 U.S. 589, 599 (1845).
5   Harro Höpfl, *Luther and Calvin on Secular Authority*, Cambridge Texts in the History of Political Thoughts, ed. and trans. Harro Höpfl (Cambridge: Cambridge University Press, 2004), xxxviii.
6   The various uses of the term *secular* occur often throughout the book. The appearances of these terms are so frequent in the book that it is not necessary to give page numbers. So far as wrestling with a Christian understanding of secular government is concerned, Luther gave far more attention to it than anyone else I have read. So far as my purpose is concerned, *Luther's use of secular had no hint of secularism.*
7   See Plato, *Republic*, Book IV (Cambridge: Cambridge University Press: 1963).
8   *Everson v. Board of Education*, 330 U.S. 1, 29 (1947) (Rutledge, W., dissenting).
9   Id. at 13.

10   Id. at 18.
11   Id. at 13.
12   Thomas Jefferson to the Danbury Baptist Association, January 1, 1802, in *Jefferson: Political Writings*, ed. Joyce Appleby and Terence Ball, Cambridge Texts in the History of Political Thought, ed. Raymond Geuss and Quentin Skinner (Cambridge: Cambridge University Press, 1999), 397 (italics added).
13   *Everson*, 330 U.S. at 16.
14   Lenni Brenner, ed., *Jefferson & Madison on Separation of Church and State: Writings on Religion and Secularism* (Fort Lee, N.J.: Barricade, 2004), back cover.
15   James Madison, Memorial and Remonstrance Against Religious Assessments, June 20, 1785, in Brenner, ed., *Jefferson & Madison on Separation of Church and State*, 71 (italics added).
16   Thomas Jefferson, Report of the Commissioners for the University of Virginia, August 4, 1818, in Brenner, ed., *Jefferson & Madison on Separation of Church and State*, 270–71 (italics added).
17   *McCollum v. Board of Education*, 333 U.S. 203, 245–46 (1948) (Reed, S., dissenting) (in-text citations removed).
18   Id. at 246 (italics added).
19   Id. at 247 (italics added).
20   Leonard W. Levy, *The Establishment Clause: Religion and the First Amendment*, 2nd ed. rev. (Chapel Hill, N.C.: The University of North Carolina Press, 1994), 72.
21   Ibid.
22   Ibid.
23   Thomas Jefferson, Report of the Commissioners for the University of Virginia, August 4, 1818, in *Jefferson: Political Writings*, ed. Joyce Appleby and Terence Ball, Cambridge Texts in the History of Political Thought, ed. Raymond Geuss and Quentin Skinner (Cambridge: Cambridge University Press, 1999), 306 (italics added).
24   Roy J. Honeywell, *Educational Work of Thomas Jefferson*, vol. 16, *Harvard Studies in Education* (New York: Russel & Russel, 1964), 249, 256.
25   Charles Eliot Norton, *The Correspondence of John Ruskin and Charles Eliot Norton*, ed. John Lewis Bradley and Ian Ousby (Cambridge: Cambridge University Press, 1987), 175–76 (italics added).
26   U. S. Constitution, art. I, § 7, cl. 2.

CHAPTER FIFTEEN

1   "Nine reasons why you should become an E.F. Hutton account executive and one reason why you shouldn't," *Princeton Alumni Weekly* 77 (September 27, 1976), 39.

NOTES

2 *Everson v. Board of Education*, 330 U.S. 1, 13 (1947).
3 Readers may find files to the original Rockfish Gap Report at the University of Virginia Library Online here: The Rockfish Gap Report, *University of Virginia Library Online Exhibits*, https://explore.lib.virginia.edu/items/show/2077, accessed February 5, 2021. Additionally, they may find information about the historical marker that was erected to commemorate the meeting at The Historical Marker Database: "Rockfish Gap Meeting," *The Historical Marker Database*, https://www.hmdb.org/m.asp?m=21831, accessed February 5, 2021.
4 Thomas Jefferson, Report of the Commissioners for the University of Virginia, August 4, 1818, in *Jefferson: Political Writings*, ed. Joyce Appleby and Terence Ball, Cambridge Texts in the History of Political Thought, ed. Raymond Geuss and Quentin Skinner (Cambridge: Cambridge University Press, 1999), 306.
5 I trace out these distinctions in much greater detail in a forthcoming book on secularism.
6 Michel Bourdeau, "Auguste Comte," *Stanford Encyclopedia of Philosophy*, May 8, 2018, http://plato.stanford.edu/entries/comte/, accessed January 10, 2019.
7 See Mary Pickering, *Auguste Comte: An Intellectual Biography*, vol. 3 (Cambridge: Cambridge University Press, 2009).
8 Speaking of Hume, for example, Jefferson writes, "Our laws, language, religion, politics and manners are so deeply laid in English foundations, that we shall never cease to consider their history as a part of ours, and to study ours in that as its origin. Every one knows that judicious matter and charms of style have rendered Hume's history the manual of every student. I remember well the enthusiasm with which I devoured it when young, and the length of time, the research and reflection which were necessary to eradicate the poison it had instilled into my mind. . . . Although all this is known, he still continues to be put into the hands of all our young people, and to infect them with the poison of his own principles of government. It is this book which has undermined the free principles of the English government, has persuaded readers of all classes that these were usurpations on the legitimate and salutary rights of the crown, and has spread universal toryism over the land" (Thomas Jefferson to Mr. Duane, Monticello, August 12, 1810, in *The Writings of Thomas Jefferson*, vol. 5 [New York: Riker, Thorne, and Co., 1854], 533–34).
9 U. S. Constitution, amend. I.
10 *American Humanist Association v. United States*, October 30, 2014, https://www.scribd.com/document/245271872/American-Humansits-v-US, accessed January 12, 2019.

SECULARISM AND THE AMERICAN REPUBLIC

11 Jack Jenkins, "Atheists Score Major Win In Federal Court," *Think Progress*, November 3, 2014, http://thinkprogress.org/justice/2014/11/03/3587801/district-court-declares-secular-humanism-a-religion/, accessed January 12, 2019.

12 Steven Dubois, "Federal Prisons Agree to Recognize Humanism as a Religion," *Seattle Times*, July 27, 2015, http://www.bigstory.ap.org/article/12cfba9ea684438baae0badef1d5b1fe/federal-prisons-agree-recognize-humanism-religion, accessed January 12, 2019.

13 Nicholas J. Little, Ronald A. Lindsay, and Tom Flynn, "Secular Humanism: Not a Religion," *Free Inquiry* 35, no.2 (February/March 2015), https://secularhumanism.org/2015/01/cont-secularism-humanism-not-a-religion/, accessed January 14, 2019.

14 Sati is a traditional Indian practice where a widow would sacrifice herself by being burned on her husband's funeral pyre.

15 Jefferson to the Danbury Baptist Association, in *Jefferson: Political Writings*, 397; *Reynolds v. United States*, 98 U.S. 145, 164 (1878).

APPENDIX I

1 Maurice Cranston, *John Locke: A Biography* (London: Longmans, Green, and Company, 1959), 20.
2 Ibid., 41.
3 Cardinal Avery Dulles, *A History of Apologetics* (San Francisco: Ignatius Press, 2005), 174.
4 John Locke, *The Reasonableness of Christianity, as Delivered in the Scriptures* (London: A. Bettesworth and C. Hitch, 1731), 26–27. Grammar and spelling have been updated to resemble modern conventions.
5 Ibid., 30–31, 52–55, 151–55, 166–67.
6 Ibid., 258.
7 Jeremy Waldron, *God, Locke, and Equality: Christian Foundations of John Locke's Political Thought* (Cambridge: Cambridge University Press, 2002), 103.
8 Locke, *The Reasonableness of Christianity*, 6.
9 John Locke, *An Essay Concerning Human Understanding* (London: Thomas Tegg, R. Milliken, Griffin, and M. Baudry, 1825), 204. Grammar and spelling have been updated according to modern conventions.
10 Ibid., 475.
11 John Locke, *A Letter Concerning Toleration* (Huddersfield: J. Brook, 1796), 22. Grammar and spelling have been updated according to modern conventions.
12 John Locke, *Two Tracts on Government*, ed. and trans. Philip Abrams (Cambridge: Cambridge University Press, 1967), 121.

NOTES

13 Ibid., 119, 121, 124.
14 Locke, *A Letter Concerning Toleration*, 2.
15 Ibid., 10–11.
16 Ibid., 12–13.
17 Ibid., 10.
18 Ibid., 12.
19 Ibid., 35.
20 Ibid., 35–37.
21 Victor Nuovo, ed., *John Locke and Christianity: Contemporary Responses to the Reasonableness of Christianity*, Key Issues, ed. Andrew Pyle (New York: Thoemmes Press, 1997), xiv.
22 Locke, *A Letter Concerning Toleration*, 37–41.
23 The church as a voluntary society would remain voluntary, regardless of a magistrate's involvement. Locke writes, "For the civil government can give no new right to the church, nor the church to the civil government: so that whether the magistrate join himself to any church, or separate from it, the church remains always as it was before, a free and voluntary society" (*A Letter Concerning Toleration*, 20–21).
24 Ibid., 18–21.
25 Ibid., 20.
26 Ibid., 25. "Our government has not only been partial in matters of religion; but those also who have suffered under that partiality, and have therefore endeavoured by their writings to vindicate their own rights and liberties, have for the most part done it upon narrow principles, suited only to the interests of their own sects" (1).
27 Ibid., 25.
28 Ibid., 21.
29 Ibid., 26.
30 Ibid., 22.
31 Ibid., 47–48. "Further, the magistrate ought not to forbid the preaching or professing of any speculative opinions in any church, because they have no manner of relation to the civil rights of the subjects. If a Roman Catholic believes that to be really the body of Christ, which another man calls bread, he does no injury thereby to his neighbour. If a Jew does not believe the New Testament to be the word of God, he does not thereby alter anything in man's civil rights. If a heathen doubt of both testaments, he is not therefore to be punished as a pernicious citizen. The power of the magistrate, and the estates of the people, may be equally secure, whether any man believes these things or no. I readily grant that these opinions are false and absurd: but the

business of the laws is not to provide for the truth of opinions, but for the safety and security of the commonwealth, and of every particular man's goods and person. And so it ought to be. For truth certainly would do well enough, if she were once made to shift for herself. She [truth] seldom has received, and I fear never will receive, much assistance from the power of great men, to whom she [truth] is but rarely known, and more rarely welcomed."

32 Ibid., 6.
33 Ibid., 53.
34 Ibid., 51.
35 Ibid., 56. "Lastly, Those are not at all to be tolerated who 'deny the being of God.' Promises, covenants, and oaths, which are the bonds of human society, can have no hold upon an atheist. The taking away of God, though but even in thought, dissolves all. Besides also, those that by their atheism undermine and destroy all religion, can have no pretense of religion whereupon to challenge the privilege of a toleration. As for other practical opinions, though not absolutely free from all error, yet if they do not tend to establish dominion over others, or civil impunity to the church in which they are taught, there can be no reason why they should not be tolerated."
36 John Locke, "The Fundamental Constitutions of Carolina," *A Collection of Several Pieces of Mr. John Locke*, 2nd ed. (London: Mr. Desmaizeaux under the direction of Anthony Collins, 1739), 1–16.
37 Locke, *A Letter Concerning Toleration*, 12–13. Public penalties and force cannot produce such believing that convinces men's minds in the light of reason. Locke acknowledges such outward symbols of profession, when coerced, is vain, but that God acknowledges faith and the inward sincerity (33). "[N]ot even Americans, subjected unto a Christian prince, are to be punished either in body or goods, for not embracing our faith and worship" (41–42).
38 Ibid., 48.
39 Steve Straub, "John Locke, Epitaph," *The Federalist Papers*, https://thefederalistpapers.org/political-philosophers/john-locke/john-locke-epitaph, accessed February 3, 2021.

APPENDIX 2

1 John Calvin, *Institutes of the Christian Religion*, 2 vols., ed. John T. McNeill (Philadelphia: Westminster Press, 1960), 4.20.4, 2:1489–92.
2 Mary-Elaine Swanson, *The Education of James Madison* (Montgomery, Ala.: Hoffman Center, 1992), 20–22, 24; see also Garrett Ward Sheldon, *The Political Philosophy of James Madison* (Baltimore: Johns Hopkins University Press, 2001), 3–4.

NOTES

3   Swanson, 24; see also Sheldon, *Political Philosophy of James Madison*, 4.
4   Irving Brant, *James Madison* (Indianapolis: Bobbs-Merrill, 1941), 62; see also Sheldon, *Political Philosophy of James Madison*, 5.
5   Swanson, 4; Brant, 60; see also Sheldon, *Political Philosophy of James Madison*, 4.
6   Sheldon, *Political Philosophy of James Madison*, 5–6; see also James Madison to Rev. Thomas Martin, August 10, 1769, in Swanson, 30; Alan Heimart and Perry Miller, *The Great Awakening* (Indianapolis: Bobbs-Merrill, 1967).
7   Swanson, 24–26; see also Sheldon, *Political Philosophy of James Madison*, 6.
8   Brant, 73, 77; see also Sheldon, *Political Philosophy of James Madison*, 6.
9   See Jeffry Morrison, *John Witherspoon and the Early American Republic* (Notre Dame: Notre Dame University Press, 2004); see also Sheldon, *Political Philosophy of James Madison*, 10–11.
10 Sheldon, *Political Philosophy of James Madison*, 6–7.
11 John Witherspoon, *Lectures on Moral Philosophy*, ed. Jack Scott (Newark, Del.: University of Delaware Press, 1982), 147; see also Sheldon, *Political Philosophy of James Madison*, 16.
12 James Madison to William Bradford, December 1, 1773, in *James Madison: A Biography in His Own Words*, ed. Merrill D. Peterson (New York: Harper and Row, 1974), 29; see also Sheldon, *Political Philosophy of James Madison*, 29.
13 Sheldon, *Political Philosophy of James Madison*, 27.
14 Ibid.
15 Ibid., 28.
16 Gaillard Hunt, *Life of James Madison* (New York: Russell and Russell, 1902), 4; Ralph Ketcham, *James Madison* (Charlottesville: University Press of Virginia, 1990), 58; see also Sheldon, *Political Philosophy of James Madison*, 27.
17 Sheldon, *Political Philosophy of James Madison*, 27–28.
18 Quoted in Jeffrey Hays Morrison, "John Witherspoon and 'The Public Interest of Religion,'" *Journal of Church and State* 41 (summer 1999), 567; see also Sheldon, *Political Philosophy of James Madison*, 28.
19 Garrett Ward Sheldon, *The History of Political Theory: Ancient Greece to Modern America*, vol. 21, American University Studies Series X: Political Science (New York: Peter Lang, 2003), 136.
20 Sheldon, *Political Philosophy of James Madison*, 29–30; see also James Madison to William Bradford, December 1, 1773, in Peterson, 28–30.
21 James Madison to William Bradford, in Peterson, 29–30; see also Sheldon, *Political Philosophy of James Madison*, 29–31.
22 Ketcham, 73; see also Sheldon, *Political Philosophy of James Madison*, 31.
23 Ibid.

24 Ibid.
25 See Sheldon, *Political Philosophy of James Madison*, 32–33.
26 James Madison, Memorial and Remonstrance Against Religious Assessments, June 20, 1785, in *Jefferson & Madison on Separation of Church and State: Writings on Religion and Secularism*, ed. Lenni Brenner (Fort Lee, N.J.: Barricade, 2004), 68.
27 Ibid., 69.
28 Ibid.
29 Ibid, 70.
30 Ibid.
31 Peterson, 93; see also Sheldon, *Political Philosophy of James Madison*, 35.
32 Ketcham, 166; see also Sheldon, *Political Philosophy of James Madison*, 35.
33 Peterson, 94; see also Sheldon, *Political Philosophy of James Madison*, 35.
34 Ketcham, 167; see also Sheldon, *Political Philosophy of James Madison*, 35.
35 Quoted in Daniel L. Dreisbach, *Religion and Politics in the Early Republic* (Lexington, Ky.: University of Kentucky Press, 1996), 117; see also Sheldon, *Political Philosophy of James Madison*, 35.
36 James Madison, *The Writings of James Madison: Comprising His Public Papers and Private Correspondence, Including Numerous Letters and Documents Now for the First Time Printed*, vol. 8, ed. Gaillard Hunt (New York: G. P. Putnam's Sons, 1906), 412.
37 Jefferson's Virginia Statute for Religious Freedom is reprinted in David L. Dreisbach, *Thomas Jefferson and the Wall of Separation Between Church and State* (New York: New York University Press, 2002), 133–35.
38 Thomas Jefferson, Draft of the Virginia Statute for Religious Freedom [1777–1779], in *Jefferson & Madison on Separation of Church and State: Writings on Religion and Secularism*, ed. Lenni Brenner (Fort Lee, N.J.: Barricade, 2004), 48.
39 Ibid., 49.
40 Ibid.
41 Ibid.
42 Ibid., 50.
43 Jefferson to Dr. Thomas Cooper, November 2, 1822, *The Writings of Thomas Jefferson*, vol. 15, ed. Albert Ellery Bergh (Washington, D.C.: Memorial ed., 1904–1905), 404, quoted in Henry Wilder Foote, *The Religion of Thomas Jefferson* (Boston: Beacon Press, 1960), 7–8; see also Garrett Ward Sheldon, *The Political Philosophy of Thomas Jefferson* (Baltimore: Johns Hopkins University Press, 1993), 110.
44 U.S. Constitution, amend. I.

NOTES

APPENDIX 3

1 James Turner, *Without God, Without Creed: The Origins of Unbelief in America*, New Studies in American Intellectual and Cultural History, ed. Thomas Bender (Baltimore: Johns Hopkins University Press, 1985), 141.
2 Isaac Kramnick and R. Laurence Moore, *The Godless Constitution: The Case Against Religious Correctness* (New York: W. W. Norton & Company, 1997), 28.
3 Philip Hamburger, *Separation of Church and State* (Cambridge: Harvard University Press, 2004), 15n23.
4 See Susan Jacoby, *Freethinkers: A History of American Secularism* (New York: Holt, 2004); as well as Andrew L. Seidel, *The Founding Myth: Why Christian Nationalism Is Un-American* (New York: Sterling, 2019).
5 Mark David Hall, *Did America Have a Christian Founding? Separating Modern Myth from Historical Truth* (Nashville: Thomas Nelson, 2019), 21.
6 Joseph O. Baker and Buster G. Smith, *American Secularism: Cultural Contours of Nonreligious Belief Systems*, Religion and Social Transformation (New York: New York University Press, 2015), 82.
7 Ibid., 8.
8 Charles Taylor, "Afterword: Apologia pro Libro sum," in *Varieties of Secularism in a Secular Age*, ed. Michael Warner, Jonathan VanAntwerpen, and Craig Calhoun (Cambridge: Harvard University Press, 2010), 300.
9 Charles Taylor, *A Secular Age* (Cambridge: Belknap Press: An Imprint of Harvard University Press, 2007), 2.
10 Ibid., 366.
11 See, for example, Richard Dawkins, *The God Delusion* (Boston: Houghton Mifflin, 2006); and Christopher Hitchens, *God Is Not Great: How Religion Poisons Everything* (New York: Grand Central, 2007).
12 See Rodney Stark, "Secularization, R.I.P.," *Sociology of Religion* 60, no. 3 (Fall 1999): 249–73.
13 Taylor, *A Secular Age*, 3.
14 Michael Warner, Jonathan VanAntwerpen, and Craig Calhoun, Editors' Introduction to *Varieties of Secularism in a Secular Age* (Cambridge: Harvard University Press, 2010), 1–2.
15 James K. A. Smith, *How (Not) to Be Secular: Reading Charles Taylor* (Grand Rapids, Mich.: Eerdmans, 2014), 3.
16 Still other publications followed Taylor's *A Secular Age*. However, they are too numerous to list here but regard the following subjects: philosophy, religion, identity, meaning, value, the faith, the gospel, the pastor, the church, apologetics, the state, law, justice, politics, education, globalization, and more.

17 Carl Trueman, "Taylor's Complex, Incomplete Historical Narrative," in *Our Secular Age: Ten Years of Reading and Applying Charles Taylor*, ed. Collin Hansen (Deerfield, Ill.: The Gospel Coalition, 2017), 21.
18 Carl R. Trueman, *The Rise and Triumph of the Modern Self: Cultural Amnesia, Expressive Individualism, and the Road to Sexual Revolution* (Wheaton: Crossway, 2020), 20.
19 See Hunter Baker, *The End of Secularism* (Wheaton: Crossway, 2009), 15; and Richard John Neuhaus, *The Naked Public Square: Religion and Democracy in America* (Grand Rapids, Mich.: Eerdmans, 1984). See also Roy A. Clouser, *The Myth of Religious Neutrality: An Essay on the Hidden Role of Religious Belief in Theories*, rev. ed. (1991; repr., Notre Dame: University of Notre Dame, 2005).
20 Paul Cliteur, *The Secular Outlook* (Oxford: Wiley-Blackwell, 2010), 3 (italics added).
21 See Steve Bruce, *Secularization: In Defence of an Unfashionable Theory* (Oxford: Oxford University Press, 2011).
22 Baker, 97.
23 Ibid., 14, 23.
24 Ibid., 16.
25 Craig Calhoun, Mark Juergensmeyer, and Jonathan VanAntwerpen, eds., *Rethinking Secularism* (Oxford: Oxford University Press, 2011), 3.
26 Ibid., 16.
27 Arnold E. Loen, *Secularization: Science without God?* trans. Margaret Kohl (London: SCM, 1967), 7, 11 (italics removed).
28 Ibid., 12.
29 Peter L. Berger, *The Many Altars of Modernity: Toward a Paradigm for Religion in a Pluralist Age* (Berlin: De Gruyter, 2014), 1.
30 Ibid., 68.
31 J. P. Moreland, *Scientism and Secularism: Learning to Respond to a Dangerous Ideology* (Wheaton: Crossway, 2018), 25.
32 Ibid.
33 Ibid., 197.
34 Jocelyn Maclure and Charles Taylor, *Secularism and Freedom of Conscience*, trans. Jane Marie Todd (Cambridge: Harvard University Press, 2011), 10.
35 Ibid., 42.
36 Ibid., 46.
37 Ibid., 47.
38 Ibid., 65.
39 Ibid., 67.
40 Ibid., 10–11.

NOTES

41 John Rawls, *Political Liberalism*, Columbia Classics in Philosophy (New York: Columbia University Press, 2005), xxiv, 4. Of course the crucial question asks what *reasonable* means.
42 For example, see Victoria Davion and Clark Wolf, eds., *The Idea of a Political Liberalism: Essays on Rawls* (Lanham, Md.: Rowman & Littlefield, 2000); and Thom Brooks and Martha C. Nussbaum, eds., *Rawls's Political Liberalism* (New York: Columbia Press, 2015).
43 Bruce Ashford and Chris Pappalardo, *One Nation Under God: A Christian Hope for American Politics* (Nashville: B&H Academic, 2015), 51–52.
44 Ibid., 46–47.
45 Ibid., 50. See also Richard J. Mouw and Sander Griffioen, *Pluralisms and Horizons: An Essay in Christian Public Philosophy* (Grand Rapids, Mich.: Eerdmans, 1993), 17–18.
46 John Perry, "Anglo-American Secular Government," in *The Oxford Handbook of Secularism*, ed. Phil Zuckerman and John R. Shook (Oxford: Oxford University Press, 2017), 126.
47 Emmet Kennedy, *Secularism and Its Opponents from Augustine to Solzhenitsyn* (New York: Palgrave Macmillan, 2006), 23, 41, 131.
48 Ibid., 2.
49 Ibid., 1–2.
50 Bruce, 1.
51 Andrew Copson, *Secularism: Politics, Religion, and Freedom* (Oxford: Oxford University Press, 2017), 1.
52 Ibid., 2.
53 Secular Democrats of America, *Restoring Constitutional Secularism and Patriotic Pluralism in the White House*, https://seculardems.org/wp-content/uploads/2020/11/SecularDemocratsofAmerica_Blueprint_BidenHarris-Transition_11-30-20_FINAL.pdf, accessed February 16, 2021.

Bibliography

Primary Sources

Adams, John. John Adams to the Officers of the First Brigade of the Third Division of the Militia of Massachusetts, October 11, 1798. In *The Works of John Adams, Second President of the United States*, Vol. 9. Edited by Charles Francis Adams. Boston: Little, Brown, and Company, 1854.

———. "Thoughts on Government" (1776). In Charles Francis Adams, *The Works of John Adams, Second President of the United States: With a Life of the Author, Notes and Illustrations*, 10 vols. Boston: Charles C. Little and James Brown, 1850–56.

Bacon, Francis. *The Advancement of Learning*, Book I. The Works of Francis Bacon. Edited by James Spedding, et al. London: Longmans and Company, 1870.

———. *The Advancement of Learning*. In *The Squashed Philosophers: The 45 Great Classics of Philosophy Abridged into Readable Little Epitomes*. Edited by Glyn Hughes. Morrisville, N.C.: Lulu, 2016.

Calvin, John. *Institutes of the Christian Religion*, 2 vols. Edited by John T. McNeill. Philadelphia: Westminster Press, 1960.

Early History of the University of Virginia as Contained in the Letters of Thomas Jefferson and Joseph C. Cabell, Hitherto Unpublished; with an Appendix, consisting of Mr. Jefferson's Bill for a Complete System of Education, and Other Illustrative Documents; and an Introduction, Comprising a Brief Historical Sketch of the University, and a Biographical Notice of Joseph C. Cabell. Richmond: J. W. Randolph, 1856.

Holyoake, George Jacob. *The Origin and Nature of Secularism: Showing That Where Freethought Commonly Ends Secularism Begins*. London: Watts & Co., 1896.

———, ed. *The Reasoner: Gazette of Secularism*, Vol. 16. London: Holyoake and Co., 1854.

Jefferson, Thomas. Draft of the Virginia Statute for Religious Freedom [1777–1779]. In *Jefferson & Madison on Separation of Church and State: Writings on Religion and Secularism*. Edited by Lenni Brenner. Fort Lee, N.J.: Barricade, 2004.

———. Report of the Commissioners for the University of Virginia, August 4, 1818. In *Jefferson & Madison on Separation of Church and State: Writings on Religion and Secularism*. Edited by Lenni Brenner. Fort Lee, N.J.: Barricade, 2004.

———. Report of the Commissioners for the University of Virginia, August 4, 1818. In *Jefferson: Political Writings*. Edited by Joyce Appleby and Terence Ball. Cambridge Texts in the History of Political Thought. Edited by Raymond Geuss and Quentin Skinner. Cambridge: Cambridge University Press, 1999.

———. Report to the President and Directors of the Literary Fund, October 7, 1822. In *Jefferson & Madison on Separation of Church and State: Writings on Religion and Secularism*. Edited by Lenni Brenner. Fort Lee, N.J.: Barricade, 2004.

———. Thomas Jefferson to Arthur S. Brockenbrough, April 21, 1825. *Founders Online: Jefferson Papers*. National Archives. https://founders.archives.gov/documents/Jefferson/98-01-02-5152.

———. Thomas Jefferson to Dr. Thomas Cooper, Monticello, November 2, 1822. In *Jefferson: Political Writings*. Edited by Joyce Appleby and Terence Ball. Cambridge Texts in the History of Political Thought. Edited by Raymond Geuss and Quentin Skinner. Cambridge: Cambridge University Press, 1999.

———. Thomas Jefferson to John Adams, April 11, 1823. In *Jefferson & Madison on Separation of Church and State: Writings on Religion and Secularism*. Edited by Lenni Brenner. Fort Lee, N.J.: Barricade, 2004.

———. Thomas Jefferson to Martha Jefferson Randolph, August 4, 1818. In *The Papers of Thomas Jefferson*. Retirement Series, Vol. 13. Edited by J. Jefferson Looney. Princeton: Princeton University Press, 2016.

———. Thomas Jefferson to Mr. Duane, Monticello, August 12, 1810. In *The Writings of Thomas Jefferson*, Vol. 5. New York: Riker, Thorne, and Co., 1854.

———. Thomas Jefferson to the Danbury Baptist Association, January 1, 1802. In *Jefferson & Madison on Separation of Church and State: Writings on Religion and Secularism*. Edited by Lenni Brenner. Fort Lee, N.J.: Barricade, 2004.

———. Thomas Jefferson to the Danbury Baptist Association, January 1, 1802. In *Jefferson: Political Writings*. Edited by Joyce Appleby and Terence Ball. Cambridge Texts in the History of Political Thought. Edited by Raymond Geuss and Quentin Skinner. Cambridge: Cambridge University Press, 1999.

John Locke. *A Letter Concerning Toleration*. Huddersfield: J. Brook, 1796.

———. *A Letter Concerning Toleration*. Edited by Mario Montuori. The Hague, Netherlands: Martinus Nijhoff, 1963.

BIBLIOGRAPHY

———. *An Essay Concerning Human Understanding*. London: Thomas Tegg, R. Milliken, Griffin, and M. Baudry, 1825.

———. *An Essay Concerning Human Understanding*. Philadelphia: Kay and Troutman, 1846.

———. "The Fundamental Constitutions of Carolina." *A Collection of Several Pieces of Mr. John Locke*, 2nd ed. London: Mr. Desmaizeaux under the direction of Anthony Collins, 1739.

———. *The Reasonableness of Christianity, as Delivered in the Scriptures*. London: A. Bettesworth and C. Hitch, 1731.

———. *Two Tracts on Government*. Edited and translated by Philip Abrams. Cambridge: Cambridge University Press, 1967.

Madison, James. James Madison to Edward Everett, March 19, 1823. In *Jefferson & Madison on Separation of Church and State: Writings on Religion and Secularism*. Edited by Lenni Brenner Fort Lee, N.J.: Barricade, 2004.

———. James Madison to Frederick Beasley, December 22, 1824. In *Jefferson & Madison on Separation of Church and State: Writings on Religion and Secularism*. Edited by Lenni Brenner Fort Lee, N.J.: Barricade, 2004.

———. James Madison to Marquis De La Fayette, November 24, 1826. In *Jefferson & Madison on Separation of Church and State: Writings on Religion and Secularism*. Edited by Lenni Brenner. Fort Lee, N.J.: Barricade, 2004.

———. James Madison to Rev. Thomas Martin, August 10, 1769. In Mary-Elaine Swanson. *The Education of James Madison*. Montgomery, Ala.: Hoffman Center, 1992.

———. James Madison to Robert Walsh, March 2, 1819. In *Jefferson & Madison on Separation of Church and State: Writings on Religion and Secularism*. Edited by Lenni Brenner. Fort Lee, N.J.: Barricade, 2004.

———. James Madison to William Bradford, December 1, 1773. In *James Madison: A Biography in His Own Words*. Edited by Merrill D. Peterson. New York: Harper and Row, 1974.

———. Memorial and Remonstrance Against Religious Assessments, June 20, 1785. In *Jefferson & Madison on Separation of Church and State: Writings on Religion and Secularism*. Edited by Lenni Brenner. Fort Lee, N.J.: Barricade, 2004.

———. *The Writings of James Madison: Comprising His Public Papers and Private Correspondence, Including Numerous Letters and Documents Now for the First Time Printed*, Vol. 8. Edited by Gaillard Hunt. New York: G. P. Putnam's Sons, 1906.

"Meeting Minutes of University of Virginia Board of Visitors, 4–5 Oct. 1824." *Founders Online*. https://founders.archives.gov/documents/Jefferson/98-01-02-4598. Accessed February 9, 2021.

Newton, Isaac. *Newton's Principia: The Mathematical Principles of Natural Philosophy.* Translated by Andrew Motte. New York: Putnam, 1850.
Paine, Thomas. *The Age of Reason.* New York: Kensington, 1988.
Plato. *Republic*, Book IV. Cambridge: Cambridge University Press: 1963.
"Quotations on the Jefferson Memorial." *Monticello.* https://www.monticello.org/site/jefferson/quotations-jefferson-memorial. Accessed September 7, 2018.
Report of the Board of Commissioners for the University of Virginia to the Virginia General Assembly [4 August] 1818. *Founders Online.* https://founders.archives.gov/documents/Madison/04-01-02-0289. Accessed January 17, 2019.
Report of the Commissioners Appointed to Fix the Site of the University of Virginia. In Roy J. Honeywell. *Educational Work of Thomas Jefferson,* Vol. 16. Harvard Studies in Education. New York: Russel & Russel, 1964.
The Historical Marker Database: "Rockfish Gap Meeting." *The Historical Marker Database.* https://www.hmdb.org/m.asp?m=21831. Accessed February 5, 2021. Internet.
The Rockfish Gap Report. *University of Virginia Library Online Exhibits.* https://explore.lib.virginia.edu/items/show/2077. Accessed February 5, 2021.
Witherspoon, John. *Lectures on Moral Philosophy.* Edited by Jack Scott. Newark, Del.: University of Delaware Press, 1982.

Secondary Sources

Adams, Herbert Baxter. *Thomas Jefferson and the University of Virginia.* Washington: Government Printing Office, 1888.
Ashford, Bruce, and Chris Pappalardo. *One Nation Under God: A Christian Hope for American Politics.* Nashville: B&H Academic, 2015.
Baker, Hunter. *The End of Secularism.* Wheaton: Crossway, 2009.
Baker, Joseph O., and Buster G. Smith. *American Secularism: Cultural Contours of Nonreligious Belief Systems.* Religion and Social Transformation. New York: New York University Press, 2015.
Berger, Peter L. *The Many Altars of Modernity: Toward a Paradigm for Religion in a Pluralist Age.* Berlin: De Gruyter, 2014.
Boudinhon, Auguste. "Secular Clergy." *The Catholic Encyclopedia,* Vol. 12. New York: Robert Appleton, 1912. http://www.newadvent.org/cathen/13675a.htm. Accessed July 17, 2018.
Bourdeau, Michel. "Auguste Comte." *Stanford Encyclopedia of Philosophy.* May 8, 2018. http://plato.stanford.edu/entries/comte/. Accessed January 10, 2019.

BIBLIOGRAPHY

Bracey, Matthew Steven, and W. Jackson Watts, eds. *The Promise of Arminian Theology: Essays in Honor of F. Leroy Forlines*. Nashville: Randall House Academic, 2016.

Brant, Irving. *James Madison*. Indianapolis: Bobbs-Merrill, 1941.

Brenner, Lenni, ed. *Jefferson & Madison on Separation of Church and State: Writings on Religion and Secularism*. Fort Lee, N.J.: Barricade, 2004.

Brooks, Thom, and Martha C. Nussbaum, eds. *Rawls's Political Liberalism*. New York: Columbia Press, 2015.

Bruce, Steve. *Secularization: In Defence of an Unfashionable Theory*. Oxford: Oxford University Press, 2011.

Calhoun, Craig, Mark Juergensmeyer, and Jonathan VanAntwerpen, eds. *Rethinking Secularism*. Oxford: Oxford University Press, 2011.

Cliteur, Paul. *The Secular Outlook*. Oxford: Wiley-Blackwell, 2010.

Clouser, Roy A. *The Myth of Religious Neutrality: An Essay on the Hidden Role of Religious Belief in Theories*, revised ed. 1991; repr., Notre Dame: University of Notre Dame, 2005.

Copson, Andrew. *Secularism: Politics, Religion, and Freedom*. Oxford: Oxford University Press, 2017.

Cranston, Maurice. *John Locke: A Biography*. London: Longmans, Green, and Company, 1959.

Davion, Victoria, and Clark Wolf, eds. *The Idea of a Political Liberalism: Essays on Rawls*. Lanham, Md.: Rowman & Littlefield, 2000.

Dawkins, Richard. *The God Delusion*. Boston: Houghton Mifflin, 2006.

Dreisbach, David L. *Religion and Politics in the Early Republic*. Lexington, Ky.: University of Kentucky Press, 1996.

———. *Thomas Jefferson and the Wall of Separation Between Church and State*. New York: New York University Press, 2002.

———. "'Sowing Useful Truths and Principles': The Danbury Baptists, Thomas Jefferson, and the 'Wall of Separation.'" *Journal of Church and State*, 39, no. 3 (1997): 455–501.

Dubois, Steven. "Federal Prisons Agree to Recognize Humanism as a Religion." *Seattle Times*. July 27, 2015. http://www.bigstory.ap.org/article/12cfba9ea6 84438baae0badef1d5b1fe/federal-prisons-agree-recognize-humanism -religion. Accessed January 12, 2019.

Dulles, Cardinal Avery. *A History of Apologetics*. San Francisco: Ignatius Press, 2005.

Feldman, Noah. *Divided By God: America's Church-State Problem—And What We Should Do About It*. New York: Farrar, Straus and Giroux, 2005.

Finke, Roger, and Rodney Stark. *The Churching of America, 1776–2005: Winners and Losers in Our Religious Economy*. New Brunswick: Rutgers University Press, 2005.

SECULARISM AND THE AMERICAN REPUBLIC

Foote, Henry Wilder. *The Religion of Thomas Jefferson.* Boston: Beacon Press, 1960.

Forlines, F. Leroy. *The Quest For Truth: Answering Life's Inescapable Questions.* Nashville: Randall House, 2001.

Forlines, F. Leroy, and J. Matthew Pinson. *The Apologetics of Leroy Forlines.* Gallatin, Tenn.: Welch College Press, 2019.

Gamble, Harry Y. *God on the Grounds: A History of Religion at Thomas Jefferson's University.* Charlottesville: University of Virginia Press, 2020.

Gaukroger, Stephen. *Francis Bacon and the Transformation of Early-Modern Philosophy.* Cambridge: Cambridge University Press, 2001.

Gaustad, Edwin S. *Sworn on the Altar of God.* Grand Rapids, Mich.: Eerdmans, 1996.

Gladstone, W. E. "The Courses of Religious Thought" (June 1876). In *The Contemporary Review*, Vol. 28, 1–26. June-November 1876. London: Henry S. King and Co., 1876.

Glanzer, Perry L., Nathan F. Alleman, and Todd C. Ream. *Restoring the Soul of the University: Unifying Christian Higher Education in a Fragmented Age.* Downers Grove: IVP, 2017.

Hall, Mark David. *Did America Have a Christian Founding? Separating Modern Myth from Historical Truth.* Nashville: Thomas Nelson, 2019.

Hamburger, Philip. *Separation of Church and State.* Cambridge: Harvard University Press, 2004.

Heimart, Alan, and Perry Miller. *The Great Awakening.* Indianapolis: Bobbs-Merrill, 1967.

Hitchens, Christopher. *God Is Not Great: How Religion Poisons Everything.* New York: Grand Central, 2007.

Honeywell, Roy J. *Educational Work of Thomas Jefferson.* Vol. 16 of the *Harvard Studies in Education.* New York: Russel & Russel, 1964.

Höpfl, Harro. *Luther and Calvin on Secular Authority.* Cambridge Texts in the History of Political Thoughts. Edited and translated by Harro Höpfl. Cambridge: Cambridge University Press, 2004.

Hunt, Gaillard. *Life of James Madison.* New York: Russell and Russell, 1902.

Jacoby, Susan. *Freethinkers: A History of American Secularism.* New York: Holt, 2004.

Jenkins, Jack. "Atheists Score Major Win In Federal Court." *Think Progress.* November 3, 2014. http://thinkprogress.org/justice/2014/11/03/3587801/district-court-declares-secular-humanism-a-religion/. Accessed January 12, 2019.

Kelly, Matt. "200 Years Ago, Jefferson Left Nothing to Chance at Rockfish Gap Conference." *The University of Virginia Today.* July 27, 2018. https://news.virginia.edu/content/200-years-ago-jefferson-left-nothing-chance-rockfish-gap-conference. Accessed February 4. 2021.

BIBLIOGRAPHY

Kennedy, Emmet. *Secularism and Its Opponents from Augustine to Solzhenitsyn.* New York: Palgrave Macmillan, 2006.

Ketcham, Ralph. *James Madison: A Biography.* Charlottesville: The University Press of Virginia, 1990.

Kramnick, Isaac, and R. Laurence Moore. *The Godless Constitution: The Case Against Religious Correctness.* New York: W. W. Norton & Company, 1997.

Lambert, Frank. *The Founding Fathers and the Place of Religion in America.* Princeton: Princeton University Press, 2003.

Laslett, Peter, ed. Introduction to John Locke, *Two Treatises of Government.* Cambridge Texts in the History of Political Thought. Cambridge: Cambridge University Press, 2003.

Levy, Leonard W. *The Establishment Clause: Religion and the First Amendment,* 2nd ed. revised. Chapel Hill, N.C.: The University of North Carolina Press, 1994.

Little, Nicholas J., Ronald A. Lindsay, and Tom Flynn. "Secular Humanism: Not a Religion." *Free Inquiry* 35, no.2 (February/March 2015). https://secular humanism.org/2015/01/cont-secularism-humanism-not-a-religion/. Accessed January 14, 2019.

Loen, Arnold E. *Secularization: Science without God?* Translated by Margaret Kohl. London: SCM, 1967.

Lyon, David. "Secularization." In *New Dictionary of Theology.* Edited by Sinclair B. Ferguson and David F. Wright. Leicester: InterVarsity, 1988.

Maclure, Jocelyn, and Charles Taylor. *Secularism and Freedom of Conscience.* Translated by Jane Marie Todd. Cambridge: Harvard University Press, 2011.

Marsden, George M. *The Soul of the American University: From Protestant Establishment to Established Nonbelief.* New York: Oxford University Press, 1994.

Marsden, George M., and Bradley J. Longfield, eds. *The Secularization of the Academy.* Oxford: Oxford University Press, 1992.

Moreland, J. P. *Scientism and Secularism: Learning to Respond to a Dangerous Ideology.* Wheaton: Crossway, 2018.

Morrison, Jeffry. *John Witherspoon and the Early American Republic.* Notre Dame: Notre Dame University Press, 2004.

Morrison, Jeffrey Hays. "John Witherspoon and 'The Public Interest of Religion.'" *Journal of Church and State* 41, no. 3 (summer 1999): 551–73.

Mouw, Richard J., and Sander Griffioen. *Pluralisms and Horizons: An Essay in Christian Public Philosophy.* Grand Rapids, Mich.: Eerdmans, 1993.

Neuhaus, Richard John. *The Naked Public Square: Religion and Democracy in America.* Grand Rapids, Mich.: Eerdmans, 1984.

SECULARISM AND THE AMERICAN REPUBLIC

"Nine reasons why you should become an E.F. Hutton account executive and one reason why you shouldn't." *Princeton Alumni Weekly* 77 (September 27, 1976).

Norton, Charles Eliot. *The Correspondence of John Ruskin and Charles Eliot Norton.* Edited by John Lewis Bradley and Ian Ousby. Cambridge: Cambridge University Press, 1987.

Nuovo, Victor, ed. *John Locke and Christianity: Contemporary Responses to the Reasonableness of Christianity.* Key Issues. Edited by Andrew Pyle. New York: Thoemmes Press, 1997.

Onuf, Peter S. "Thomas Jefferson's Prayer for the Future: A Look Back at His Forward-Looking Mission for the University." *University of Virginia Magazine.* Spring 2017. https://uvamagazine.org/articles/thomas_jeffersons_prayer_for_the_future. Accessed February 4, 2021.

Perry, John. "Anglo-American Secular Government." In *The Oxford Handbook of Secularism.* Edited by Phil Zuckerman and John R. Shook. Oxford: Oxford University Press, 2017.

Peterson, Merrill D., ed. *James Madison: A Biography in His Own Words.* New York: Harper and Row, 1974.

Pickering, Mary. *Auguste Comte: An Intellectual Biography,* Vol. 3. New York: Cambridge, 2009.

Ragosta, John A., Peter S. Onuf, and Andrew J. O'Shaughnessy. *The Founding of Thomas Jefferson's University.* Charlottesville: University of Virginia Press, 2019.

Randall, Henry Stephens. *The Life of Thomas Jefferson,* Vol. 3. Philadelphia: J. B. Lippincott, 1871.

Rawls, John. *Political Liberalism.* Columbia Classics in Philosophy. New York: Columbia University Press, 2005.

Read, James H. *Power versus Liberty: Madison, Hamilton, Wilson, and Jefferson.* Charlottesville: The University Press of Virginia, 2000.

Roberts, Jon H., and James Turner. *The Sacred and the Secular University.* Princeton: Princeton University Press, 2000.

Rosenberg, Alex. *Philosophy of Science: A Contemporary Introduction.* London: Routledge, 2000.

Scott, Eugenie C. "Creationism, Ideology, and Science." In *The Flight from Science and Reason,* Edited by Paul R. Gross, Norman Levitt, and Martin W. Lewis. Baltimore: Johns Hopkins University Press, 1996.

Scott, Gary. *Faith and the Presidency from George Washington to George W. Bush.* Oxford: Oxford University Press, 2006.

BIBLIOGRAPHY

Secular Democrats of America. *Restoring Constitutional Secularism and Patriotic Pluralism in the White House.* https://seculardems.org/wpcontent/uploads/2020/11/SecularDemocratsofAmerica_Blueprint_BidenHarrisTransition_113020_FINAL.pdf?utm_source=Albert+Mohler&utm_campaign=eaf2956e9aEMAIL_CAMPAIGN_2019_04_08_09_12_COPY_01&utm_medium=email&utm_term=0_b041ba0d12-eaf2956e9a-308485057&mc_cid=eaf2956e9a. Accessed February 16, 2021.

Seidel, Andrew L. *The Founding Myth: Why Christian Nationalism Is Un-American.* New York: Sterling, 2019.

Sheldon, Garrett Ward. "Liberalism, Classicism, and Christianity in Jefferson's Political Thought." In *Religion and Political Culture in Jefferson's Virginia.* Edited by Garrett Ward Sheldon and Daniel L. Dreisbach. Lanham, Md.: Rowman & Littlefield, 2000.

———. *The History of Political Theory: Ancient Greece to Modern America*, Vol. 21. American University Studies Series X: Political Science. New York: Peter Lang, 2003.

———. *The Political Philosophy of James Madison.* Baltimore: Johns Hopkins University Press, 2001.

———. *The Political Philosophy of Thomas Jefferson.* Baltimore: The Johns Hopkins University Press, 1993.

Smith, James K. A. *How (Not) to Be Secular: Reading Charles Taylor.* Grand Rapids, Mich.: Eerdmans, 2014.

Stark, Rodney. "Secularization, R.I.P." *Sociology of Religion* 60, no. 3 (Fall 1999): 249–73.

Straub, Steve. "John Locke, Epitaph." *The Federalist Papers.* https://thefederalistpapers.org/political-philosophers/john-locke/john-locke-epitaph. Accessed February 3, 2021.

Sommerville, C. John. *The Decline of the Secular University.* Oxford: Oxford University Press, 2006.

Swanson, Mary-Elaine. *The Education of James Madison.* Montgomery, Ala.: Hoffman Center, 1992.

Taylor, Charles. *A Secular Age.* Cambridge: Belknap Press: An Imprint of Harvard University Press, 2007.

———. "Afterword: Apologia pro Libro sum." In *Varieties of Secularism in a Secular Age.* Edited by Michael Warner, Jonathan VanAntwerpen, and Craig Calhoun. Cambridge: Harvard University Press, 2010.

"The Campaign for Secularism." *Free Inquiry* 28, no. 3 (April/May 2008).

Thompson, Seymour D., and Leonard A. Jones, eds. *American Law Review* 32. St. Louis: Review, 1898.

Trueman, Carl. "Taylor's Complex, Incomplete Historical Narrative." In *Our Secular Age: Ten Years of Reading and Applying Charles Taylor*. Edited by Collin Hansen. Deerfield, Ill.: The Gospel Coalition, 2017.

Trueman, Carl R. *The Rise and Triumph of the Modern Self: Cultural Amnesia, Expressive Individualism, and the Road to Sexual Revolution*. Wheaton: Crossway, 2020.

Tuckness, Alex. "Locke's Political Philosophy." *Stanford Encyclopedia of Philosophy*. January 11, 2016. https://plato.stanford.edu/entries/locke-political/. Accessed August 17, 2018.

Turner, James. *Without God, Without Creed: The Origins of Unbelief in America*. New Studies in American Intellectual and Cultural History. Edited by Thomas Bender. Baltimore: Johns Hopkins University Press, 1985.

Waggoner, Michael D. *Sacred and Secular Tensions in Higher Education*. New York: Routledge, 2011.

Waldron, Jeremy. *God, Locke, and Equality: Christian Foundations of John Locke's Political Thought*. Cambridge: Cambridge University Press, 2002.

Warner, Michael, Jonathan VanAntwerpen, and Craig Calhoun. Editors' Introduction to *Varieties of Secularism in a Secular Age*. Cambridge: Harvard University Press, 2010.

Weber, Alfred. *History of Philosophy*. Translated by Frank Thilly. New York: Charles Scribner's Sons, 1896.

Young, Warren C. "Secularism." In *Baker's Dictionary of Theology*. Edited by Everett F. Harrison. Grand Rapids, Mich.: Baker, 1960.

About the Author

F. Leroy Forlines (1926–2020) was Professor Emeritus of Theology at Welch College, where he served more than fifty years, much of that time as Dean of Students. After concluding his studies at Welch, he received the M.A. from Winona Lake School of Theology, the B.D. from Northern Baptist Theological Seminary, and the Th.M. from Chicago Graduate School of Theology. Forlines has influenced generations of leaders through his many publications, including *Biblical Ethics*, *Systematics*, *The Quest for Truth*, *Classical Arminianism*, and his commentary on Romans. Forlines was married to his wife, Fay, from 1956 until his death in 2020. Their two sons, Jonathan and James, live and work in Middle Tennessee.

About the Editor

Matthew Steven Bracey is Vice Provost for Academic Administration and Assistant Professor of Theology and Culture at Welch College. He holds a B.A. degree in history from Welch College, an M.T.S. from Beeson Divinity School, and a Juris Doctor (J.D.) from Cumberland School of Law of Samford University, and he is ABD for his Ph.D. in Christian Ethics and Public Policy at Southern Baptist Theological Seminary. He has written widely, including contributing chapters to *Sexuality, Gender, and the Church* and *The Promise of Arminian Theology*, which he also co-edited. Bracey is a co-founder and Senior Editor of the Helwys Society Forum. He and his wife Sarah have been married for ten years.

Name Index

Adams, Herbert Baxter, 142–43, 149–51, 304
Adams, John, xvii, 15–18, 33, 40, 45, 49, 80, 82, 143, 252, 282n20, 301–02
Arminius, Jacobus, 229
Ashford, Bruce, 266, 304
Bacon, Francis, xvii, 18–19, 21–24, 33, 37, 301, 306
Baker, Hunter, 259–60, 264, 304
Baker, Joseph O., 254, 304
Baubérot, Jean, 269
Beasley, Frederick, 174, 177, 303
Berger, Peter, 261–63, 266, 304
Black, Hugo, xix–xxii, xxiv–xxvi, 50–57, 59–63, 68–69, 73, 75–81, 92–93, 103, 108, 110–12, 118, 124, 128, 135, 139–40, 152–53, 172, 180–81, 186, 188, 194–95, 198, 208, 219, 270
Blake, William, 257
Bourdeau, Michel, 213, 304
Bradford, William, 241, 303
Bradlaugh, Charles, 7, 12
Brennan, William, Jr., xvi, 5
Brenner, Lenni, xviii, 3, 37–38, 196, 283n19, 284n7, 301–03, 305
Brockenbrough, Arthur Spicer, 167, 169–70, 172–74, 176–77, 302
Bruce, Steve, 259, 269, 305
Burton, Howard, 50, 81

Cabell, Joseph C., 142, 301
Calhoun, Craig, 256, 261–63, 305, 309–10
Calvin, John, 16, 229, 301, 306
Catron, John, 58
Cliteur, Paul, 259–61, 305
Cocke, J. H., 142
Comte, Auguste, 213, 304, 308
Constantine, 121–22
Cooper, Thomas, 167, 169, 176, 202, 302
Copson, Andrew, 269–70, 305
Cranston, Maurice, 224, 305
Cromwell, Oliver, 224
Darwin, Charles, 36, 215, 257
Davies, Myles, 11
Dawkins, Richard, 255, 305
Dewey, John, 91
Douglas, William O., 50
Dreisbach, Daniel, 131, 309
Dubois, Steven, 215, 305
Dulles, Cardinal Avery, 225, 305
Edwards, Jonathan, 16, 240
Everett, Edward, 173–76, 303
Feldman, Noah, xviii, 36, 120, 305
Flynn, Tom, 215, 307
Frankfurter, Felix, xxii, 50, 75, 81–101, 110, 117, 280n16, 281n1, 281n21, 281n24, 282n4
Freud, Sigmund, 257
Frost, Robert, 100

Gamble, Harry Y., xxviii–xxix, 274n17, 306
Gaustad, Edwin, xxvii, 18, 40–43, 45, 142–43, 145, 147, 154, 285n1, 286n12, 306
Gee, Edward, 11
Gladstone, William, 13, 306
Grant, Ulysses S., 89–91
Haggerty, Ancer, 214–15
Hall, Mark David, 253–54, 306
Hansen, Collin, 257, 259, 310
Henry, Patrick, xx, xxiv, xxvii, 54–55, 57, 68, 74, 83, 94, 116–17, 119, 121–24, 126, 134, 179, 181, 194, 200, 205, 208
Hitchins, Christopher, 255, 306
Holden, Jason Michael, 214–15
Holyoake, George Jacob, xiii, xvii, 6–8, 11–13, 15, 36, 38, 49, 65, 125, 191, 196, 212, 250, 252, 269, 301
Honeywell, Roy, 203, 286n25, 304, 306
Höpfl, Harro, 9, 306
Hume, David, 214, 291n8
Huxley, Thomas H., 125
Ingersoll, Robert, 8, 191, 212, 250, 252
Jackson, Robert H., xxi–xxiii, 50, 63–70, 76, 81, 92–93, 101–08, 273n6, 279n1, 281n18
Jacoby, Susan, xviii, 35–37, 252–54, 306
Jarratt, Devereux, 149
Jefferson, Thomas, ix, xiii, xvi–xxi, xxiii–xxxi, 3, 5–6, 15, 18, 22, 33, 35–46, 49–50, 52, 54–57, 61–63, 68–69, 71–76, 78–79, 81, 83, 86, 95, 99–100, 109–12, 115–17, 120, 124–77, 179–88, 193, 195–205, 207–10, 213–14, 217–19, 236, 244–48, 251–52, 260, 265–66, 270, 283n10, 283n20, 285n12, 291n8, 301–06, 308–09

Jenkins, Jack, 215, 306
Juergensmeyer, Mark, 261–64, 305
Kant, Immanuel, 214, 268
Kennedy, Emmet, 268, 307
King George III, 31
Kramnick, Isaac, xvi, 3, 17, 25–28, 251–53, 307
La Fayette, Marquis De, 116, 170, 303
Lambert, Frank, 3–4, 16–18, 307
Laslett, Peter, 27, 307
Levy, Leonard, xxvii, 201–03, 285n1, 307
Lincoln, Abraham, 133, 252
Lindsay, Ronald, 215, 307
Little, Nicholas, 215, 307
Locke, John, xvi–xviii, 16–18, 25–33, 37, 49, 120, 223–34, 251, 267, 277n31, 293n23, 294n37, 302–03, 305, 307–10
Loen, Arnold E., 262, 307
Luther, Martin, 9–10, 16, 49, 192, 289n6, 306
Maclure, Jocelyn, 264–65, 307
Madison, Frances Taylor, 237
Madison, James, xvi, xviii–xxi, xxiv, xxx–xxxi, 3, 37–38, 41, 54–57, 61–62, 68–69, 71–72, 74–75, 82–83, 86, 89, 95, 100, 110–12, 115–28, 131, 134–35, 139, 142–43, 152–54, 163–64, 173–77, 179, 181–88, 193–97, 199–200, 204–05, 207–09, 236–45, 247–48, 265, 270, 301–09
Mann, Horace, 84, 86
Marsden, George, xxvii, 146, 159, 286n12, 307
Martin, Thomas, 237–38, 303
Marx, Karl, 257
McCollum, Vashti, 77, 102–03, 105
McReynolds, James, 70

NAME INDEX

Mill, John Stuart, 241
Monroe, James, 142–43
Moore, R. Laurence, xvi, 3, 17, 25–28, 251–53, 307
Moreland, J. P., 262–63, 307
Murphy, Frank, 50
Murrin, John, 16–17
Neuhaus, Richard John, 259–60, 307
Newton, Isaac, xvii, 18, 22–25, 33, 37, 42, 45, 304
Nietzche, Friedrich, 257
Noah, Mordecai, 245
Norton, Charles Eliot, 204, 308
Onuf, Peter, xxviii, 308
O'Shaughnessy, Andrew, xxviii, 308
Owen, John, 224
Paine, Thomas, 36, 150, 236, 252, 304
Pappalardo, Chris, 266, 304
Penn, William, 241
Perry, John, xvii, 267–69, 272, 308
Prynne, William, 11
Ragosta, John, xxviii, 308
Randall, Henry Stephens, xxvii, 308
Randolph, Martha Jefferson, 153, 302
Rawls, John, 265–67, 305, 308
Reed, Stanley Forman, xxii–xxiii, 50, 76, 92–93, 109–12, 164–66, 198–201, 273n8, 282n36, 287n22, 290n17
Reynolds, George, 133–34
Robertson, Donald, 237–38
Root, Elihu, 100
Rousseau, Jean-Jacques, 257
Ruskin, John, 204, 308
Rutledge, Wiley, xxi, 50, 68–73, 81, 133, 181, 186, 193, 273n5, 278n1,

280n9, 280n15, 284n8, 289n6, 289n8, 289n14
Scott, Eugenie, 29, 308
Seidel, Andrew, 252, 309
Sheldon, Garrett, ix–xi, xvi, xviii, 26, 28, 235, 309
Shelley, Percy Bysshe, 257
Shook, John R., 267, 308
Smith, Buster G., 254, 304
Smith, James K. A., 256–57, 309
Stark, Rodney, 256, 305, 309
Strauss, Leo, 25
Taylor, Charles, 254–58, 261, 264–65, 297n16, 298n34, 307, 309–10
Taylor, Jeremy, 224
Trist, Nicholas Philip, 213
Trueman, Carl, 257–59, 310
Tuckness, Alex, 25, 31, 310
Turner, James, 9, 250–51, 254–55, 258, 308, 310
VanAntwerpen, Jonathan, 256, 261–63, 305, 309–10
Vinson, Fred M., 50
Waite, Morrison, xxv, 134–40, 179–80, 217–19, 270
Walsh, Robert, 182, 184, 188, 303
Warner, Michael, 256, 309–10
Watson, David, 142
Watts, Charles, 7–8
Wenner, George U., 95
Whitefield, George, 240
Williams, Roger, 6, 251
Witherspoon, John, 238, 240, 304, 307
Young, Brigham, 133–34
Young, Warren C., 6, 191, 310
Zuckerman, Phil, 267, 308

Subject Index

A Bill Establishing a Provision for Teachers of the Christian Religion, xx, xxiv, 54–55, 68, 74, 83, 94, 116–17, 119, 121–24, 126, 134, 179, 181, 194, 200, 205, 208
A Bill for the Establishment of an University, 143
A Letter Concerning Toleration, 25, 33, 228, 293n23, 294n37, 302
Abington School District v. Schempp, xvi, 5, 10, 192, 275n9, 275n17, 289n3
Agnosticism, Agnostic, 8, 12, 44, 46, 125, 204, 210–11, 213, 250
Albemarle Academy, 142, 173
American Humanist Association, 214–15, 291n10
American Secular Union, 8
An Essay Concerning Human Understanding, 29, 303
Atheism, Atheist, 6–7, 12, 21, 28, 33, 44, 46, 90–92, 102–03, 105, 120, 149–51, 204, 210–11, 213, 231, 236, 250, 255–56, 294n35, 306
Biblical Languages (Hebrew, Greek, Latin), xxvi, 147, 157, 184, 197, 203, 209, 286n12
Biden-Harris Administration, 271, 309
Bill of Rights, xxi, 36, 55, 58–59, 76, 89, 127–28, 137, 145, 193–94, 279n17
Blaine Amendment, 91

British Secular Movement, 6–7, 12, 38, 49, 125, 191
Cantwell v. Connecticut, 59
Central College, 142, 173
Champaign Board of Education, Champaign School District, 76, 78, 81, 83, 85, 97–99, 111
Champaign Council on Religious Education, 78
Charlottesville, VA, 143, 173–76, 247
Church-State Accommodation, xxx, 52, 60, 68, 71–73, 79, 81–84, 87–88, 90, 93, 95, 97, 101–02, 109, 112, 140–41, 143–45, 147–48, 152–53, 166–67, 169, 172–73, 175–77, 181, 184, 186, 188, 191, 193, 196, 200, 205, 208, 247, 259
Church-State Relations, xviii, xx–xxi, xxiv, xxvi, xxx–xxxi, 7, 50, 52, 55, 68, 75–76, 78, 81, 99–100, 102, 110, 115, 117, 124, 129, 143, 154, 163, 168, 171–72, 181–82, 186–88, 193, 195–98, 200, 204–07, 209, 219, 223, 228, 230, 251–52, 258
Civil, xxv, 5, 9–10, 33, 36, 38, 52, 56, 118–19, 122, 125, 129, 131, 134–38, 160, 183, 192, 218, 228–32, 234, 238, 271, 293n23, 293n31, 294n35
Congress, xxi, 5, 18, 55, 58–59, 73, 76, 84, 128, 135–36, 138, 162, 164, 180, 193, 205, 214, 247, 257, 279n17

317

Constitutional Convention, 16–18, 127
Danbury Baptist Association, xix, xxii–xxvi, 55, 61, 63, 74, 83, 99, 111–12, 128–36, 139, 141, 148, 152, 154–55, 159, 165, 179–80, 182–83, 185, 188, 195, 199–200, 204–05, 209, 219, 302, 305
Declaration of Independence, 15, 37, 39, 124, 236, 278n5
Deism, Deist, 14, 23, 41, 45, 120, 150, 226, 236, 256, 283n10
Divinity Schools, xxvii, xxix, 160–61, 166, 169, 171, 174, 185
Doctrine of Incorporation, xxi, 59, 62, 73, 76, 84
Education, xv–xvi, xviii, xxii–xxiii, xxvi, xxxi, 12, 19, 42, 45, 50–51, 65–66, 68–73, 75, 77–78, 81–96, 99–101, 103–04, 106–12, 118, 141, 143–45, 148, 153, 155, 158–60, 162, 164–66, 168, 171, 176–77, 182, 184, 187, 198–200, 203–04, 206–07, 209–12, 214, 216–19, 223–24, 232, 234, 236–37, 239, 242, 260, 267–68, 297n16, 301, 303–04, 306, 309–10
Empiricism, Empiricist, Empirical, xvii–xviii, 19, 21, 28–29, 211, 224–26, 262, 268
Epistemological Atheism, 28
Epistemological Empiricism, 213
Epistemological Secularism, 212, 250, 255, 268
Establishment Clause, xxi, xxvii, 5, 58–61, 63, 68, 76, 79–80, 83, 111, 128, 132, 139, 186, 195, 201, 215, 247–48, 307
Evangelical, 234, 237, 244, 263
Everson v. Board of Education, xix–xxii, xxiv–xxvi, xxx–xxxi, 49–52, 55, 57–59, 61–64, 70, 73–76, 78–80, 82–83, 86, 90, 94, 100, 109–10, 112, 115, 118, 124, 128, 133–35, 139, 144, 147, 152, 155, 163, 165, 172, 179–181, 183, 185–88, 193–96, 199, 204, 208, 273n5, 278n1, 279n1, 279n12, 279n19, 279n21, 280nn10–11, 280n15, 283n18, 284n4, 284n8, 284n11, 284n24, 289nn5–6, 289n8, 289n14, 290n13, 291n2

Federalism, 59, 85, 89, 100
First Amendment, ix, xix–xxi, xxiii–xxiv, xxvii, 5, 7, 49–52, 54–55, 57–63, 67, 69, 71, 73–77, 79–81, 83–84, 86–89, 94, 100, 103, 109–10, 124, 126–29, 132–35, 139–41, 145, 148–49, 159, 162, 164–65, 180–81, 183–84, 186, 188, 193–96, 201, 207–08, 210, 214, 236, 244, 246–48, 254, 260, 279n17, 307
Fourteenth Amendment, 58–59, 76–77, 79–80, 84–85, 194
Free Exercise Clause, 59, 68, 83, 128, 132, 244, 246, 248
Fundamental Constitutions of Carolina, 232, 303
Fundamental Orders of Connecticut, 3
Great Awakening, The, 238, 240, 306
Humanism, Humanist, xxxi, 16, 72, 206–07, 212, 214–16, 218, 305–07
Indoctrination, 65, 88
Interfaith Conference on Federation, 95–97
Jefferson Memorial Monument, 38
Leicester Secular Society, 191
Liberty of Conscience, ix, xxxi, 229, 235, 238, 244, 261, 264–65, 269–70, 307
Memorial and Remonstrance Against Religious Assessments, xviii–xix,

SUBJECT INDEX

xxi, xxiv, 55, 61–62, 82–83, 111, 116–17, 126, 131, 139, 153, 179, 187, 194–95, 200, 205, 208, 236, 242–43, 270, 303

McCollum v. Board of Education, xix–xx, xxii, xxiv–xxvi, xxx–xxxi, 50, 62, 74–76, 79, 81–83, 85–86, 90, 93–94, 101, 108–12, 115, 117, 128, 133–34, 139, 144, 147, 152, 155, 163–65, 179–81, 183, 185–87, 193, 196, 198–201, 204, 207–08, 217, 273n6, 280n1, 280n3, 280nn11–12, 280n15, 281n1, 281n21, 281n24, 282n4, 287n22, 287n25, 289n5, 290n17

Morrill Anti-Bigamy Act, 133, 180

Natural Law, xviii, 25, 31, 225, 231

No Religious Test Clause, 5

Nonsectarian, xxvi, 86–87, 150–51, 153, 155, 157–60, 166, 174–77, 184, 187, 218

Oregon's Compulsory Education Act, 70

Peace of Westphalia, 11

Permoli v. Municipality No. 1 of City of New Orleans, 58, 279n17, 289n4

Persecution, xx, 52–56, 61–62, 73, 83, 122–23, 225, 229, 239, 243

Personal Liberty, xviii, 226–27, 229

Pierce v. Society of Sisters, 70–71, 280n13

Pluralism, 259–67, 271, 304, 307, 309

Political Liberty, xviii, 226–27

Popular Secularism, 8, 212–13, 250, 255, 268

President-Directors Report/Report to the President and Directors of the Literary Fund, xxvi–xxviii, xxx, 110, 147–48, 155–59, 162–65, 167–68, 170–71, 184–85, 187, 199, 205, 218–19, 274n17, 302

Princeton College, 237–40

Professor of Divinity, 145–48, 152, 157, 168–69, 174, 184, 197, 202, 210

Professor of Ethics, xxvi, xxix, 147–48, 157, 169, 184, 197, 203, 209

Proselytize, 67, 104

Quarterly Christian Spectator, The, 11

Reasonableness of Christianity, as Delivered in the Scriptures, The, 225, 303, 308

Religious Establishment, xx–xxi, xxv, xxix, xxxi, 52–56, 58–59, 61–63, 66, 73, 83–84, 101, 109, 118, 122, 133, 144, 148, 154–55, 159–60, 162, 172, 177, 182–84, 186–87, 196, 235–36, 239, 241, 243, 245, 248, 253, 258–59, 270–71

Religious Liberty, ix, xiii, xvi, xviii–xix, xxiv–xxv, xxxi, 53, 55–59, 67, 71–73, 84, 87, 117, 119, 124–26, 130–35, 137, 139–40, 143–46, 148, 162, 180–81, 183–185, 188, 195, 208, 217, 228, 231, 235–48, 266, 270–72, 279n17

Religious Unbelief, 251, 255

Revelation, 16, 123, 224–25, 233

Reynolds v. United States, xxv, xxx, 133–34, 136–40, 165, 179–80, 188, 195, 208, 217, 270, 284n9, 284n12, 284nn16–17, 288n1, 292n15

Rockfish Gap Report/Report of the Commissioners for the University of Virginia, xxvi–xxviii, xxx, 111–12, 141–46, 151–58, 161, 164, 167, 170–71, 173, 184–85, 187, 197–98, 200–01, 203, 205, 207–10, 218–19, 285n8, 285n12, 291n3, 302, 304

Sacred, xxii, 9–10, 16, 39, 42, 105, 138, 161–62, 240, 256, 258, 308, 310

Scientism, 262–63, 307

Sectarian, xxii, 6, 81, 84, 86–87,

319

90–93, 101, 105, 108, 144, 146, 152, 158–60, 163, 166, 175
Secular Authorities, 9, 16–17, 192, 306
Secular Democrats of America, 271, 309
Secular Government, 9–10, 38, 49, 192, 252–53, 267, 289n6, 308
Secular State, 4, 16, 223, 251–52, 257–58
Sherbert v. Verner, 192, 289n3
Supreme Court, ix, xvi, xix–xxii, xxx, 5, 10, 50–52, 59–60, 62–64, 68, 70, 72–73, 75–77, 79–82, 87, 89–90, 99–110, 115, 117, 124, 127, 133–34, 136, 145, 148, 154, 164, 179–81, 186, 188, 192–201, 204–05, 207–08, 210, 217, 219, 234, 250, 279n17
Tabula rasa, 30
Temporal, 7, 9–10, 33, 39, 56, 66, 70, 87, 94–95, 122, 124, 161, 192
Tripoli, Treaty of, 4–5
Two Tracts on Government, 303
Two Treatises of Government, The, 25, 307
Unitarian, Unitarianism, 14, 41, 120, 150
United States Constitution, ix, xi, xxi, xxxi, 3–4, 6–7, 16–18, 25, 36, 58, 68, 71–72, 76–77, 80–81, 89, 91, 94, 98–100, 102, 108, 127, 129, 131, 135, 137, 145, 149, 152, 158, 192, 197, 201–04, 212, 235–36, 251–54, 271, 273n4, 275n8, 276n5, 279n11, 279n18, 279n20, 280n2, 281n20, 281n23, 284n3, 287n18, 288n2, 290n26, 291n9, 296n44
University of Virginia, xiii, xvi, xxvi–xxix, 109–11, 141–46, 148–49, 154–55, 163–64, 167–70, 173–74, 177, 181–82, 184, 187, 193, 197–201, 203–05, 207, 210, 213, 218–19, 291n3, 301–04, 306–08
Virginia Statute for Religious Freedom, xix, xxiv, xxvii, 43, 55–57, 61–62, 74, 83, 116, 124, 126, 131, 134–37, 139, 141, 152, 162, 164, 179, 181, 185, 187–88, 195, 200, 205, 208, 210, 236, 244–47, 270, 301
Wall of Separation, xix–xx, xxiii–xxiv, 45, 50–51, 61, 63, 73, 79, 83, 99, 108, 111, 127–28, 132–33, 136, 139–40, 148, 154–55, 159, 165, 180–82, 184, 186–87, 194–95, 199–200, 204, 260, 305
Weltlich, 9–10, 192